FROM DALI TO BURRELL

Other books by Jack Webster:

THE DONS (1978)
A GRAIN OF TRUTH (1981)
GORDON STRACHAN (1984)
ANOTHER GRAIN OF TRUTH (1988)
'TIS BETTER TO TRAVEL (1989)
ALISTAIR MACLEAN: A LIFE (1991)
FAMOUS SHIPS OF THE CLYDE (1993)
THE FLYING SCOTS (1994)
THE EXPRESS YEARS (1994)
IN THE DRIVING SEAT (1996)
THE HERALD YEARS (1996)
WEBSTER'S WORLD (1997)

Television Films:

WEBSTER'S ROUP (1985)
AS TIME GOES BY (1987)
NORTHERN LIGHTS (1989)
WEBSTER GOES WEST (1991)
THE GLORY OF GOTHENBURG (1993)
JOHN BROWN: THE MAN WHO DREW A LEGEND (1994)
WALKING BACK TO HAPPINESS (1996)

JACK
WEBSTER

from DALI *to* BURRELL

THE TOM HONEYMAN STORY

B&W PUBLISHING

First published 1997
by B&W Publishing Ltd., Edinburgh
ISBN 1 873631 82 0

British Library Cataloguing in Publication Data:
A catalogue record for this book is available
from the British Library.

Cover photograph:
Salvador Dali and Tom Honeyman
at Port Lligat (1963)

Back Cover:
Portrait of T. J. Honeyman (1931)
by G. Leslie Hunter

Printed by Werner Söderström

CONTENTS

ILLUSTRATIONS

I should like to thank the following for their kind permission to reproduce the illustrations in this book:

Black & white photographs:

All photographs courtesy of Margaret Wilson, except those of:
Sir William Burrell—courtesy of Glasgow Museums: The Burrell Collection
Sir Patrick Dollan—courtesy of the *Herald* Picture Archive.

Colour plates:

Portrait of Alexander Reid by Vincent van Gogh
Glasgow Museums: Art Gallery & Museum, Kelvingrove

Empress Eugénie on the Beach at Trouville by Eugène Boudin
Glasgow Museums: The Burrell Collection

Mrs T. J. Honeyman by Wyndham Lewis
Private Collection; Photograph: William Hardie Gallery

Le Château de Médan by Paul Cézanne
Glasgow Museums: The Burrell Collection

Flower Seller by Pablo Picasso
Glasgow Museums: Art Gallery & Museum, Kelvingrove;
Copyright © Succession Picasso/DACS 1997

State Visit of Queen Victoria by Sir John Lavery
Glasgow Museums: Art Gallery & Museum, Kelvingrove

The Marne at Chennevieres by Camille Pissarro
The National Gallery of Scotland

Flowers in a Chinese Vase by G. Leslie Hunter
Glasgow Museums: Art Gallery & Museum, Kelvingrove

Dr Honeyman by Emilio Coia; Private Collection

The Rehearsal by Edgar Degas
Glasgow Museums: The Burrell Collection

Head of a Young Girl by Henri Matisse
Glasgow Museums: Art Gallery & Museum, Kelvingrove;
Copyright © Succession H. Matisse/DACS 1997

"We're at the Front all right!" by T. J. Honeyman; Private Collection

Portrait of William McInnes by G. Leslie Hunter
Glasgow Museums: Art Gallery & Museum, Kelvingrove

The Pool of London by André Derain
Photograph: Tate Gallery;
Copyright © ADAGP, Paris and DACS, London 1997

Christ of St John of the Cross by Salvador Dali
Glasgow Museums: The St Mungo Museum of Religious Life and Art

Portrait of T. J. Honeyman by G. Leslie Hunter; Private Collection

MY THANKS

Many witnesses of Tom Honeyman's life and work co-operated to provide this portrait of the man, not least his daughter Margaret, whose help was invaluable.

For one part of his life I have drawn substantially on his own book, *Art and Audacity*, which was published by Collins in 1971, shortly before he died. A thesis by Anne Marie Millar was also a useful guide.

My thanks are due to all these sources. But there is one man above all without whom a publication of this technical quality would not have been possible, at least at such an affordable price.

Colin Clark, a London-Scot who combines distinction with chronic modesty, was more than happy to provide the financial backing which enabled me to include, among other things, the costly business of colour reproduction.

It was Mr Clark's own way of repaying the debt he felt he owed to Dr Honeyman—a personal tribute to the man who devoted so much time to the moulding of his early enthusiasm for art.

JACK WEBSTER

Glasgow, November 1997

I

WHO WAS TOM HONEYMAN?

WHEN Glasgow stepped out of the shadows to become European City of Culture in 1990 there was much celebration at the highest level of artistic expression. The breadth of that culture was reflected in the fact that major stars from Luciano Pavarotti to Frank Sinatra beat a path to the Dear Green Place and, in a city which had prided itself in a certain macho resistance to the finer points of life, a curious transformation took place.

Indeed, Pavarotti and Sinatra became symbols of that change inasmuch as the great Italian tenor had just opened the eyes and ears of a vastly wider world to the pleasures of operatic music with his rendering of Puccini's "Nessum Dorma" as the theme song of football's World Cup that year; and Ol' Blue Eyes extended the soccer connection by raising the roof of Ibrox stadium on a damp and miserable summer's eve with one of his most inspired performances.

Quite perceptibly, the self-protective barriers with which the human race will insist on dividing itself showed signs of crumbling. Perhaps culture was not, after all, some élitist privilege but a joy for anyone who was prepared to meet it half way. Men on building sites could be heard in imitation of Pavarotti, having already gone to see him at the Scottish Exhibition Centre and given a good old Glasgow greeting of "Gaun yersel, Luciano!"

While there has long been a sound artistic base to the city, dating back to the Glasgow Boys and beyond, the more recent story had been one of washing away the industrial grime (hopefully along with the inferiority complex) and reaching out for a better image in the wider world.

In the groping analysis of how Glasgow came to be European City of Culture, there was a general conclusion that the arrival of the Burrell Collection had been very much the catalyst. There had been a lot of talking and planning, much pride and celebration. But as the credits for 1990 were claimed and the kudos distributed, it seemed to me that the name of one man had been shamefully overlooked.

Hardly anyone had mentioned the name of Dr Tom Honeyman, former Director of Glasgow Art Galleries and Museums. Yet was it not this distinguished son of the city more than anyone who so popularised art among ordinary folk that they would queue for hours to see the latest exhibition?

Was it not Tom Honeyman who negotiated with his old acquaintance, Salvador Dali, and persuaded him not only to sell his much publicised "Christ of St John of the Cross" but to grant those reproduction rights which have since brought the city a small fortune?

And, if we were so convinced of the Burrell significance, had we forgotten that Sir William Burrell himself made it fairly plain that it was the work of Tom Honeyman more than any other factor which persuaded him that the famous collection should go to Glasgow rather than Edinburgh or London?

Even before all that, the former pupil of Queen's Park School had rendered such a breadth of service to the city that, in 1943, he became only the second recipient of Glasgow's highest honour, the St Mungo Prize, bestowed on the person who has done most to promote the city's interests in the previous three years.

Honeyman was part of that coincidence of brilliant Glaswegians which included men like Denis Brogan, Professor of Political Science at Cambridge, James Bridie, famous playwright and moving spirit in the foundation of the Citizens' Theatre, and Walter Elliot, a man of such statesmanlike qualities as to raise forecasts of a future Prime Minister.

Just as Bridie had given up being a doctor at Glasgow's Victoria Infirmary to gain fame as a playwright, so did Honeyman give up medical practice in Dennistoun to devote himself to art. It was part of a tradition which became fashionable at the time, taken up by such as that other distinguished doctor-writer, A. J. Cronin.

Having also been a doctor in the First World War, Honeyman moved to London as an art dealer and came to know everyone from Dali to Matisse and Picasso before returning to mastermind the art culture of Glasgow. When Bridie called on him, as an old friend, to help him found the Citizens' Theatre, it was just another indication of the scope of one who had already staged early Bridie plays in both Glasgow and London before they became well known.

As a stocky man of plain talking and great good humour, a showman for his city, he was not afraid to cross swords with bumbling bureaucracy which frustrated so many of his ambitions for Glasgow. But at his eightieth birthday party in the Central Hotel, Glasgow, Tom Honeyman expressed much of his true personality and outlook when he told the assembled guests: "Whatever you do in life, do it gloriously!"

It was the fitting climax to the extraordinary life of a Scottish character now much forgotten. The stature of the man could be gauged from the assessment of Sir Denis Brogan, one of the most brilliant academics of the century, who said, "Tom Honeyman has been the most interesting Glasgow man active in public life since the First World War."

By chance, as a feature writer on the *Daily Express*, I interviewed him in the closing weeks of his life and absorbed enough of the man to sense his significance.

Then, wandering by Kelvingrove one day, I came upon his memorial garden, within sight of the university where he was both student and Rector, the Western Infirmary where he was a houseman, and the Art Gallery which was the centre of his achievements for the city.

Sadly, I discovered the memorial plaque was frequently obscured nowadays by the assembled winos who have found a rendezvous; though even with his life-long commitment to temperance, Dr Honeyman had the sense of humour which would have appreciated the irony.

The fate of that memorial may be no more than a symbol of what has happened to the man who was not only denied his pedestal in the Year of Culture but continues to be ignored in an information age which, paradoxically, is tending to leave its heritage behind.

We began with a question of "Who was Tom Honeyman?" If the first chink in the veil of neglect has appeared, it is just the beginning of a fascinating personal story.

II

MYSTERY MAN IN BUENOS AIRES

TOM HONEYMAN was born in Glasgow on 10th June 1891 and, apart from military service in the First World War and ten years in London, his home was always in the native city.

The family origins, however, were on the eastern side of Scotland, stretching from the Kingdom of Fife to the Moray coast. His paternal grandfather, Sandy Honeyman, was an esteemed townsman of Ladybank in Fife, at one time a substantial building contractor who not only put up the parish church but specialised in railway bridges, building them all over Scotland as a subcontractor to larger companies.

By the time his grandchildren encountered Sandy, he had become a quietly reserved old man, in sharp contrast to his earlier days when, by all accounts, he had been the picture of warm geniality. The years between had been a sorry tale of the drink, which saw his business stature reduced to the borderline of poverty, when superior homes would be pointed out as the ones "where Grandpa and Granny used to live".

By then, a modest but-and-ben was the destination for the Honeyman grandchildren who nevertheless set out with much excitement on the railway journey to Fife, which meant crossing the Forth Bridge, passing through Kirkcaldy, with its funny smell of linoleum, and a comic wee place called Kingskettle (Who was the king and what did he have for tea? asked the children), before reaching Granny's place, with the novelty of its dry closet at the bottom of the garden.

Primitive perhaps; but then we are going back to the days when Queen Victoria was still on the throne! Granny Honeyman ran a sweetie shop from the front room of Clare Cottage, a favourite with the schoolchildren and employing her own system of incentives. A religious woman, she would produce an alluring bottle of confectionery as bait for the grandchildren to learn their psalms. Success brought the freedom of as big a handful as could be extracted through the neck of the bottle.

But there was a moral to the exercise for those who would grab to the point of greed. She didn't need to put it into words but implicit in the look was the lesson that you get more out of life if you pick and choose with more discretion and less selfishness.

The records show the coincidence that Sandy and Janet Honeyman (she came from Aberdeenshire) were actually born on the same day, were naturally married on the same day and evidently prayed that they would die on the same day. Having reached the fine old age of eighty-six, Janet finally passed away and, on the day she died, old Sandy simply crumpled up and followed her a few weeks later. Despite all the hardship and sorrow, such were the loving bonds of marriage in a bygone age.

Far from the Kingdom of Fife, on the other hand, Tom Honeyman's mother came from the rolling farmlands of Morayshire, in the community of Dunphail, where her father was plain John Smith, local blacksmith and smallholder. Because of distance and expense, visits to the maternal grandparents were less frequent for Tom Honeyman and his six brothers and one sister but no less exciting. The rail journey north could be tedious in cold weather, though in those far-off days the carriages were heated with unsightly iron boxes filled with coal.

Tom Honeyman would recall the interminable walk to church

in Morayshire, a monotony made bearable only by the awaited novelty of watching the elders taking the collection with those brass ladles at the end of long poles.

Though the sermons made little impression on the child mind, Tom did like the minister, the Rev Mr Watt, a scholarly man with a distant look of sadness about him. Within a few years the long arm of coincidence was to offer some clue to that sadness when Tom Honeyman set out, as a teenager in 1908, to work his passage to the River Plate aboard a tramp steamer.

Held up in Buenos Aires for several weeks, he observed one day a shabby-looking man who came to the galley door and asked if there was any chance of a job. He was a down-and-out and seemed to want home to Britain. Detecting young Honeyman's accent, he began to question him till it became clear that he knew much of his family background. Was his mother's name Elspeth Smith? Did he know Dunphail, Elgin, Forres? Did he know the smiddy and had he ever met the parish minister? But he refused to give his own name.

Young Honeyman liked him and wished he were coming on the homeward trip. He wrote to his mother and gave as much detail as he knew. And when he reached home he was further questioned and shown photographs of a man who was almost certainly the down-and-out of Buenos Aires before his decline.

The minister came round, listened to the story and knew that Tom Honeyman had met his son George who, under a cloud, had vanished twelve years earlier and was never to be seen again.

Meanwhile, Grandpa Smith applied his powerful arms to the music of the anvil, a joy to see at the shoeing of a horse, though the treat was discouraged as far as the children were concerned because of the old man's adventurous language.

Once again, in the background of Tom Honeyman's genes, the demon drink raised its horns as old John Smith would head off to market in the certainty that his homeward journey would be at the mercy of a wise old horse with a sure-footed sense of direction.

Unlike the other grandfather, however, whose alcoholic adventures inclined towards joviality and benevolence, John Smith became quarrelsome and difficult to handle. For all the attack on his liver, he survived till eighty-seven and ended his days near daughter Elspeth, or Elsie as she was known, and the Honeyman grandchildren on the South Side of Glasgow.

Long before that, however, Elsie had escaped the family home at Dunphail and gone to Aberdeen where she trained as a teacher before heading to her one and only job in Lerwick. That was where she met Tom Honeyman's father, another Tom, whose home town of Ladybank was a well-known railway junction. As a result, he left school and started work with the North British Railways, qualifying as an engine-driver and gaining a reputation for looking after the welfare of his fellow men. He was a hard-working, diligent man who could do with little sleep.

In any railway emergency, in the dead of night and in all weathers, the first call was always for Tom Honeyman. Among other things, "You're sure to find him sober," folk said, an ironic comment when you considered the paternal example.

In the light of that family history, however, Tom had given his mother a solemn promise that he would keep away from the drink. In fact he did more than that. Very early in his career he took an interest in the temperance movement which had begun to exert an influence upon British society that would be hard to understand a century later. With the Independent Order of Good Templars imported from America, Thomas Roberts founded a lodge in Glasgow and the movement was then in full swing in Scotland.

When the Liberal Party was in power in the land, its young bloods like Lloyd George and Winston Churchill cultivated the temperance vote and appeared on its platforms. The pioneers of the Labour movement, Keir Hardie, Philip Snowdon, Arthur Henderson and others, were to graduate into politics from their training in public speaking about the temperance movement.

Even then it was ridiculed and the initials of the Independent Order (IOGT) were hijacked for the waggish version of "I Often Get Tight". The faithful recovered the situation by declaring "I Owe God Thanks".

A wave of enthusiasm sweeping through Fife caught the senior Tom Honeyman on its crest and he was initiated into one of its lodges, attracted by the obligations as well as the missionary purpose and becoming absorbed in the big idea of social reform.

All the while he was gaining promotion and driving goods trains to Glasgow, where he would save on lodging money by sleeping in a surfaceman's hut at Cowlairs.

He never lost his affection for the old North British Railways and in later years, when emerging from the tunnel which stretches northward from Queen Street Station, he would alert his children to the sight of an old engine which had taken its solemn place in railway history and was ending its days in shunting operations at Cowlairs Junction. The engine was none other than that which plunged into the river with all its passengers in the Tay Bridge Disaster of 1879.

Tom Honeyman's heart was warming more and more to the idea of becoming a full-time worker in the temperance movement, a role for which he was already being marked out by those in search of young men of promise. Finally he stepped from the footplate to the temperance platform, donned a silk hat and frock-coat and was still wearing that elegant garb long after it had been abandoned by the doctors and businessmen of the city.

As a full-time temperance man, Tom was given a territory stretching from Dundee to the Orkney and Shetland Islands, charged with the opening of new lodges, stimulating those already in existence, collecting subscriptions for missionary work at home and abroad and, as part of the propaganda for total abstinence, taking his place as a lay preacher.

That took him into many a manse in the North as a welcome guest, including the home of the young Peter Fraser, destined to be Prime Minister of New Zealand. When the Premier, on visiting Scotland at the start of the Second World War, was fêted by the Royal Glasgow Institute of the Fine Arts, he caused some exasperation by showing less interest in the paintings than in what had happened to people like Tom Honeyman!

With much of his work in the northern isles, it was not unnatural that he should meet his future wife in Shetland—introduced to Elsie Smith by her minister on a windy day at a street corner in Lerwick. The wedding took place at Dunphail, an occasion when the bride's father was told for once in his life exactly how things were to be done. To old John Smith the idea of a wedding without drink was an affront to his idea of hospitality and contrary to all decent practice. He evidently consoled himself with the thought that there was no accounting for taste, which extended to his daughter's selection of a husband—and their joint resolution that no hard liquor would cross their doorstep.

They made their home in Dundee, where their first two children were born, before the job took them to Glasgow. The house at 11 Stevenson Street was stretched to accommodate the mounting family of seven sons before the only daughter arrived, prompting father Honeyman to announce, "Now boys, there are seven of you and each of you has a sister." Young Tom's first impression was that his mother had produced a litter of seven girls!

In those days at the turn of the century an annual treat for Glasgow children was a visit to Hengler's Circus, originally at Waterloo Street and then in Sauchiehall Street, and the Honeyman beds would subsequently be tested to their limits as the amateur trapeze artists balanced and bounded their way to make-believe.

Another feature of Glasgow's entertainment in those days

was Bostock's Zoo in New City Road. Mr Bostock came from a long line of showmen and happened to be sympathetic to Tom Honeyman and the temperance movement. So there were free passes for the Honeyman children. Not long before the zoo was finally closed and the animals dispersed, the lioness created history by giving birth to four cubs. They didn't survive but were stuffed and expertly mounted. Two were given to the Glasgow Museum and the other two were given to Mr Honeyman for sale at a charity bazaar. But they failed to find a buyer and for years they reposed on a bookcase in the Honeyman house, eventually going to a museum.

Father Honeyman had a connection with concerts in the city, especially those run on Saturday evenings by the Good Templar Philharmonic Association and the Glasgow Abstainers' Union. That was how he gained the acquaintance of Scottish singers and comedians who would become household names in later years, people like Harry Lauder and W. F. Frame.

III

HARRY LAUDER IN PANTO

THE HONEYMAN family used to go to the Clyde resort of Millport for their summer holidays and there you would find them ranged along the front row when W. F. Frame came to entertain. Young Tom remembered "The Man You Know", as he was billed, launching into a roistering song about the tipple, breaking his flow of patter to address his father across the footlights with "Ay, it wouldna suit you, Mr Honeyman, but we had a rare night's fun."

Mrs Honeyman had her way of identifying the eight children at a distance. She dressed them all in bright red jerseys, which evidently made the Honeyman children a feature of the summer season in Millport. During those holidays Mr Honeyman travelled to work in Glasgow. When he came back at the weekend it warmed his heart, as the island steamer circled the bay, to spot the line of red jerseys coming along the pier to meet him.

When they moved house to Battlefield Crescent young Tom Honeyman became a pupil at Queen's Park School, where his academic attainments were no more than average. Before a properly qualified art teacher arrived, there was only a visiting drawing master whose one hour per week cost parents 2s. 6d. if they wished the privilege.

There was another optional class for elocution and it is

interesting, in view of Honeyman's later achievements in both art and oratory, to trace those first influences which sprang from his parents' decision to afford him the extra classes.

In art, the man handed out engravings after the greater or lesser masters from which they had to make slavish copies. This was how young Tom Honeyman was introduced to Landseer and other Victorians and gained some distinction with his copies of a special favourite, "Dignity and Impudence". He won a competition prize of five shillings for "The Head of a Horse" but the money went into the family holiday fund and left him with an early impression that the artist's lot was a hard one.

Mr Vallance, the elocution man, was large and distinguished looking and taught the full range of gestures as well as voice. At the end-of-term concert in the Dixon Halls, on the South Side of Glasgow, the eight-year-old Tom Honeyman was dressed in white blouse and velvet breeks for his big moment. Drawing much mirth with his initial bowing to the audience, he proceeded to recite:

My name is Tommy and I hate
That fellow of my sister Kate
He's bigger than I am, and you see
He keeps on looking down at me
He's older and he's mighty fly
But he's a kid, and so am I

Young Tom didn't think he had been as funny as the audience seemed to find him. But from such nonsense a distinguished orator began his career.

Though the children were all sent to piano lessons, and Mrs Honeyman had a reputation as a fine singer, they were not a musical family. But they were a fairly religious one, attending Langside Hill Church, first in the little brick building inside

Queen's Park, at the foot of Langside Hill, and then in the big church which still faces the monument of the Battle of Langside.

The minister, the Rev D. F. Mackenzie, was known as a fine preacher but what stuck in the mind of Tom Honeyman was an incident in 1901 when they were being given their introduction to the moving pictures. At a Sunday School soirée the film included shots of the Boer War, with men throwing themselves in the air and falling face down in dramatic fashion. As a pacifist, Mr Mackenzie ordered the performance to be stopped, sparking off a hullabaloo and near-riot in the young audience.

Tom Honeyman set down some thoughts of his childhood visits to Langside Church, proving that even in more religious times boys were always boys.

He wrote: "I have sat through sermons which I never heard, my thoughts wandering all the time. After a visit to the circus I would imagine myself swinging from the chandeliers, landing with a great shout of '*Voilà!*' on the pulpit steps. I have looked at the faces of old men, speculating on what they must have looked like when they were boys. I have had my share of writing parodies of hymns, twisting Bible texts to mean something very far removed from the writer's intention."

Giving the flavour of the times, Tom Honeyman used to describe the young doctor who set up his plate near their home and treated brother Gilbert as his very first patient. Dr Douglas Russell looked every inch the medic of his day, wearing silk hat and morning coat or frock-coat, a handsome man with an elegant walk, quiet of speech but always thoroughly interested in what you had to say.

With the illnesses of the time, there were spells when he was seldom out of the house, not least when three of the Honeyman boys were removed to Belvedere hospital suffering from scarlet fever, which was a scourge in the first half of the century. Dr Russell eventually became a consultant physician at the Victoria

Infirmary and part of his significance in Tom Honeyman's memory was that his eventual successor in the practice was a Dr O. H. Mavor, who would become a close friend, better known as James Bridie, the famous playwright.

With thoughts of a university career ahead for young Tom, a deficiency in Latin brought him the coaching of a Mr Bell, a former civil servant of some standing, talented and cultured but written off as a provider for his family by a fatal attraction for the booze.

But Mr Bell was a charming and entertaining instructor and, what's more, he had an attractive daughter who seemed to know everyone that mattered in the acting profession. She worked in a piano warehouse which had a theatre ticket agency and she had access to complimentary tickets. Thus, once again, Tom Honeyman found the influence which would lead him to the theatrical experience. He was enchanted by everything he saw and grasped every opportunity to attend the theatre and the music hall, sometimes in secret.

While the so-called legitimate theatre was approved of at home, the pantomime and music hall were regarded as dangers which threatened the morals.

Tom Honeyman saw his first pantomime in 1905, at the age of fourteen, when Harry Lauder appeared at Glasgow's Theatre Royal. That gained approval only because Lauder had served his apprenticeship as an entertainer under the banner of the temperance movement and was on friendly terms with his father, who held him in high regard but felt he had rather fallen from grace in deserting the concert platform for this lesser form of entertainment.

That pantomime, incidentally, was *Aladdin*, which featured one of Harry Lauder's greatest songs, "I Love a Lassie", guaranteed to prolong the performance in what later came to be known as a show-stopper. Whereas a liberal education in those days was generally to do with books, Tom Honeyman's pursuit of knowledge had much to do with the analysis of vaudeville performance from his seat in the gods. In examining how theatrical talent had influenced the lives and leisure times of the masses, he was able to draw on personal experience of every great name of the day, from George Robey and George Formby to Houdini, the Great Lafayette and Scotland's own remarkable Dr Walford Bodie.

At the academic level it seemed as if Tom would be the first in the family to follow a university career. The fact that his parents had him marked out for the ministry may have dated back to a childhood incident when, in reply to a visitor who asked what he wanted to be when he grew up, he had said: "A minister on Sunday and a joiner through the week."

By the time he had his first man-to-man talk with his father, however, he had plucked up enough courage to say that he didn't want to be a minister. When he added that he wanted to follow his older brother and go to sea, a crisis point had been reached and much pressure was brought from all directions.

All right, he would aim for the university, even though he had not been applying himself too diligently to examinations.

But for three summers before reaching university he did in fact go to sea and give some vent to that side of his ambition. In 1906 he was sailing with the Laird Line to Northern Ireland before signing on for a longer trip to what he thought was the Mediterranean. The fact that the destination was the port of Montevideo didn't say much for his knowledge of geography. While still sixteen, he signed on at Ardrossan and sailed on the *SS Zamorra*, bound for the River Plate.

As a steward on an old ship, facing incredibly heavy weather among other hazards, Tom Honeyman would find himself growing up within the miserable period of the thirty-seven days it took to reach South America. In Montevideo, as the cargo of coal was unloaded into lighters, a gang of tough but cheerful ruffians came aboard every morning. Tom Honeyman was fascinated by their behaviour. At the midday break, the heavers produced huge steaks of meat, brushed the dust off their shovels and used them as frying pans over buckets pierced to act as ovens. They were enjoying a huge picnic and nobody bothered about the fire risk.

For weeks, they lay in Buenos Aires while stevedores and agents held conferences and the skipper developed an attack of delirium tremens. The young Scot was to discover how fearsome a business it is to control the DTs, and for a time it seemed to spread like a contagious disease through the *SS Zamorra*. He and the second engineer were the only ones to escape.

If Tom missed the chance to venture forth and see a great city in the course of development, he was also spared the sordid pleasures of the Boca dockland district.

IV

TRAGEDY OF BROTHER ALEX

BY the time he returned to Glasgow his parents had moved house from Millbrae, on the South Side, to 160 Hill Street, Garnethill, and his father had chosen Cowcaddens Church to cater for their spiritual needs.

It was there that he met a man who would play another significant role in his career. Duncan Macdonald's family had come down to Glasgow from the Highlands in a well-worn tradition of people who were often bewildered and intimidated by the roar of the city. Survival and occasional success were the rewards of those who gained immunity to poisonous influences, a situation which Tom Honeyman recognised so clearly from Edwin Muir's autobiographical narrative, *The Story and the Fable.*

Though his humble beginnings and basic education gave no hint of what lay ahead, Duncan Macdonald would rise to be an art dealer of international reputation, largely responsible for tempting Tom Honeyman in the same direction.

In the beginning, however, they merely became close friends at Cowcaddens Church, persuaded into the choir more for the purpose of making up numbers than adding by way of vocal merit. One of the ministers at Cowcaddens around that time was the Rev James Robertson, known as the Singing Minister, as well as being the father of a man who would become one of the personalities in the early life of television, the craggy J. Fyfe Robertson.

With Tom's father so often away from home and deeply absorbed in his work, it fell to his mother to guide the affairs of the family at Hill Street.

Eldest son Alex had always wanted to be an engineer so it was Mrs Honeyman who trekked around Glasgow to see if she could find him an apprenticeship. From then onwards Alex became self-reliant, planning to qualify as a marine engineer, joining the Clan Line and intending to look for greater opportunities in the Colonies.

He sailed to Africa and India, always returning with gifts for the whole family, but confided in brother Tom that his next voyage would be his last. He had discovered that the big jobs were on shore. In fact there was an impressive-looking government postal packet awaiting him which would confirm that he had gained a post in the Sudan.

Before he would even know about his success, however, tragedy struck. An official turned up on the doorstep one day with a cable from the captain of the *SS Clan Sutherland* to say that engineer Alex Honeyman had been accidentally killed. Tom Honeyman wrote down his feelings:

"To report it as sad or tragic can do little more than reveal that there are experiences for which there are no terms of definition or description. It was painful to feel the silences of my father and to see the effect of mental numbness on my mother's face."

The effect on Tom Honeyman himself was profound. His faith in an all-wise Creator had already been dented by his contact with some clever and amicable people whose lives were untouched by religious belief and church connection. Now, very privately, he wrote off God, keeping it quiet because he did not want to add to the family's sorrows or to upset the image of a God-fearing, God-loving household.

Nothing about the whole tragedy made any sense to him and it took a long time before he could relax the feeling. That happened only when someone quoted to him an A. J. Balfour observation, to the effect that a religion small enough to come within the range of our understanding would never be large enough for our needs.

Alex had been the perfect brother, writing unfailingly from abroad and making it clear, in those days when it was hard for families like the Honeymans to put a boy through university, that he would take over part of that burden for Tom. He believed that students needed proper relaxation and should not be out earning money to cover their educational costs. Ironically, Alex's clothes and effects were delivered by embarrassed shipmates in October 1909, just as Tom was about to matriculate at Glasgow University.

It was a long time before they would persuade Mrs Honeyman to snap out of her depression, but in time she resumed her domestic authority and steeped herself in the affairs of Glasgow Parish Council, looking after the welfare of boarded-out Glasgow children and feeling that foster parents offered the best solution to the problems of broken homes and neglected children.

The Hill Street house was bigger than any of the earlier ones, while the street itself was well known for its theatrical boarding houses. Many distinguished actors and actresses of the day would be staying nearby, forming friendships with landladies which brought them back time and again, even when they could have afforded more luxurious quarters.

This theatrical environment may have had something to do with the future career of Walter, the youngest of the seven Honeyman sons, who would rise to prominence as a theatrical producer in London's West End under the name of Murray Macdonald, the surname being taken from his own middle name and the Murray being borrowed from a well-known railway timetable of the day!

Murray would surface again later but the bug of theatre was infecting the entire family, to the extent that they were staging performances in the Hill Street house. These would take the form of one-act plays presented to groups of friends and relatives, coerced into the limited space of the largest room in the house, with the stage confined around the area of the oriel window.

These humble family efforts would eventually grow into an amateur dramatic company known as the Albany Players. Despite economic strains, Tom Honeyman developed a substantial interest in the theatre through his visits to the King's Theatre with his mother. They were mainly to be found in the gallery but if funds allowed they would promote themselves to the stalls. It was a side of his life which would gain more and more significance as the years went by.

With some curious, even mysterious interruptions, the period from 1909 until 1916 was largely taken up with the affairs of Glasgow University, the gates of which he entered with a certain lack of enthusiasm. It was a period of much activity around the world, taking in the first ghastly years of the so-called Great War.

Tom Honeyman would see service in that war. But within his first week at university, indifference had given way to enthusiasm, even excitement, as a whole new kind of life began to open up.

V

THE BODIE PLOT

TO SPEND YEARS studying for one profession only to give it up for something entirely different seems an odd diversion, especially for those who have had a financial struggle to get there in the first place.

Tom Honeyman was just one of many distinguished graduates who fell into this category, seeking to justify himself by saying the infinite varieties and absurdities of the medical course provided a first-class liberal education which was in itself an ample preparation for any job of work.

One of his university teachers, Professor T. K. Monro, published a book called *The Physician as Man of Letters, Science and Action*, in which he dealt with the impressive list of doctors and surgeons who gained distinction in other pursuits. Tom Honeyman would come to have personal knowledge of several of those people, including Sir Seymour Haden, the English surgeon who founded the Royal Hospital for Incurables and went on, as an eminent etcher, to found the Royal Society for Painter-Etchers and Engravers; Henry Tonks, a Fellow of the Royal College of Surgeons who gave up medicine and became Slade Professor of Fine Art at London University; and Sir Augustus Donnell, a doctor who preceded Sir Kenneth Clark as Director of the National Gallery in London.

Nearer home, as young Honeyman embarked on his medical course at Glasgow University, he found himself hard on the heels of two of the most distinguished names to emerge from that university this century.

One of them was Osborne Henry Mavor, who would become James Bridie, famous playwright. The other was Walter Elliot, who went on to be an eminent politician, Secretary of State for Scotland (1936-38), Minister of Health (1938-40) and widely tipped as a future Prime Minister. Honeyman marvelled at the universality of Elliot, who could match the variety with brilliance in so many directions.

In his private life, Walter Elliot had a less fortunate start. Straight from their wedding in Glasgow, he and his bride went honeymooning on the Isle of Skye, with hopes of climbing in the Cuillins. Together, on the first day, they slipped and fell and when Elliot regained consciousness, he looked around for his young bride. Crawling over to where she lay, he found her already dead. For his second marriage he spend the rest of his life with Katharine Tennant, a member of the Glasgow family which owned the world's biggest chemical works, that complex in the East End of the city which eventually became the basis of the company we now know as ICI. Baroness Elliot, as she became, had the distinction of being the first life peeress, sent to the Lords by Prime Minister Harold Macmillan in 1958.

When Honeyman arrived at Gilmorehill, Mavor and Elliot were the natural leaders who seemed to determine the line of action in most student adventures, from rectorial elections to the *Glasgow University Magazine.*

A few years later they were to be followed by yet another medical man who would reach fame elsewhere. Archibald Joseph Cronin, who came from Cardross, Dunbartonshire, was fortunate enough to acquire the peptic ulcer which drove him to recuperate on the shores of Loch Fyne, where he discovered he could write.

As A. J. Cronin, he had an immediate success with his autobiographical novel, *Hatter's Castle,* and went on to a string of triumphs, not least with the series of medical stories which gave rise to the popular *Dr Finlay's Casebook* on television.

Absorbing the fascinating characters around him, Tom Honeyman was also coping with the financial restrictions of his studenthood. A three-course lunch at the Union may have cost a modest ninepence (less than four pence in modern money) but there was still the need to carry a snack lunch from home.

Seeking a quiet place to eat it, he found an ideal location in the Art Gallery, just across Kelvingrove Park from the university.

Lunch had to be taken surreptitiously between tours by attendants and, even though the place was quieter around midday, it was prudent to be seen at least gazing at the pictures in the gallery. Fate has its wily ways, as can be gathered from the fact that Tom Honeyman began to be more and more aware of what he was viewing. His favourites were the 19th century narrative paintings, such as Millais' "The Ornithologist" and Pettie's "Two Strings to Her Bow".

He thought Rembrandt's "Man in Armour" was wonderful, though he later confessed he thought that that was the right kind of view to take! Actually, he could have seen very little art in the picture since it was quite filthy, as later events would prove. The Dutch Room, packed with paintings, generally left him unmoved but the Italian Room was much more exciting. If Whistler's portrait of Thomas Carlyle was a special favourite, much of the painting left him cold and he was to decide that aesthetic standard hardly existed at the time.

The Kelvingrove Gallery and Museum had opened as recently as 1902, following the International Exhibition of the previous year, so the novelty of it was still fresh.

Away from his lunchtimes—and although unable to afford the wide range of student activity—Tom seldom missed the student rags. The most notorious event was the "Bodie Riot", involving an extraordinary character known as Dr Walford Bodie MD, a vaudeville entertainer whose old home in Macduff, in the North-east, can still be seen.

With a combination of hypnotism, manipulative surgery and electrical stunts, Doctor Bodie undertook to give a new lease of life to the incurable. In the course of a civil action, he admitted he had no medical qualification and that the initials MD stood for nothing more than "Merry Devil".

Tom Honeyman had nevertheless shared the public's fascination with Bodie, though he still went on to play a minor part in the Riot. Despite his friendship with James Bridie, he felt the playwright's account of that uproar, as given in his autobiography, was neither accurate nor fair. Honeyman gave his own version of it.

Walford Bodie was due to appear at the Coliseum Music Hall in Glasgow, having previously adopted a critical attitude to the medical profession. Students of the university decided to register their protest and did so on the Monday evening by staging a demonstration which wrecked Bodie's act.

The showman's response was to castigate the "Carnegie Cads" as he called them, a reference to the financial assistance available to students from the trust funds of Andrew Carnegie, the Scottish-American philanthropist. This was too much for the budding medics. They planned to assemble at the first house on the Thursday for what would be a "peaceful gathering", a coded message to bring along the usual rectorial ammunition, which meant that peaceful was spelled "peasful".

The earlier acts were greeted with ovations which must have astounded them. Then the curtain rose on Doctor Bodie, as the flamboyant figure made his entrance amid glittering paraphernalia, accompanied by his charming lady assistant, La Belle Electra. Then the storm broke.

The din and dust of flying missiles was overwhelming, with the ammunition of animal and vegetable creating a scene of pandemonium. As the curtain was dropped to save further damage, the students rushed the stage and ripped a hole in it, only to be faced with a body of stalwart policemen who had already been alerted to the situation.

As the second house was abandoned, arrests were made and the students reassembled outside the theatre, the lust for blood unappeased as they resolved to march upon the citadels of other practising charlatans while they were at it. The marching song arose spontaneously as "Bodie, Bodie, Bodie, Quack, Quack, Quack!" but the other targets were now in sight.

A prime victim would be the notorious "Professor" Eastbourne, who claimed to cure all manner of venereal diseases, known and unknown. Though he lived in luxury in Helensburgh, he consulted in rooms at Berkeley Street, Glasgow. Eastbourne was indeed a menace, not above resorting to blackmail with his scared and miserable young victims by threatening to send the bill to their fathers. He eventually got his deserts. Some years later, while acting as a relief medical officer at Barlinnie Prison, Tom Honeyman administered to a sick inmate who turned out to be none other than the notorious "Professor".

Reflecting on that theatrical spree which developed into an orgy, Tom would confess to qualms and regrets over what happened that night. Indeed his sympathies switched to the side of Bodie. As he stood there, one man against the mob, there was a sense of shame in what was going on. Student life would always have its juvenile excesses but that riot was said to have broken Doctor Bodie completely.

Tom Honeyman later pointed out that the man had never claimed to be anything other than a showman, versatile in ventriloquism, hypnotism and cage-of-death electrical stunts. He met Bodie several years later and, while he was not much impressed by his personality, he found his range of experience a matter of considerable interest. Bodie had said he bore ill-will to no-one. It was just one of those breaks. While Tom had no time for Eastbourne, he did feel sorry that the Bodie Riot had ever taken place.

Such was the temperature of student life in the years leading up to the First World War, involving many a young man who would see little more of life—and indicating that that earlier generation had nothing to learn from some of the wild adventures more commonly associated with universities in the middle part of the century.

Tom Honeyman regarded himself lucky to have been around in that particular period. The only fly in the ointment was that lack of pocket money, in which department he continued to be less well provided than most of his contemporaries.

VI

NIGHT OF THE 'TITANIC'

THE QUESTION of remuneration crops up as a recurring theme, almost a complex, in much of Tom Honeyman's recollection. While many a student of his day had to augment the income to save parental embarrassment, he acknowledged that most of them seemed better equipped to do so without losing sight of the main objective—the professional examinations and the eventual degree.

Perhaps he was excusing himself for some unexplained blanks in his university career when he wrote: "I found it difficult to resist outside interests, especially if they were remunerative. I believe now that I was cheating myself with the belief that my main consideration was to ease the financial problems at home. Actually many things were happening around me and I was curious and eager to add to experience and did not seem aware of the fact that I was running in and out of dead-ends."

Among his money-earning efforts was a job of "holding copy" at the *Glasgow Herald*. That is to say, he was an assistant proof-reader. It was an interesting enough job, more mechanical than creative but calling for the accuracy and intelligence which newspaper editors expected to find in students.

From seven in the evening till well past midnight, at the old *Herald* offices in Mitchell Street, Tom would find himself reading all kinds of scripts, however illegible, and sniffing at smelling salts just to keep himself awake. He worked for three nights a week at a pay-rate of 3s. 10d. per night, less than 20p today.

On one of those nights, in April of 1912, he was working away at his proofreading when the wires began to buzz with news of the *Titanic* disaster. He recorded his impressions:

"When the incredible news came through, an indefinable sensation of unutterable horror seemed to travel through the building. I walked home in the darkness in the company of dreadful images of people struggling for life and losing it. My father, who called me a greeting from his room, had difficulty in accepting the news as fact. When he did so, I heard him say, 'I hope W. T. Stead is saved.' But his hope was not realised."

Stead was the famous journalist and reformer who wrote *If Christ Came to Chicago* and *The Americanisation of the World.*

Tom Honeyman found himself drifting into the company of painters and sculptors, whose studio gossip stimulated him to an awareness of territory worth exploring. This led him to an evening class at Glasgow School of Art for which he managed to gain reimbursement of his class fee. The School of Art had been completed around the same time as the Art Gallery but, whereas he regarded the latter as fifty years behind the times, with little distinction as a work of art, the School was a masterpiece, fifty years ahead of its time.

The Principal of the Art School was Francis Newbery, a kenspeckle figure in sugar-loaf hat, with deliberate gait and alert attitude as he walked along Sauchiehall Street. More significantly, as head of the previous School of Art, he had helped raise funds for the new one—and is said to have been the person who persuaded a young Charles Rennie Mackintosh to enter the competition for its architecture. The rest of that story is history.

Newbery welcomed Tom Honeyman graciously and expressed the view that a course in art would be a worthwhile addition to the medical curriculum. Honeyman let him down badly with irregular attendance. At home they were amused by one of his charcoal drawings, a nude model, which was hung close to the telephone and suffered the indignity of being used as a scribbling pad for telephone numbers!

But if Tom was lacking diligence in his art studies, he was causing more concern at home with a lack of application to his medical course. It wasn't a case of failing examinations but simply that he wasn't sitting them.

With his mother serving on some social committees along with the mother of O. H. Mavor, his hero, some allowance was made through the fact that the future James Bridie was not exactly setting the scholastic heather on fire either. When Mavor's failure in anatomy was turned to success, however, there was trouble in store for Honeyman.

VII

THE MISSING YEARS

TOM HONEYMAN had entered a strangely wayward phase of his life, a two-year period in which he deserted his medical studies and began wandering far from home. His proofreading on the *Glasgow Herald* extended to writing doggerel for Christmas and greetings cards before he found himself in Bradford, tempted by another student who was making big money in selling correspondence courses. Long tramps at weekends took him into the fascination of the Bronte country as he sought to straighten out his life.

Those Sundays on the Yorkshire moors gave him some hint of what people meant when they spoke of "purpose in the art of living". Searching in vain for some signposts in his life, he followed one which took him to London, finding distaste in the work he was doing. He realised he was landing many youngsters with the financial burden of a correspondence course even after they had given it up. Ironically, he was also urging them to do something he had failed to do himself. That was when Tom Honeyman came to the conclusion that would echo along the years as he rose to eminence: When a job becomes distasteful, QUIT.

Arriving in London with £3.10s in his pocket, he managed to survive the first few weeks, during which he discovered the art galleries of the capital. Then he found a job selling fire extinguishers, along with a colleague who would become well-known as a member of parliament, as well as Lord Provost of Edinburgh. He was the unmistakable figure of the future Sir Will Y. Darling.

From his base in the beautiful Dorset village of Wimborne he cycled round the countryside till an accident landed him in hospital. That was when he came to reflect on how far from home he really was. His boss discovered his background and promptly sent him to work in Scotland, based in the Moray Firth town of Buckie. There he succeeded in selling fire extinguishers not only to farmers but even to the Buckie Fire Brigade!

That was the poignant moment when his mother appeared on the scene and he agreed it was time to get his life together again and resume his medical studies at Glasgow University. That was when the prodigal son returned to the fold, buckled down to his course and, emerging from this grey area of his life, promised his father that he would respect the principles of total abstinence for which the family stood so firmly. Whatever the truth of those mystery years, Tom had seen enough of alcoholic consequences to place him on the side of temperance and he had no difficulty in supporting the family tradition for the rest of his life.

This time there would be no vacation jobs to earn money. Instead he would spend the time in laboratories and libraries—and that was what he was doing when the First World War broke out in August 1914, a year after his return. In the general rush to join the army, medical students within sight of their finals were rejected, since qualified doctors would soon be in demand. Within a year, hospitals were being staffed by house surgeons and final-year students in round-the-clock marathons for which the only stimulants were endless cups of tea and mild flirtations with nurses in the kitchen. Tom's room at the Western Infirmary became a minor picture gallery, decorated with recently published etchings by Bone, Cameron, Bauer and McBey. What is more, he was once again in touch with Duncan Macdonald, whose first step towards that international reputation as an art dealer had been a junior assistant's job with George Davidson of Sauchiehall Street.

They dealt mainly in the work of living Scottish artists, with E. A. Hornel and W. A. Gibson the best sellers. Now and then a Raeburn portrait would crop up and an Old Master might pass through their hands. Tom knew very little about the firm until a craze for etchings began to afflict Glasgow businessmen and doctors. In his final year he made his very first art purchase, an etching by the highly talented Aberdeenshire painter, James McBey. Guided by his old friend Duncan, he would then pick up etchings by the famous Swedish artist Anders Zorn, not that he could ever afford these purchases. But credit was long and, in the certainty that the value would have risen within six months, there was no real risk involved.

That was how he was able to decorate his room at the Western and acquire an unwarranted reputation as an expert on art. By arrangement with Duncan Macdonald, he had to be ready to part with his treasures on demand, having made a profit even before they were paid for. It was an easy way to make money and Tom Honeyman later acknowledged that it had virtually marked his entry to the realms of art dealing.

He recalled acquiring two fine prints by Zorn, a self-portrait and "The Swan", a lovely nude. The staff nurse accepted his invitation to see them but, to his surprise, then expressed indignation and was convinced his motives in displaying the picture of a nude were wickedly ulterior. It was some time before he came to appreciate the hidden meaning behind "Come up and see my etchings sometime!"

With the onset of the First World War the bottom fell out of the art market and Duncan Macdonald found his job in jeopardy. Rejected for the army on medical grounds, he moved to Nelson's, a small firm in Edinburgh. Tom Honeyman would join him at studio parties in the capital but this time the social intercourse did not divert him from the main job in hand.

In 1916 he gained his degree in medicine and surgery and was immediately posted to the Royal Army Medical Corps. His uniform was made by Richard Gunn, brother of the famous portrait painter James Gunn, and when he arrived at the depot at Ripon in Yorkshire, he encountered another well-known name in the camp adjutant who was John Glaister, destined to follow his worthy father as Professor of Forensic Medicine at Glasgow.

In a fortnight at Ripon he was licked into presentable shape and dispatched to the Salonika front, as a doctor in the 42nd General Hospital. Before leaving, he had suggested to a young lady called Victoria Catherine Burnett, a minister's daughter, that they might get married when the war was over. In the interests of the concert party in Salonika, the same Cath sent out a regular flow of entertainment material, not least a new book by Robert Service, *Rhymes of a Red Cross Man*, from which Tom extracted "Soulful Sam", a party piece which was to last him for years.

For all the vast number of soldiers in the First World War, there were endless stories about the coincidence of meetings. When Tom Honeyman succumbed to an attack of fever, the man who came to take his place was Professor A. J. Ballantyne, a distinguished ophthalmic surgeon from Glasgow who had taught him the little he knew about the eyes. Then one of his RAMC sergeants turned out to be Christopher Grieve, later to be known as Hugh MacDiarmid, one of Scotland's greatest poets.

VIII

WHY FRANK WAS SELLING BRICKS

WHEN the First World War ended in 1918, Tom Honeyman was demobilised without delay. Glasgow University was desperately short of teaching staff and he was appointed assistant to Professor Noel Paton in 1919. If his qualifications as a teacher were not robust, he did have a loud voice and he would jest about covering ignorance with belligerence. Not that he was joking entirely. Indeed he would often make the point that he had known many examples where emphasis had been used as a substitute for argument.

Nevertheless he was happy in his work, adoring his new chief, whereas he had been rather scared of Noel Paton when he was a student. The basic pay for a university assistant in the early 1920s was £150 per annum but Tom realised that, to follow through his plans for marriage, he should have a spell in general practice while keeping a foot in the academic field.

He gained a staff appointment at Glasgow Royal Infirmary, held a part-time assistantship to the Professor of Medicine, Walter K. Hunter, and had a busy general practice in the Dennistoun-Bridgeton district of the city. He and Cath were now married and had set up their first home in Dennistoun.

He recorded that the financial rewards of hospital work were very nominal but that his private practice was "quite lucrative".

As a man of energy and ambition he had his sights set on becoming a consultant and, towards that end, moved house across town to Lynedoch Place in the West End, which could have been classed as Glasgow's Harley Street of the time.

About his happy time at the Royal Infirmary, he made a number of observations, the first of which would be heartily endorsed by those of us who arrived in Glasgow from the fresh fields of places like Foresterhill in Aberdeen, where hospitals were untroubled by the hazards of industrial grime.

Honeyman merely emphasised the fact that the Royal Infirmary in Glasgow was built in the wrong place. Apart from its distressing effect on Glasgow Cathedral nearby, the structure was so solidly permanent that it was soon out of date. The outside noise from passing traffic was so acute in his time that when the chief did his rounds, all windows had to be closed.

All that apart, Honeyman was appalled that, when they planned the building, the powers-that-be rejected all efforts to retain the original ward where the great Joseph Lister made his discovery of antiseptic surgery. With a little foresight they would have had a wonderful memorial to a great man, an attraction for doctors and surgeons from all over the world.

When they finally demolished the Lister Ward, a well-known character in the pathology laboratory, Frank the attendant, embarked on a private enterprise of his own. Sending bricks to the many people who wrote and asked him for a memento of the historic ward, he soon found he was on to a good thing. But as the requests continued to pour in, the bricks ran out. Frank was not to be denied his lucrative enterprise, however. It was not difficult to find bricks in Glasgow and for a long time afterwards, until someone tumbled to his fraudulent scheme, Frank did a roaring business in Lister bricks!

Tom Honeyman appreciated the humour of the situation and said it reminded him of the story from his art-dealing days:

"Corot in his lifetime painted 5000 pictures, of which no fewer than 6000 are in the State of New York."

When the Honeymans moved to Lynedoch Place they would count among their neighbours Dr O. H. Mavor who had given up his general practice in Langside and was now on the visiting staff of the Victoria Infirmary. By the time of renewing this acquaintance from university days, Mavor was already gaining fame as playwright James Bridie and had some difficulty in deciding whether and when he should give up medicine altogether. Honeyman thought he should have done it sooner. There was much pressure on Bridie to move south and Honeyman made the point that it would have been greatly to his financial benefit to be operating from the centre of things, theatrically speaking. However, the man himself never departed from the conviction that he could best help to revive the theatre in Scotland by staying there.

Despite the pressure of professional work, Tom Honeyman was devoting a lot of his own time and thought to the amateur stage. His only sister, who became Queenie McPherson, took an active part in producing for the Milngavie Players while his younger brother, who would turn professional as Murray Macdonald, was gaining a reputation in Glasgow for squeezing a surprising amount of quality out of bad old plays and very bad actors.

The Albany Players, having been founded by Murray, continued as a family concern even after he had departed the Scottish scene. In putting on his first Scottish production of Bridie's *What It Is To Be Young*, Tom played the part of an irascible old general and so terrified his seven-year-old daughter that she would hardly speak to him for days. It may have seemed a fairly localised production but it did have the privilege of being seen by C. B. Cochran, the leading London impresario of the day.

His role in amateur dramatics no doubt helped to develop Tom Honeyman's skills in public speaking. In pinpointing the platform on which he practised his art, we discover much about the way

Glaswegians used to spend their Sunday evenings in the days before television and bingo.

The manager of the Glasgow Corporation Halls, Walter Freer, ran a series of Pleasant Sunday Evenings, as they were called, when crowds of 3000 would turn out at the St Andrews Halls. The popularity became so great that they had to be extended to the Coliseum Theatre on the South Side. Those concerts featured singers and instrumentalists and sometimes a well-known star on the way down; but there was always a speaker on some topical issue and that was where Tom gained his experience of facing a large audience.

It was his gateway to the public platform which was liable in years to come to take him anywhere from Glasgow to New York.

IX

THE VAN GOGH CONNECTION

TOM HONEYMAN'S renewal of contact with Duncan Macdonald, dating back to choir days at Cowcaddens Church, was another of those quirks of fate which somehow point the way to our destiny. By 1926 both men were happily married, Honeyman practising as a doctor in the East End of Glasgow and Macdonald now returning from Edinburgh to join the art business of Reid and Lefevre in West George Street.

By chance, Tom Honeyman was the family doctor of McNeill Reid, whose father, Alexander Reid, founded this prestigious firm and was still in evidence when Dr Tom began to frequent the West George Street premises. It was some time later before he realised the full significance of Alex Reid, a man with whom he had merely exchanged courteous greetings. The fact that this gentleman had mixed in the Paris art set of Van Gogh and Toulouse-Lautrec—and had named his son after his friend Whistler (James Abbott McNeill)—were revelations in store.

More immediately, old Alexander Reid had reached the conclusion that art dealing in a big way in Scotland was likely to peter out. The family businesses which had produced fortunes for their owners were now becoming public companies and in many cases control was passing to London. The new generation of wealthy families was either not interested in art or was so often in London spending its leisure time that it was easier to look at pictures there, and in greater variety.

With the death of Alexander Reid in 1928, at the age of seventy-three, his son McNeill, along with partner Duncan Macdonald, went ahead with the intended move south. They would continue in Glasgow for the remainder of the lease so they would have to find someone to run the Scottish end of the business. The man for the job, they agreed, was Dr Tom Honeyman.

When the proposition was put to him he was clearly faced with the dilemma of a man who was making his way successfully in medicine, with thoughts of becoming a consultant, but was now confronted with an entirely new opportunity in life.

Was it a risk worth taking? Artist friend James McBey was among those who gave encouragement, as did his own wife Cath. The people most in need of convincing were Tom's parents, especially his mother, who believed that giving up medicine for any other profession was nothing short of insanity. He took her for a long walk and recalled how he had kept his promise to go back to his medical studies and to see that his name would one day be seen on a brass plate in the West End of Glasgow. But now there was another opportunity beckoning, with the prospect of travel and fresh adventure.

His mother sighed and smiled and said: "I suppose it's the dark streak in you!"

Thus Tom Honeyman gave up his career in medicine and became an art dealer in 1929. But to gain the full flavour of what was in store, we need to pick up the story of the company he was joining: Reid and Lefevre. That means examining more closely the remarkable life story of the same Alexander Reid who gave his name to the company.

Reid was born in Glasgow in 1854 and became an apprentice in his father's prosperous firm of Kay and Reid who were frame-makers, carvers and gilders, art dealers in a very small way, but most of all ships' outfitters. They provided the wooden furnishings and those elaborate figureheads for the steamships then being built in large numbers on the River Clyde.

The elder of two sons in the business, Alex was mainly interested in the picture-dealing side, which he tried to develop as his personal concern, though with considerable opposition from his father. In 1882, however, the workshop at 97 Dumbarton Road was destroyed by fire and James Reid discovered to his horror that he had been negligent about insurance and was liable for the losses out of his own pocket, including compensation for clients who had deposited paintings for sale. Facing financial ruin, he chose to put the firm into liquidation, knowing he was past the stage of rebuilding it and that his sons did not have the will to do so.

Meanwhile, young Alex, who had started painting and wanted to be an art dealer, decided that the way to advance such a career was to head for Paris, which he did in 1886. Settling into his new environment, he found work with the art dealing firm of Boussod and Valedon at its premises on the Boulevard des Italiens. But the fascinating part of this appointment was the discovery that the young manager was a chap called Theo Van Gogh, who had moved from Holland to Paris the previous year and was already making the acquaintance of the contemporary French artists. He had met several of the Impressionist circle and was now getting to know the younger members of the post-Impressionist generation, who were bringing in their pictures in the hope of a sale and would gather in the gallery to discuss what they were doing.

Young Reid was thus well placed not only to see a broad range of nineteenth century painting but to eavesdrop on the conversation of some great names in the making. With his own painting ambitions, he gained much advice about the free academies where he could work. As if all this were not enough for a young Glasgow man seeking to make his way in a strange city, his boss suggested he should share an apartment with his brother, the still unknown and penniless Vincent Van Gogh!

Thus the Glaswegian moved into rooms at 6 Place d'Anvers, with the man destined to become one of the greatest names in the history of art. This daily involvement with the Van Gogh brothers, at home and at work, brought him an ever wider circle of connections in the art world. Alexander Reid was now mixing with people like Toulouse-Lautrec and Emile Bernard, visiting galleries, museums and exhibitions and meeting up with Gauguin just before he left for Martinique.

Reid and Van Gogh used to spend their Sundays on painting expeditions in the suburbs of Paris and on one such outing, in the autumn of 1887, they were on their way to Gare St Lazare when they saw a basketful of gloriously red apples outside a shop. As they stopped for a closer look, Vincent said he would love to paint those apples.

"Then why not go in and buy them?" asked the Glaswegian.

"I haven't enough money," said Van Gogh.

So Alex Reid bought the basket of apples and suggested they could be delivered to the studio. But Van Gogh was having none of it. The urge upon him was so strong that he grabbed the basket and rushed off to the studio, leaving his friend to go painting on his own. When Alex Reid arrived back at the end of the day Van Gogh presented him with his painting of the apples. After all, he had bought them.

The two men were having their separate troubles, Vincent constantly out of money and Alex Reid having fallen out with his sweetheart. One day Reid opened up his heart to Van Gogh who promptly suggested a suicide pact! On reflection, it presaged things to come. But the canny Scot had retained enough sense to know that nothing quite merited such a drastic solution and he prepared to face the future more boldly.

During 1887 Van Gogh painted at least two, and possibly four, portraits of his Glasgow friend, giving him one as a present. On a visit back home, Alex Reid took with him both the portrait and the picture of the apples. They were left for safe-keeping with his father, who apparently thought they were no good—and promptly disposed of them both to a passing French dealer for £10!

It was left to Alexander Reid's son, McNeill, to retrieve the situation. In a catalogue published in 1928 (the year of his father's death), there were numerous Van Gogh items listed as "self-portrait". But the likeness between the artist and his Glasgow flatmate was really quite astonishing and McNeill Reid managed to identify two of them as being portraits of his father. They had been in the possession of Van Gogh's nephew, son of Theo, from whom he succeeded in making a purchase.

So a Van Gogh painting of Alexander Reid thus found its way back to his family. How it finally landed in Glasgow Art Gallery is a matter to which we shall return.

Vincent Van Gogh's idealism led him into numerous conflicts and the friendship with Alex Reid did not escape. The Dutchman thought dealers should be investing their profits in young artists and, because of Reid's good contacts with influential industrialists back home, he felt the Scot could do more to convince them of the potential importance of his Parisian friends.

But Reid had a good idea of what those collectors would buy and was cautious of committing himself to such a purpose. Van Gogh's resentment of Reid's caution was intensified when he discovered that he was accumulating a collection of the work of Monticelli for very little, when it had been the Van Gogh brothers who aroused his interest in the first place, knowing these paintings were bound to rise steeply in value.

If Vincent had survived, however, he would have seen what Alex Reid did to promote the cause of those French painters of the Impressionist and post-Impressionist generations in the years ahead.

Sadly he died in 1890 at the age of thirty-seven, by which time the only picture sold in his lifetime fetched 400 francs. The circumstances leading to his early death became one of the great tragic tales. On leaving his flat-sharing adventure with Alex Reid, he took Lautrec's advice and went off to paint the Provençal landscape at Arles. Having invited Gauguin to found a community of artists there, he entered into a fierce quarrel, threatened Gauguin with a razor and, in a fit of remorse, proceeded to cut off part of his own ear.

He was sent to an asylum but just as he was beginning to gain some recognition, he shot himself at the scene of his last painting, "Cornfields with Flight of Birds". Theo was so distraught that he went into decline and died within six months.

As for the Van Gogh portrait of Alexander Reid, an interesting postscript to the story is provided by Lord Macfarlane of Bearsden, distinguished Scottish businessman and generous patron of the arts.

At a much later date, McNeill Reid and family decided to sell the portrait of his father and earnestly hoped that it would land back in his native Glasgow.

As an outside observer whose opinions were much respected, Lord Macfarlane was asked to accompany Trevor Walden, then Glasgow's Art Gallery Director, to assist in the clinching of a deal. The painting was to be seen at the Lefevre Gallery in London, the successor to Alexander Reid's gallery in Glasgow. Lord Macfarlane ascertained that the asking price was £179,000 but suggested a slightly modified £169,000, which was promptly accepted. He realised that Glasgow had a bargain.

There was no time like the present for transporting it back to its new home so Lord Macfarlane and Trevor Walden wrapped it up and took it with them for the return flight to Glasgow. They booked a seat in the plane from Heathrow and travelled north with the parcel perched between them, that middle seat having been booked in the name of a man called Vincent! The stewardess remarked on the unusual shape of her booked passenger and joked: "Is that an Old Master you have there?" Little did she know!

So the Van Gogh portrait of Alexander Reid arrived back in Glasgow in 1975 and has remained on show at the Kelvingrove Gallery to this day, appropriately at the far end of that room which was named after Dr T. J. Honeyman.

Just as every picture tells a story, you can stand before that image of Alex Reid and marvel at the coincidence of a young man from Glasgow who goes to sample the life of Paris in the 1880s and finds himself in daily domestic contact with one of the greatest artists who ever lived.

X

UNION OF REID AND LEFEVRE

BY the end of 1888 Alexander Reid was back home in Glasgow, having brought with him some of the works of artists like Degas, Corot, Courbet, Daumier and Boudin. But he was not alone in having failed to recognise the genius of his former flatmate. Indeed, even as the literature and mounting values began to surround the name of Vincent Van Gogh, Alex Reid was still surprised that they could be talking about his old friend.

A portrait drawing of Van Gogh had been completed by A. S. R. Hartrick, who wrote: "We thought him a little cracked but harmless, interesting and certainly amusing at times."

With those Paris years of concentrated experience behind him, Reid now felt ready to open his own gallery in Glasgow, which he did in March 1889. He gave it the rather grand name of the Societé des Beaux-Arts, which was to be found at 227 West George Street. It later moved to 124 St Vincent Street and finally to better premises at 117 West George Street. Apart from his art dealing in Scotland, you would find him, in 1892 for example, holding an exhibition of the great French Impressionists in Old Bond Street, London. On that occasion, there were works by Pissarro and Sisley, no fewer than seven by Degas and quite a number by Monticelli.

Back in Glasgow, he was doing brisk business by selling the work of contemporary Scottish artists like Guthrie, McTaggart,

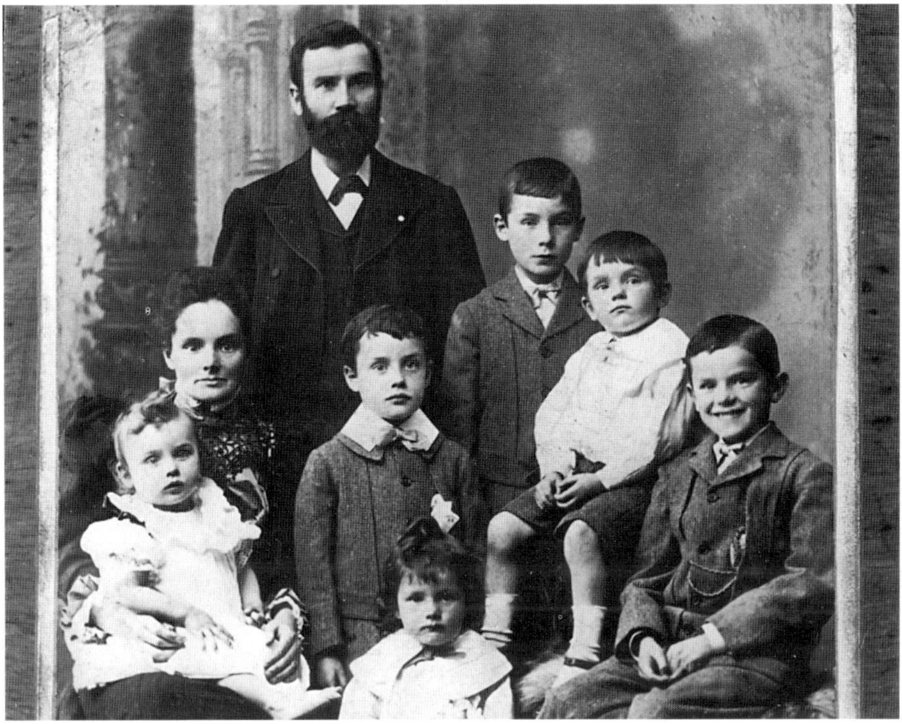

Tom and Elsie Honeyman with their six sons. Young Tom, seated, 2nd on right

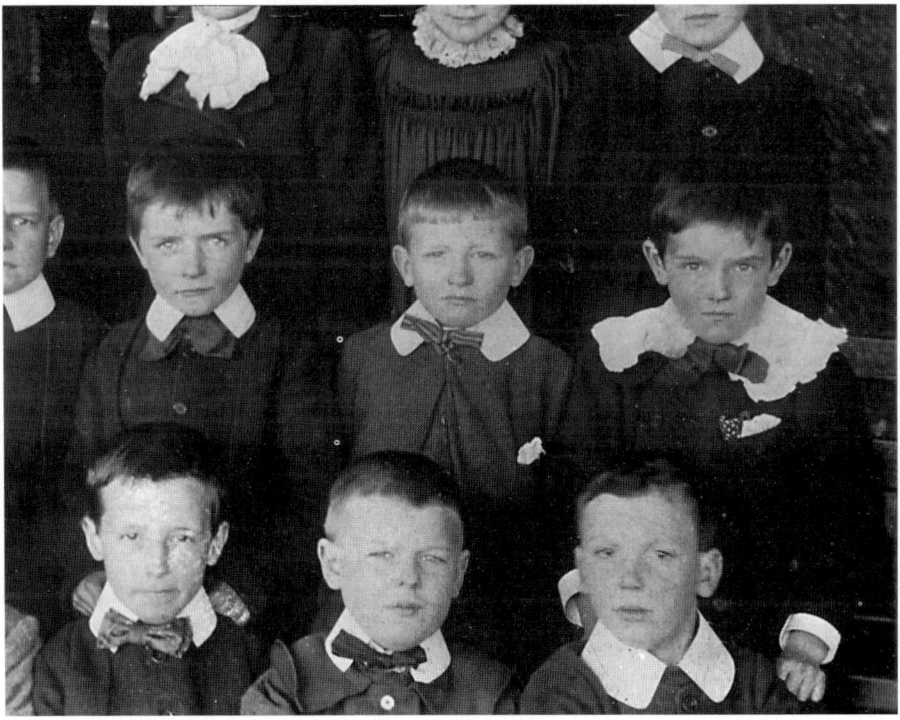

Queen's Park School. Tom, extreme right, middle row

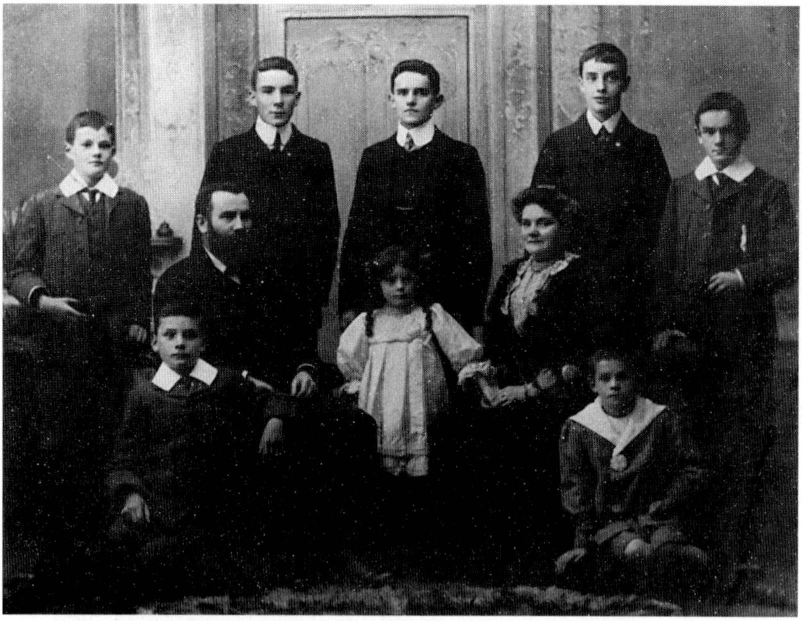

Honeyman family complete with sister Queenie.
Back row: Doddie, Gibbie, Alex, Willie, Tom
Middle row: 'Pa', Queenie, 'Ma'
Front row: Allan, Walter

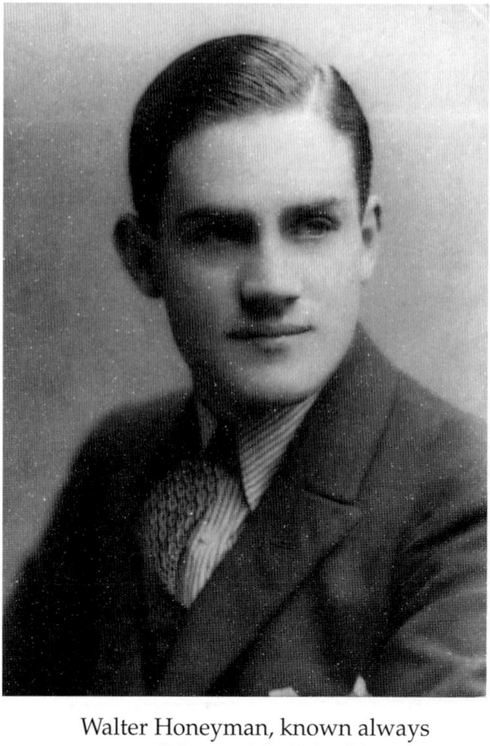

Walter Honeyman, known always as Murray MacDonald, theatrical producer

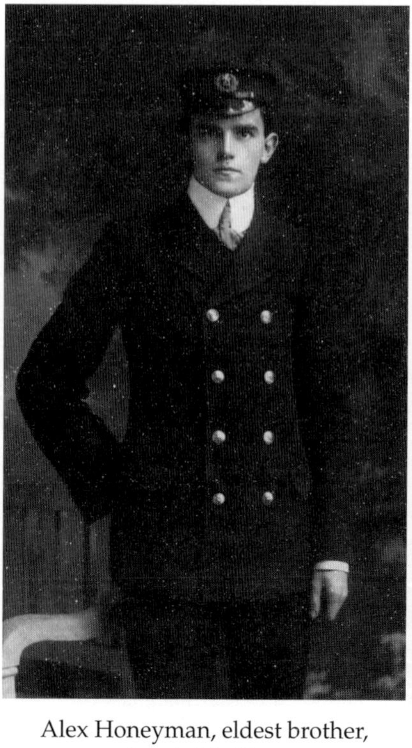

Alex Honeyman, eldest brother, devoted to Tom. Died in an accident in 1909

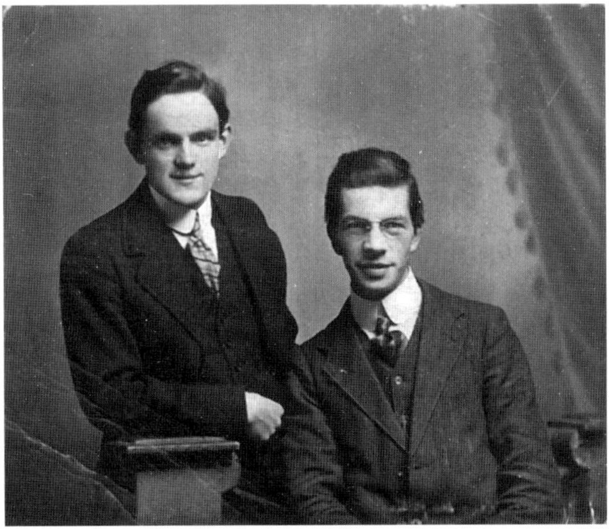

left:
Young friends and later partners in *Reid & Lefevre*—
Tom Honeyman and Duncan Macdonald

below:
Newly graduated—
Dr. Tom John Honeyman in 1916

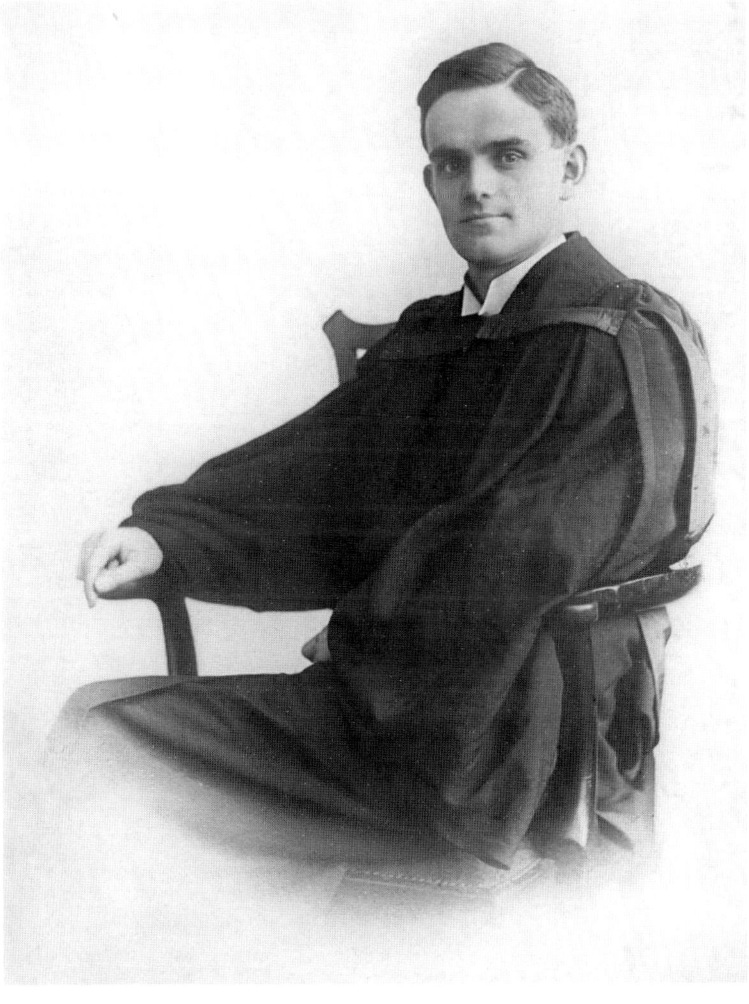

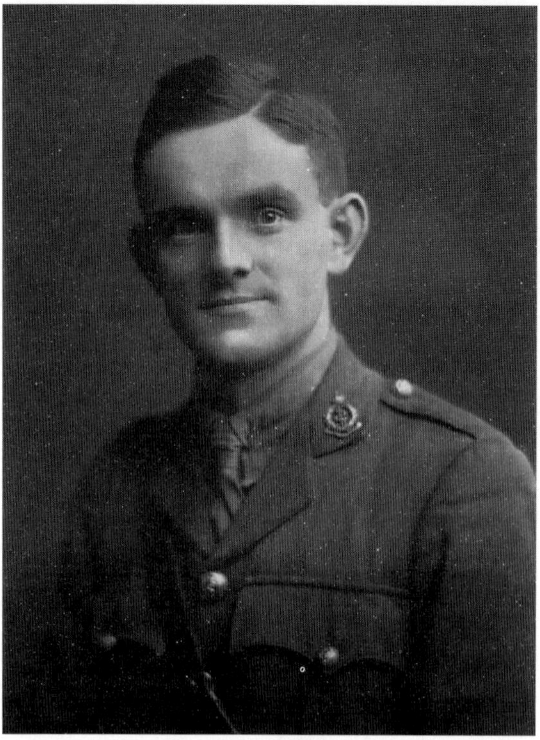

left:
Captain, Royal Army Medical Corps, 1916

below:
Dressing up as Army Chaplain!
Salonika

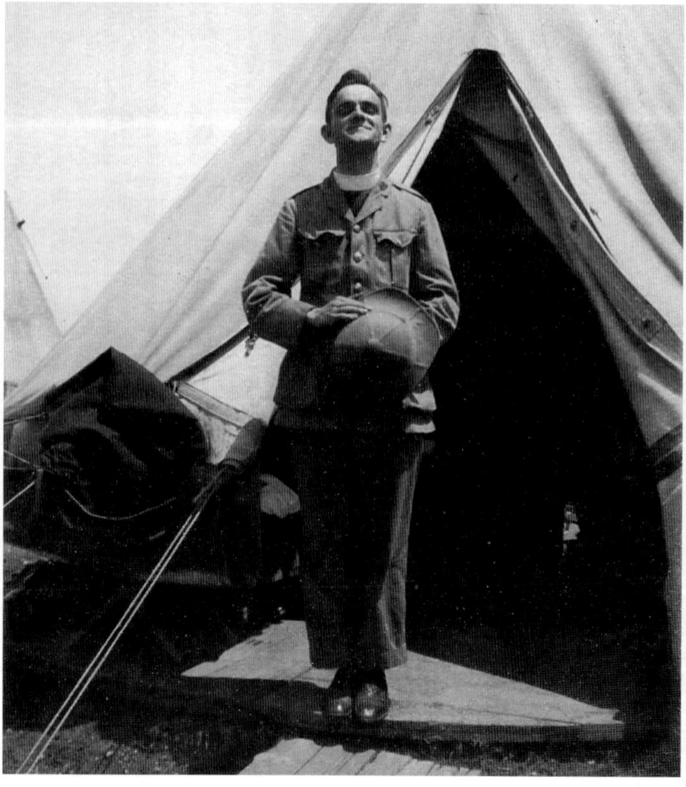

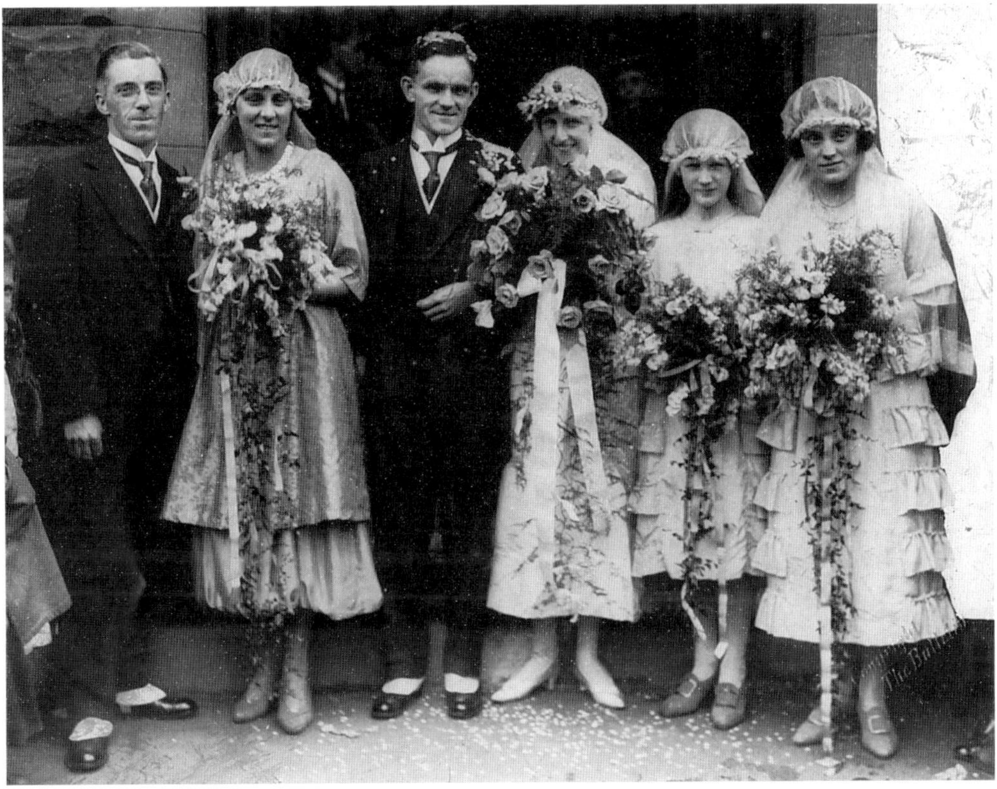

Wedding Group, 24th June, 1920
Best Man: Wilgus Grant
Bridesmaids: Edith Drysdale (best friend), Bride's sister Isabel, Bride's sister-in-law, Queenie

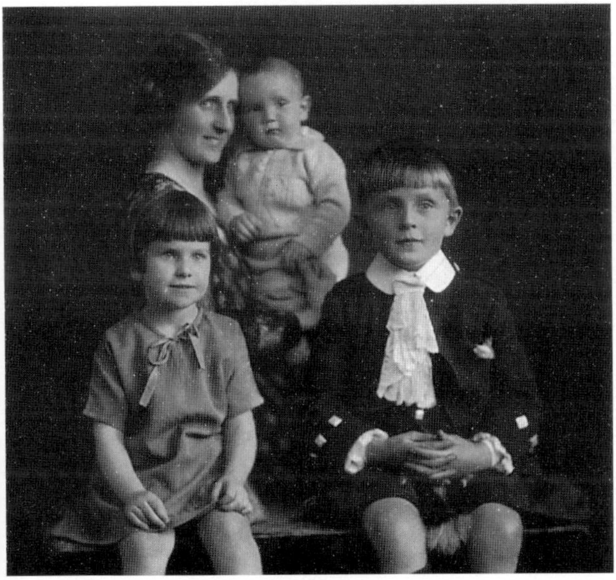

Cathie with baby Grant,
Margaret and Tim

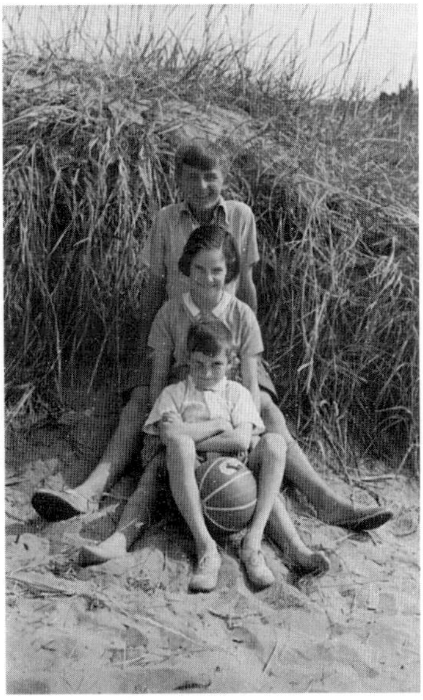

Honeyman children on holiday
at St. Andrews

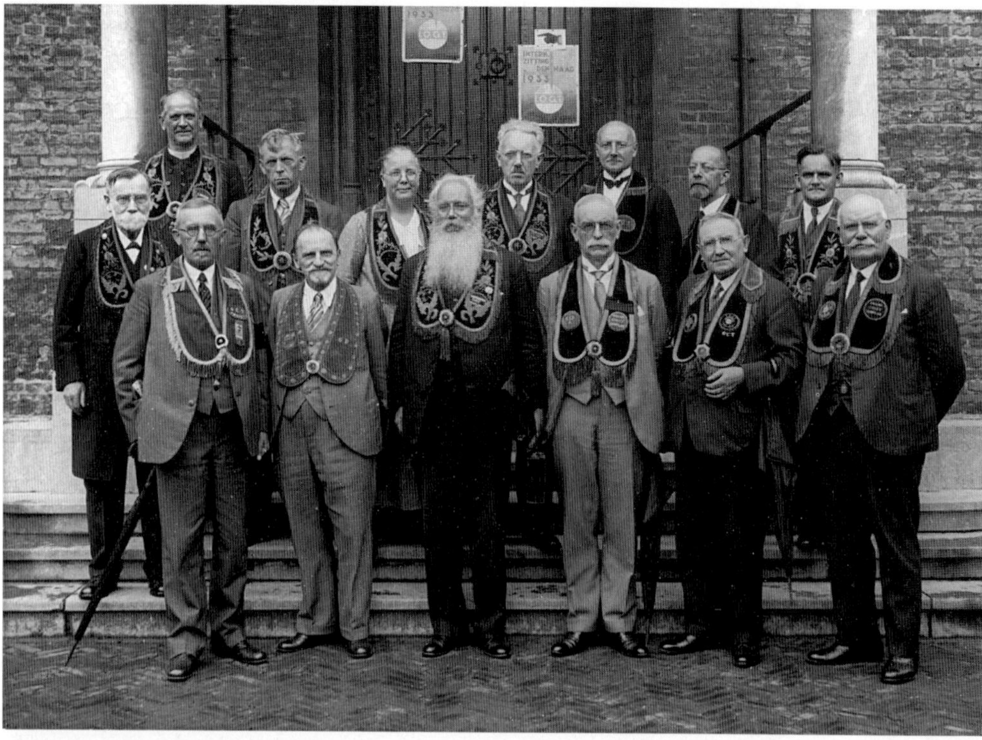

International Order of Good Templars Conference attended by father Tom Honeyman (far left) and son Dr. Tom (back row, far right)

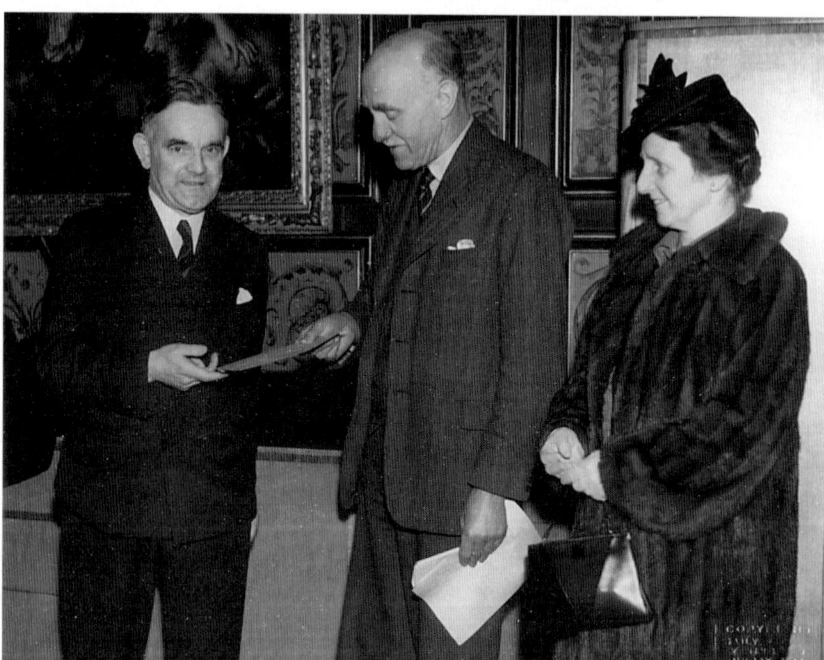

T.J. and wife with Sir James Welsh, Lord Provost of Glasgow, presenting St. Mungo Prize Certificate to T.J. in 1943

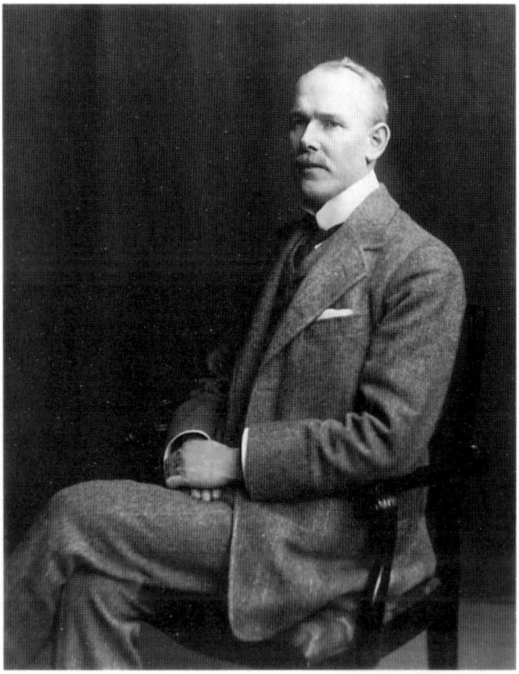

left:
Sir William Burrell

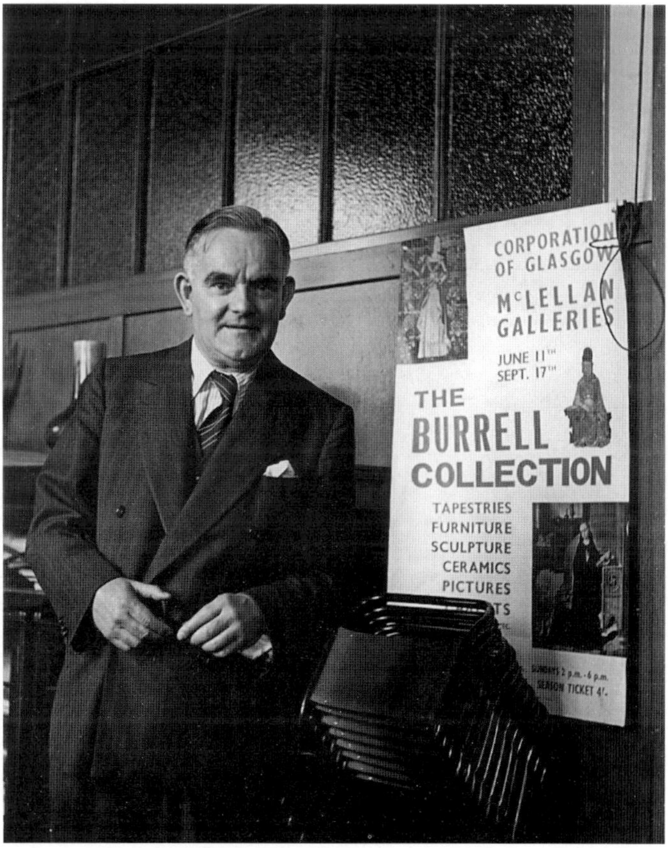

below:
T.J. advertising the first
Burrell Exhibition at
McLellan Galleries, 1949

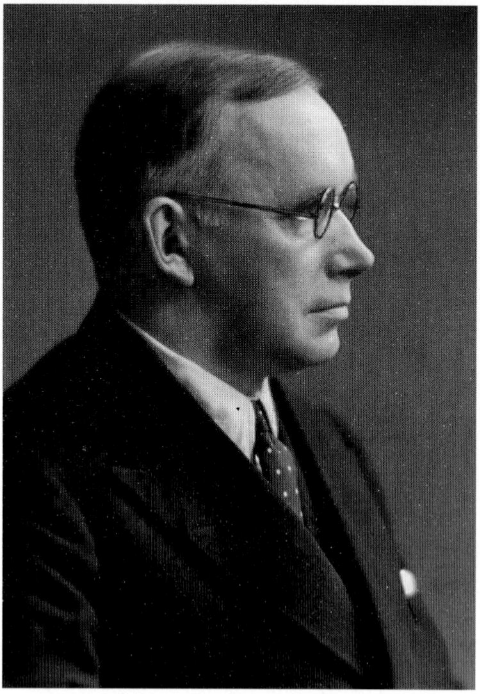

Dr. Osborne H. Mavor (James Bridie)

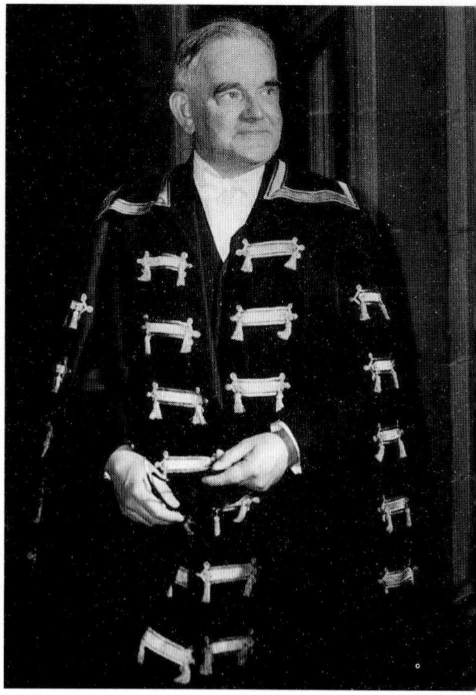

Lord Rector, 1953-1956

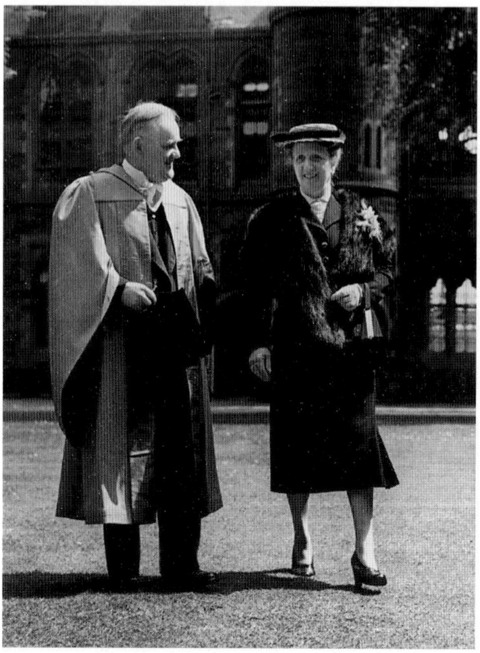

Dr. & Mrs. Honeyman at Glasgow University after LL. D. conferred on T.J. in 1956

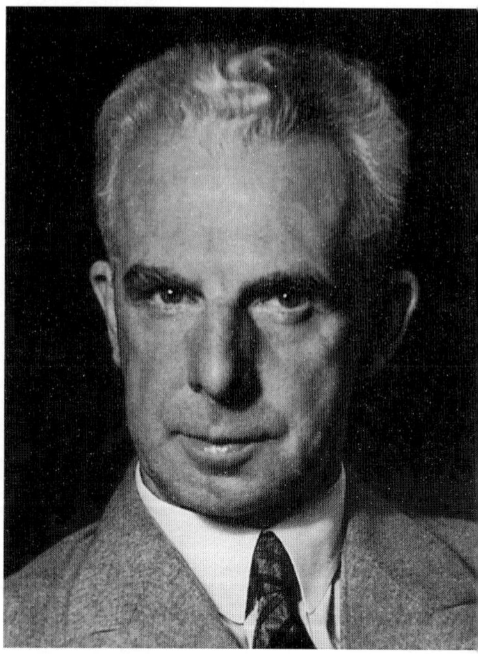

Sir Patrick Dollan, Lord Provost of Glasgow, 1938-1941

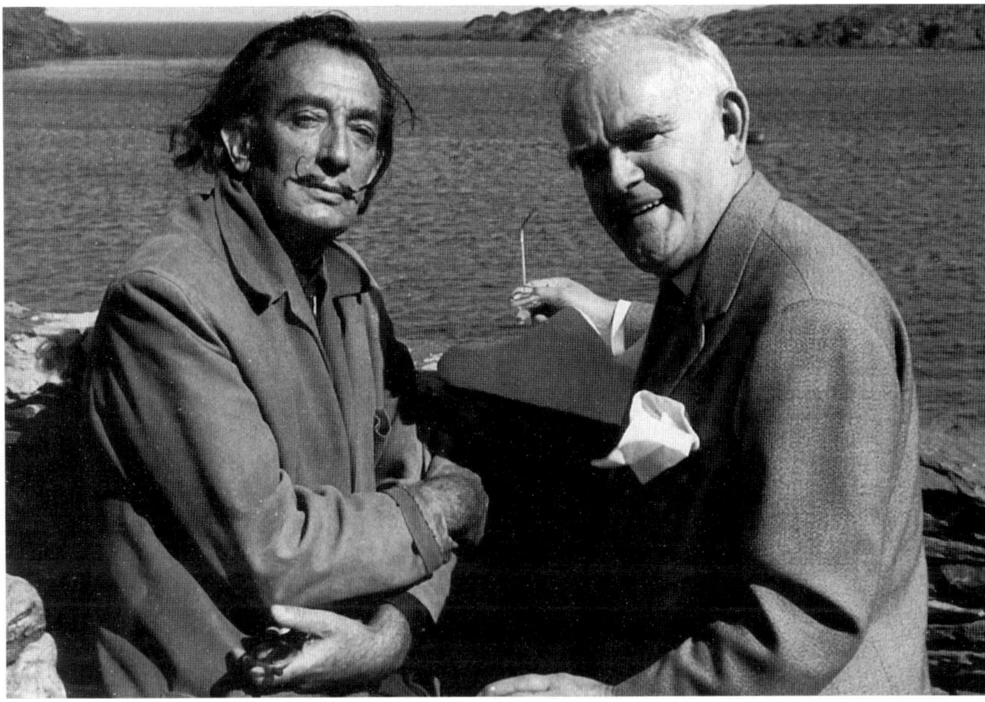

Salvador Dali and T.J. at Port Lligat, 1963

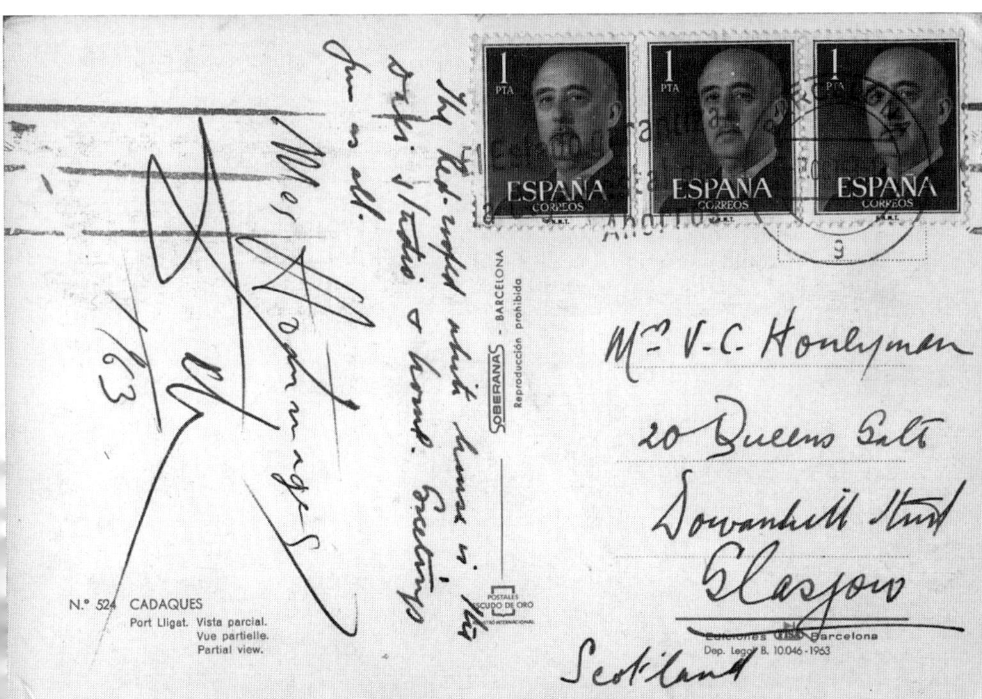

Postcard from T.J. to his wife with greetings also from Salvador Dali

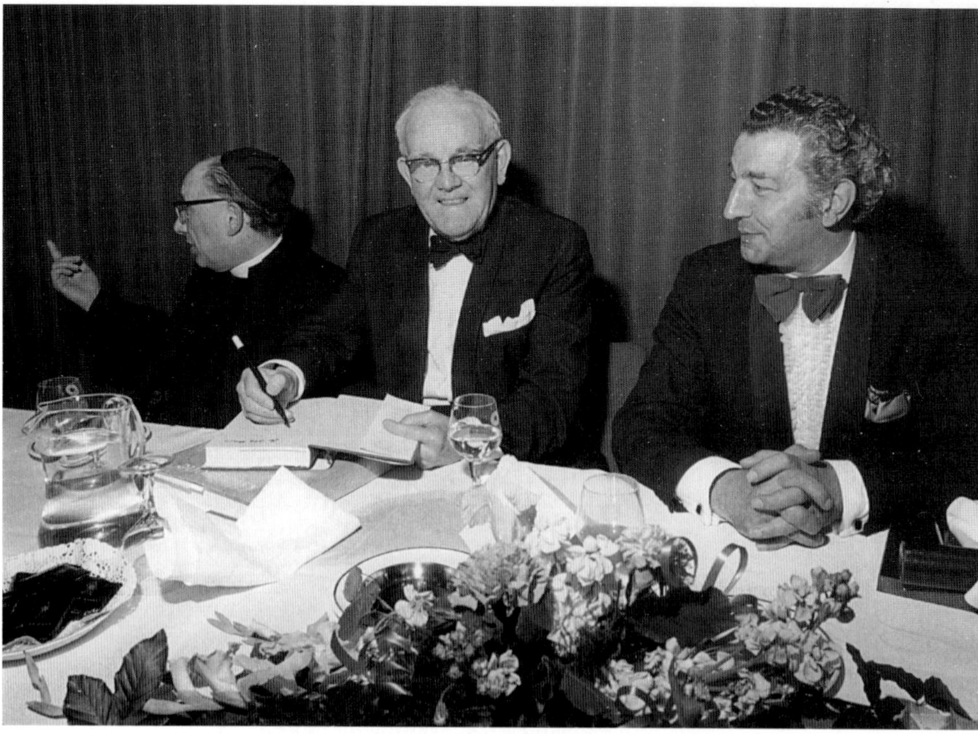

T.J. signing copies of his book *Art & Audacity* with Rev. I. K. Cosgrove (left) and Emilio Coia (right) at T.J.'s 80th birthday party

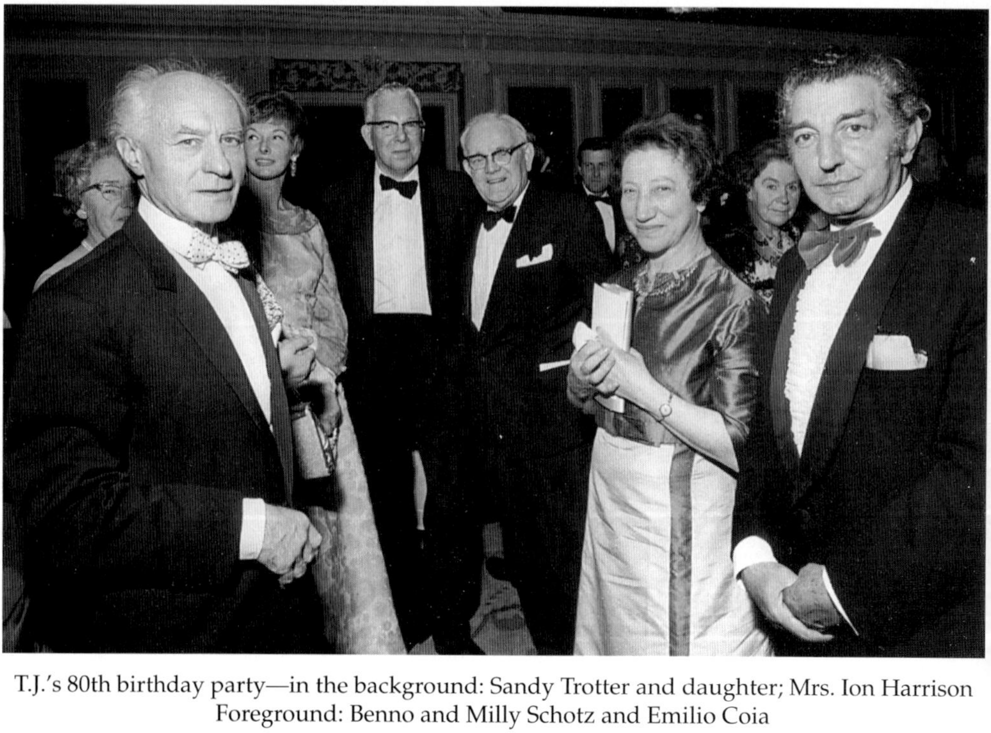

T.J.'s 80th birthday party—in the background: Sandy Trotter and daughter; Mrs. Ion Harrison
Foreground: Benno and Milly Schotz and Emilio Coia

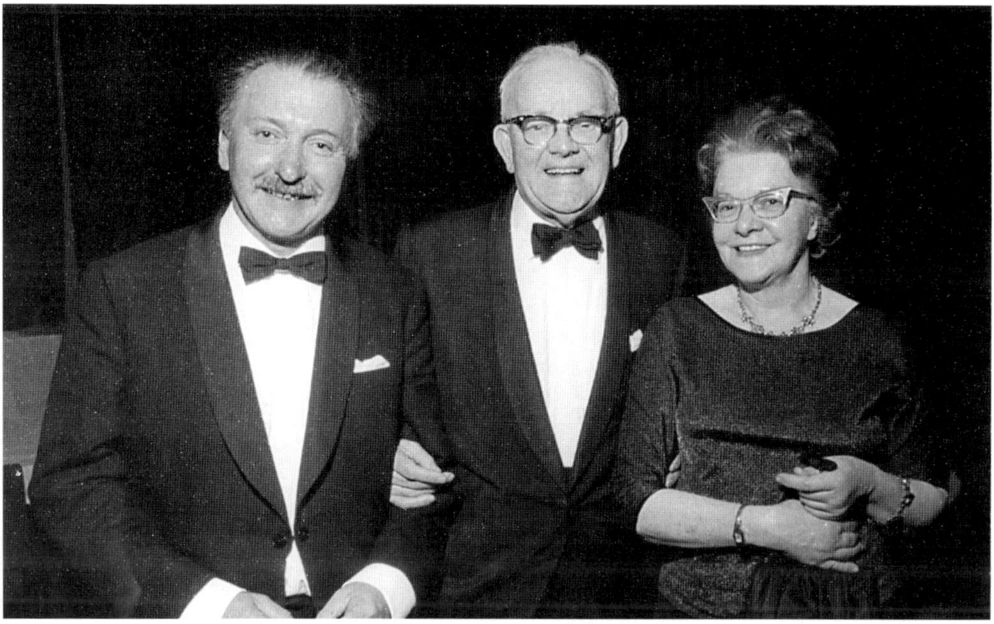

T.J. with Mr. & Mrs. Harry Maclean—Harry was Head of Conservation Dept. and Isabel was T.J.'s secretary at Kelvingrove Art Galleries

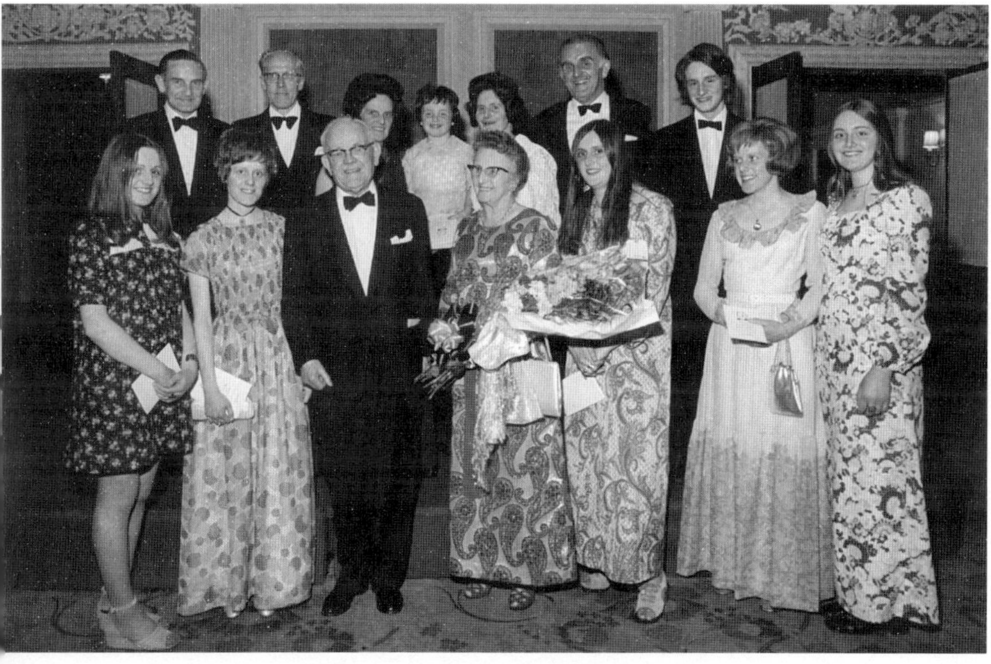

Family group at T.J.'s 80th birthday party.
Back row: Grant (son); Jim (son-in-law); Margaret (daughter); Pamela (Grant's daughter); Sheila (daughter-in-law); Tim (son); Tommy (Tim's son)
Front row: Sally (Tim's daughter); Elizabeth (Margaret's daughter); T.J.H.; V.C.H; Anne (Tim's eldest); Seonaid (Margaret's daughter); Rosemary (Tim's 2nd daughter)

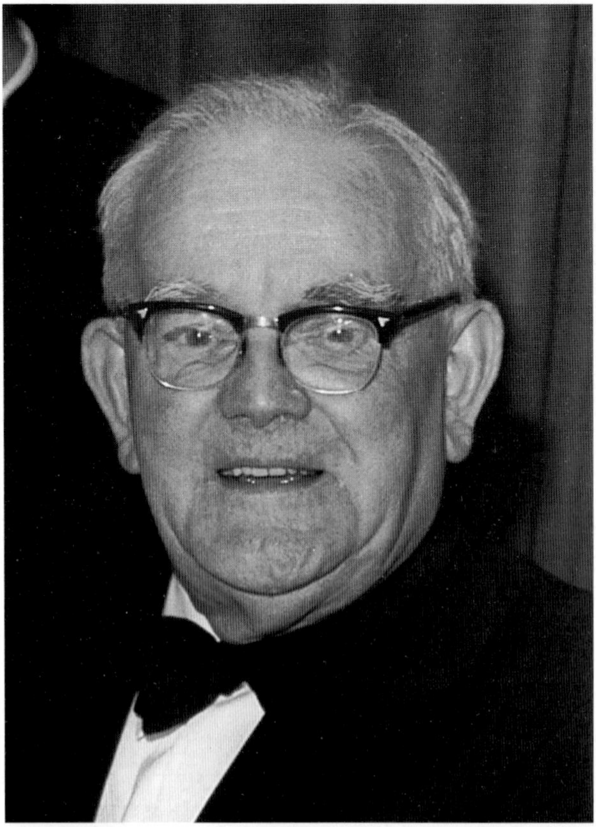

left:
T.J. at his 80th birthday party

below:
Memorial Garden to Tom John Honeyman in Kelvingrove Park. Statue by Benno Schotz and benches in honour of both Tom and Cathie.
Wall Plaque by Avril Gibb

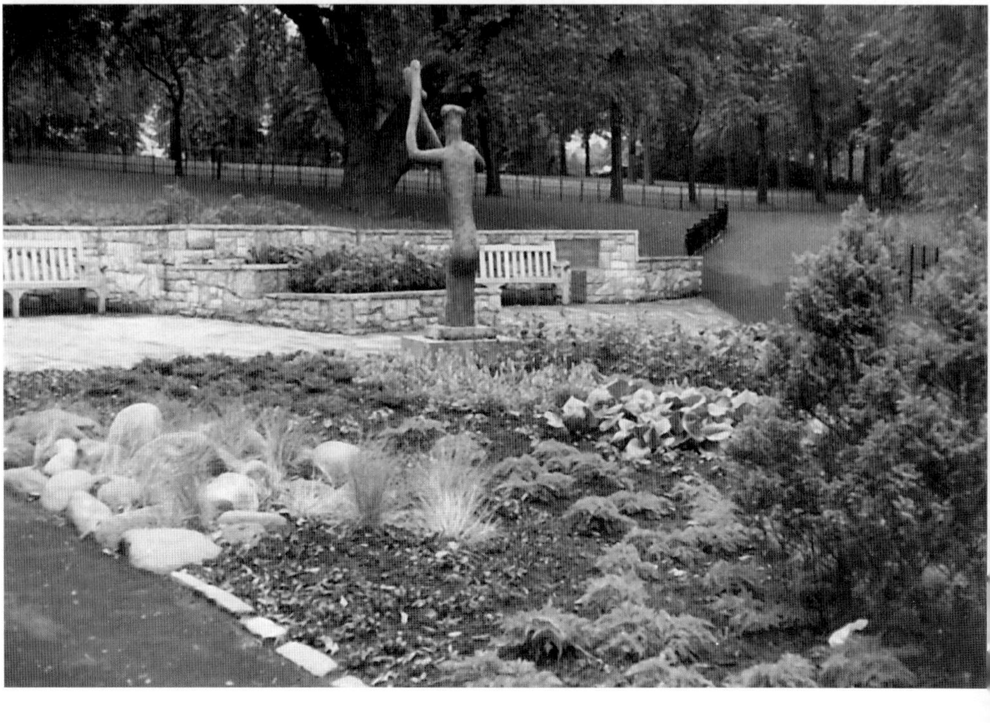

Lavery and, later, by Leslie Hunter, J. D. Fergusson and S. J. Peploe, most of whom he had known before he went to Paris.

Having met Whistler in the French capital, he became a very close friend and sold many of the artist's most important works to Scottish collectors. That was how Whistler became godfather to Alex Reid's son.

Reid had to work hard at interesting Scottish shipbuilders and industrialists in his foreign paintings but soon he was establishing links with men like William Burrell, W. A. Coats, J. Cowan, Arthur Kay, C. J. Galloway and Alexander Young. Yet it was 1920 before he could persuade Burrell, a good friend as well as an important client, to buy a painting by Degas. It has to be said, however, that the Glasgow shipowner did end up with no fewer than twenty of them.

By the end of the First World War, Reid's younger clients, such as the brothers David and William Cargill, Leonard Gow, William McInnes and Mrs R. A. Workman, were looking for paintings more recent than the works of the Impressionists.

Alex Reid had been running his gallery jointly with his brother William, on whose death in 1913 he persuaded his own son, McNeill, to give up his engineering career and come into the family business. This was a significant move since it was McNeill Reid who would set the firm on the road to international fame.

Meanwhile, in London, the Lefevre Gallery was being run by the latest member of this French family, Ernest Lefevre, who had started working with his father around the 1890s and inherited the business in 1915. In the post-war boom in art, more and more London galleries were beginning to show modern French works, with numerous one-man shows featuring names like Matisse, Picasso, Van Gogh, Gauguin and Cézanne. Ernest Lefevre was among those now being affected by this swing in artistic taste.

McNeill Reid used to tell a story of how, one day in 1922, he saw Degas' "Portrait of Duranty" in the window of a Paris gallery. He went in to ask the price, was told it was £1100 and took back a photograph for his father's approval before clinching the deal.

Alex Reid, however, took the view that the only person likely to buy such a picture was William Burrell, that name which would rise to such prominence in later years but was then not much known to the Scottish public. So if Burrell turned it down, they might be stuck with it for long enough. To his great disappointment, McNeill Reid had to cancel the deal.

Ernest Lefevre then spotted the picture and bought it to include in a show at his London gallery in May 1923. It found a buyer all right: William Burrell from Scotland! He even bought two other works by Degas at the same time. It was not hard to imagine Alex Reid's annoyance and frustration that a man who had been a long-time friend as well as customer had done such business with a rival dealer, especially when the deal could have been his own.

But it wasn't all one way. Lefevre had been receiving visits from a young Paris dealer called Etienne Bignou, who had inherited a gallery from his stepfather in Rue la Boetie and was bringing good marketable pictures over to London. Lefevre and Bignou were doing keen business together until one day the latter arrived in London to find that Lefevre had gone to Glasgow with an associate.

Bignou decided to follow them to Scotland, discovered they were staying at Glasgow's Central Hotel and turned out his usual group of pictures for sale. Lefevre made the mistake of thinking that, with Bignou so far off his usual beat, he would sell at lower prices rather than transport the pictures back to Paris.

But Bignou remembered that Alex Reid had a gallery in Glasgow, went round to see him—and was delighted when the Scot agreed to pay the full asking price. Ernest Lefevre went back to London nursing a bruised pride.

Unwilling to be caught up in such rivalry, however, Etienne Bignou decided to encourage an association between his two clients. There would be something in it for both, since Lefevre didn't have Reid's contacts among French dealers and artists and Reid could see the wisdom of having a gallery in London. The outcome of all this was that the two families went into partnership and, in April of 1926, they formed Messrs Alexander Reid and Lefevre Ltd, a new company which took over the premises at 1a King Street in St James's, already occupied by the Lefevre Gallery.

Alex Reid was by then nearly seventy and, having no wish to move to London himself, left all negotiation to his son. So the directors of the new company were Ernest Lefevre, McNeill Reid, Etienne Bignou and Tom Honeyman's old friend, Duncan Macdonald. Alex Reid stayed on to look after the Glasgow premises in West George Street and it was after his death in 1928 that Dr Honeyman was wooed from his medical practice to branch out on that new career as an art dealer.

XI

GOODBYE TO MEDICINE

WITH the fascinating tale of Alexander Reid now established, we can safely return to the Honeyman household in Glasgow, where Tom and Cath now had three children—Tim, who was born in 1921, Margaret in 1923 and Grant in 1926. Dr Honeyman was adjusting to the fact that his evenings were his own once more, though it took some time to rid himself of the feeling that every phone-call must be for the doctor. By coincidence, his last obstetric act before quitting medicine was to bring McNeill Reid's youngest son into the world.

In his new role, Tom Honeyman persuaded good friend James McBey to give him a confident start in his new life by providing his first show. The Aberdonian worked hard through that summer to oblige and such was the popularity of his watercolours that this inaugural venture produced a complete sell-out.

On the day Honeyman accepted McNeill Reid's offer of a new career, McBey happened to be in Glasgow doing some portraits. He also happened to be in the North British Hotel (now the Copthorne) where the meeting was taking place—and sketched the two men from an adjoining table. Now he had given a splendid send-off to the new career.

Tom Honeyman was no sooner tempted to think that art dealing was the easiest and most lucrative pursuit ever known than the economic slump which started in America came tumbling about his ears.

He was soon wondering if it had been a foolhardy decision to give up the security of medicine for this. Anything which looked like a luxury business was heading for a lean time; but the die was cast and he simply had to get on with it.

He forged ahead with his second exhibition, again involving an artist he had known for some time: Benno Schotz, the Estonian who spent most of his life in Scotland and became the Queen's Sculptor as well as receiving the freedom of Glasgow.

In all truth, since the heyday of the Glasgow School at the tail-end of the century, painting in Scotland had not produced much of note, with the exceptions of the men Honeyman had dubbed "The Scottish Colourists"—Samuel Peploe, Leslie Hunter and Francis Cadell. That other distinguished colourist, J. D. Fergusson, another man with a medical background, was still in France and did not return to Scotland until 1940. Independent painters like Sivell, McGlashan and Cowie were acknowledged as vital, with traditional sources of Italian or Spanish, but nothing in the way of a School arose from their lead.

So the history of the eighties and nineties of the previous century showed no sign of repeating itself and the only prospect of a place in the sun was to be found in London. Discussions on matters like these were endless and brought Honeyman into contact with many artists and patrons, most of all perhaps Leslie Hunter, a man he had first met in 1924 and who opened up for him channels of research to complement his own self-education in art which he was then undergoing.

Learning the tricks of the art-dealing trade as quickly as he could, Tom Honeyman listened a lot, talked less than usual, undertook a bit of journalism and tried to adapt to his new way of life.

Though his partners, Reid and Macdonald, were now in London, he was not at all isolated as he held the fort in Glasgow. Along with their French colleague, Etienne Bignou, the Scots pair were frequently in Glasgow, discussing future plans, reporting on new acquisitions and the "possibles" which had not yet been acquired. The search for important pictures was never-ending.

Honeyman judged that Bignou's accounts of secret missions to Europe were highly seasoned but he nevertheless regarded him as an extraordinary man who had more to do with the pattern of his own experience in art between 1929 and 1939 than perhaps anyone else.

The overall plan, of course, was to head south to London and expand into the international market. Tom Honeyman reviewed his two years in charge of the Glasgow gallery, during which he had tried to help those Scottish artists trying to retain their freedom. Far too many, he felt, had been driven into the teaching profession and were therefore unable to devote themselves to full-time art.

The most provocative of the younger Scottish artists, he judged, were Archibald McGlashan and Robert Sivell, who graduated from the group of rebels to become, in time, full members of the Royal Scottish Academy. Sivell was captured by the Aberdeen School of Art, where he proclaimed the truths of art as he saw them, while McGlashan, more erratic but more entertaining, continued to pursue his independent future.

XII

HEADING FOR LONDON

WHEN the lease of the gallery in West George Street expired in the early part of 1931, Tom Honeyman was all set for the move from Glasgow to London. Son Tim and daughter Margaret, aged ten and eight, would have to stay on for a further year of Scottish education, moving out to Hamilton to stay with Tom's brother Alan while attending Hamilton Academy.

Only younger son Grant was with his parents as they headed south to their first London home, which was in Maresfield Gardens, Hampstead. Aged five, Grant attended a local preparatory school, to which most of the pupils seemed to be delivered by luxury motor car. Instead of keeping up with the Joneses, the lad chose to boast of poverty. His dad was too poor to own a car and didn't even use a bus. But he could run faster than any bus. On top of being a sprinter he was also a prizefighter, an actor, a preacher and much more. All of this delivered in a strong Glasgow accent which intrigued the silver-spooned Londoners no end!

By Christmas, however, when the two older children came down for the holidays, Margaret was giggling in the taxi all the way from Euston Station to Hampstead. "Just listen to Grant," she was saying. "He's awfully English!" In all truth, Margaret and Tim couldn't wait to join the rest of the family in Hampstead.

Tom Honeyman made his way each morning to his new place

of work at 1a King Street, near the corner of St James's Square, on the same side of the street and just a few doors away from Christie's, the famous London auctioneers. That property was to suffer in the blitz of the Second World War, when they moved to New Bond Street and later to Bruton Street. But it was always King Street in Honeyman's time and, although the firm was officially known as Alexander Reid and Lefevre, it was generally reduced to "the Lefevre Gallery", as it had been known in London before the amalgamation, and as so often happens in that kind of situation.

The King Street premises were high and narrow, with two rooms on the ground floor and one upstairs devoted to exhibitions. The upstairs room was sometimes used for clandestine meetings and would also serve as a rendezvous for the occasional amorous adventure. The offices were on the fourth floor and the caretaker's apartment on the one above that. William Rowe was the man's name, a leftover from the old Lefevre days who didn't take kindly to the new regime.

With his duties including the hanging of exhibitions, he had difficulty in concealing his contempt for the Modern School of painting. An ex-Army man, he would hark back to the days when "them paintings was art". His large cat was not usually seen till Saturdays, when she would appear from upstairs with a penetrating look which seemed to say: "You've had the place all week. The weekend is mine so get out!" As William locked the door behind them, he would lift the cat on his shoulders and ascend to their secret lair at the top of the building.

The Lefevre Gallery in London was now very much a Scottish stronghold. Miss Miller, the very sound book-keeper-cashier, had gone south with McNeill Reid and Duncan Macdonald. She was replaced in Glasgow by Miss Crawford, who in turn was to join the southward trek. Miss Crawford found it easy to work with Tom and McNeill, but was afraid of Duncan.

Duncan Macdonald was not the most popular of people and

despite his long friendship with Tom, there were frequent differences of opinion. The three men were in discussion in the larger gallery one day when Jack Beddington, an occasional after-lunch visitor, came in with some friends. They were in mellow mood and, viewing the trio from the doorway, he exclaimed: "Three bloody Scots who came to compel the English to buy French paintings. There's Reid, who the whole world likes. There's Macdonald, who can sell you a Modigliani when you only want a box of cigars. And there's Honeyman, the only one of the three who knows anything about art!" Despite the jocular nature of the remark, Macdonald was not at all pleased. In fairness, he had to put up with a good deal of jealousy from their business rivals. Despite a rather basic education, he had certainly raised himself to the status of a major international dealer.

In the division of work, McNeill Reid looked after the financial side, Honeyman and Macdonald were mainly promoting the sales while it was left to Bignou in France to take the lead in finding the pictures. In the intricacies of art dealing, personal judgement becomes a vital factor and Tom Honeyman would find himself in Canada or the United States with the responsibility of taking a risk without reference to his colleagues in London. McNeill Reid would do the same when pursuing business in France.

Whatever they bought abroad, they would be sure that Macdonald would express some doubt if not downright disapproval. But it would usually end up in good humour and agreement, Macdonald having made his point.

Tom Honeyman used to recall the first time he set eyes on Cézanne's "The House of Zola", later renamed "Le Château de Médan". He had come across it in New York, liked it immediately and argued to himself that, although it was an early Cézanne, it had a historical significance.

Encouraged by Georges Keller of the Carstairs Gallery in New York, he concluded an exchange deal which involved a Toulouse-

Lautrec for which they had persistently failed to find a buyer. When the picture was brought to London Macdonald, true to form, showed a lack of enthusiasm. However, Honeyman was ready to assure him he need have no worries. He was prepared to make it his own investment and would simply keep it. But Macdonald soon retracted and took the picture into stock.

In his personal enthusiasm, Tom Honeyman thought it was one which should go to the National Gallery but the then Director, Sir Kenneth Clark, felt it was too early an example. Then Honeyman heard the disturbing rumour that its authenticity was in doubt. But he was soon to become more acquainted with that gentle pastime of "sneer and smear". Sometimes it was innocently done, sometimes not. ("Have you seen the Cézanne at Lefevre's?"—"Yes, but are you sure it's a Cézanne?")

Honeyman used to raise the question of whether it was more irresponsible to say a work of art was not genuine when it was, than to say it was genuine when it was not.

Then one day Sir William Burrell from Glasgow turned up at the King Street gallery. His chief passion in French painting had become Degas, of whose works he now had twenty. He had never bought a Cézanne and was not interested in the post-Impressionists, but he did like "The House of Zola" and bought it for £3800. It was taken to Glasgow and became the only Cézanne in the Burrell Collection.

After Honeyman moved to London in 1931, his first important exhibitions was "Thirty Years of Pablo Picasso", which he regarded as a baptism of fire. The foreword to the catalogue was written by Maud Dale, first wife of Chester Dale and the lady who played a major part in the creation of the world-famous Chester Dale Collection.

Maud was an enthusiastic student of the Modern School in Paris, where Tom Honeyman had met her two years earlier. Before the Chester Dale Collection was distributed on loan to museums in Chicago, Philadelphia and New York, most of it was housed in the Chester Dale home at East 79th Street, New York. (It became the Rosenberg Gallery.)

Now mixing in a vastly different society, Cath and Tom Honeyman found themselves on a visit to that house and setting eyes on a range of work the like of which they had never seen in one house.

Tom made a note of the items which showed there were nine Picassos, six each of Matisse, Modigliani, Cézanne, Renoir, Degas, Braque and Vlaminck, three each of Courbet, Gauguin, Van Gogh and Toulouse-Lautrec, two or more of Manet, Monet, Pissarro, Sisley, Utrillo and Dufy, and examples of every other artist, major and minor, in a hundred years of French painting.

In her introduction to the Picasso exhibition at the Lefevre, Maud Dale had opened by saying: "Who is Picasso and what is he?"

It was Honeyman's job to find as many answers as possible. Among his gatherings he had a letter said to have been written by Picasso himself and which helped to enlighten the puzzled visitor. The conclusion of the letter, however, was more witty than helpful: "What is art?" he posed. "If I knew, I should take care not to reveal it. I do not seek. I find."

But he did say: "Often the picture expresses much more than the author wishes to translate. Stupefied, the author contemplates the unexpected, unforeseen results."

Honeyman was intrigued to be rubbing shoulders with the art critics of London and to be having encounters, however brief, with people like Augustus John. He became a good friend of *The Scotsman's* art critic in London, Douglas Percy Bliss, a friendship which survived many differences of opinion in later years when they both headed north, Honeyman to be Director of Glasgow Art Galleries and Museums and Bliss to be head of Glasgow School of Art. Neither had an easy furrow to plough in those appointments.

XIII

THE VOICE OF J. B. PRIESTLEY

TOM HONEYMAN was learning the tricks of the trade and discovering the tricks of the customers as well. You had to be on your toes. He had always found it a pleasure to meet scholars engaged on research or compiling the complete catalogue of an artist's work. But in some cases, after giving much co-operation to such people, he was staggered to find that the "scholar" had used that introduction to a collector to make a business approach. He was further alerted to the situation when a leading European authority seeking admission to the celebrated Barnes Foundation in America received a reply saying: "This institution is not open to dealers masquerading as scholars."

There was also the kind of person who liked to have pictures on approval, without the slightest intention of buying. A selection would be hung in a West End apartment or a hotel room for the night and once the party was over and the desired effect had been achieved, the pictures were returned with appropriate regrets.

Customers were soon assessed. There was the type who could not buy without bargaining. Honeyman was often amazed at successful businessmen who, when they reached the dealer's private room, seemed to think no-one was entitled to a bargain but themselves. As in all dealing, he learned the lesson of raising the asking price as a preliminary to the subsequent skirmish.

At Lefevre they specialised in 19th and 20th century French artists and were not at any time involved with the Old Masters.

Attending sales of art work, whether in London or America, he and his colleagues hardly ever went forth with commissions to buy. They preferred to negotiate, not because it was more lucrative but because it was more fun. Unlike Picasso, they thought that seeking was more enterprising than finding.

A friend from Scotland came to visit him at King Street one day, having seen something which interested him at Christie's. Honeyman was surprised when the man added: "I don't suppose there is any use in me trying to get it. The ring will keep me out." He had difficulty in persuading the man that he knew of no such practice. It was genuinely his experience that dealing firms followed their own independent lines in the auction room.

It was at a sale of French paintings at Christie's that Tom Honeyman heard a voice he recognised. When a typical example by Corot was knocked down for £60 and the auctioneer asked for the buyer's name, the man behind him called, "Priestley". Honeyman turned to confirm that it was the famous playwright himself.

Soon his heart went out to him, however, when he realised that J. B., believing he had just beaten the dealers to a bargain, had in fact succeeded in buying himself a fake!

But he would gain from experience in building a collection because when he met him many years later, he found that Priestley had some beautiful possessions, reflecting a catholic and experienced taste. He had already endeared himself to Honeyman with *The Good Companions* in 1929, reviving memories of his happy stay in Bradford in 1912. He had lived in the same kind of lodgings and knew the same kind of people.

One thing led to another. Priestley dedicated that book to fellow novelist, Hugh Walpole, another distinguished name to enter his orbit. It was Walpole who advised Honeyman to regard his pronounced Scottish accent as a business asset. With minor exceptions, he found this to be true.

He first became acquainted with Walpole's appearance at one of his exhibitions as a dealer in Glasgow when he displayed the novelist's portrait in bronze by Benno Schotz. He had plenty time to study the bronze and when he met him in the flesh he rather saw him through Schotz's eyes.

Walpole turned out to be a kindly man who went out of his way to do a good turn. It was easy to persuade him to make the only meaningful gesture to a struggling artist: he bought the paintings and talked about them. On their meetings at King Street, Honeyman found his judgement to be more reliable than that of the so-called connoisseurs.

In the ongoing need to sell pictures, Tom Honeyman and Duncan Macdonald were doing their best to cultivate people who were achieving fame and fortune in literature and drama. But many were elusive and suspicious, and, in any case, times were still difficult following the disastrous slump of 1929, from which recovery proved as alarmingly slow as it did in the 1990s.

London dealers had a responsibility to the painters and sculptors for whom they acted as agents and Duncan Macdonald was putting in a massive effort on their behalf, at a time when private and public patronage was at a very low ebb. Other dealers were doing the same.

In the case of Maurice Lambert, it was J. B. Priestley who came to the rescue with a commission for sculpture, as part of the interior decoration of the Duchess Theatre. Because of his particular closeness to Lambert and to Wyndham Lewis, Tom knew how thin a time they were having financially, not unlike himself in that period of the early thirties.

He tried to cultivate A. J. Cronin, with that same ulterior motive of adding to the list of clients at the Lefevre Gallery.

But in the altered circumstances of his life, since he quit

medicine through ill-health and was set on the road to fame and fortune with his rather brooding *Hatter's Castle*, Cronin had developed something of a suspicion complex, sensing that Honeyman and Macdonald were after his money. Of course he was right. But, as with many another customer of the Lefevre men, he would most likely have prospered by succumbing to the sales pitch of his fellow Scots.

With the economic situation improving, Tom and Cath moved the family out of Hampstead and over to Harrow-on-the-Hill, on the other side of that hill from the famous school. And with a delightful garden at their disposal, life began to take on the kind of attractive pattern they had envisaged when they moved south.

This was especially true at weekends when tea in the garden on a Sunday afternoon became quite an institution during the summer months, which stretched decidedly longer than they had known in Scotland. Much of this leisure was caught on 16mm film which showed the visits of friends old and new who would join in those Honeyman gatherings. Some of the shots were quite unique.

For example, you would find well-known Scots actors of the day, like Jimmy Woodburn and Jimmy Gibson, both of whom had toured America in the part of John Brown, appearing with Helen Hayes, who was the Queen in Laurence Houseman's *Victoria Regina*. Another Scottish theatrical figure of her day, Elliot Mason, was a regular visitor, she who had done so much, along with Tyrone Guthrie, to keep Scottish theatre alive in the early days of the Scottish National Players, before going south in the wake of Guthrie.

So a whole array of painters, sculptors, writers and men and women of the theatre were to make these summers at Harrow quite memorable.

Meanwhile Tom Honeyman was leading a busy life as an art dealer, embarking on annual trips to the United States and Canada and with shorter rushes to the Continent. Sometimes there seemed a need to have a *pied-à-terre* in town to save so many late-night journeys out to Harrow and a solution was found in conjunction with Tom's theatrical brother, Murray Macdonald. For if Tom was coming up in the world, so too was Murray. With Laurier Lister, later noted for his revues with Joyce Grenfell and Max Adrian, he had his eye on a flat in Harley Street, which would give them a good address for their future assault on the London West End.

Of course Harley Street was reserved almost exclusively for the medical profession—and that was where brother Tom came in handy. Murray and Laurier Lister acquired their flat, Tom secured his in-town-tonight accommodation—and used to joke that he had made history by achieving a Harley Street address five years after ceasing to be a practising physician.

He was, however, very happy with the way his life was shaping, the pleasures and excitements of the art dealing business turning out to be just as he had anticipated.

XIV

VIEW FROM THE BRIDGE

WITH the economic depression fading away and prospects looking good, the gallery began to take risks and was proving popular with young artists. A one-man show at the Lefevre was something to seek after.

Tom Honeyman was gradually sorting out his accumulated experience into two conclusions. Firstly, it was stimulating to have a part in the building of private and public art collections. Similarly, there was a lot of satisfaction in helping a living artist through those early attempts to find a place in the sun. Within such heady activity the friendships were formed.

Maurice Lambert and his wife Olga were among favourite visitors to the Honeyman home and Tom would find himself mixing with Maurice's famous brother, composer and conductor Constance Lambert, at parties in Wyndham Lewis's flat in Bloomsbury. Coming from a humble background in Glasgow, Tom would look around and marvel at the kind of company he was keeping, even if his main contribution to the night was in helping the casualties to find their way home. He would study the solid stoutness of Constance Lambert, whose marriage to a dainty lady from the Far East drew the comment from his own mother that they were like "the hulk and the barnacle". Lambert was to die far too young, gone by 1951 at the age of forty-six.

Honeyman was strongly drawn to the personality of Wyndham Lewis, who was not only a famous portrait painter but, as a writer, could find himself compared by some critics to James Joyce.

He was constantly in and out of the Lefevre Gallery and the doctor within the art dealer was able to observe that the man had a persecution psychosis (something more than a neurosis) which would occasionally obtrude itself.

One of the family treasures was Lewis's portrait of Cath Honeyman. As she sat in the same chair as many a celebrated subject, Cath was charmed by his gentleness and the brilliance of his conversation. Tom was fascinated by his extraordinary talent and concluded he had never encountered a more vigorous mind. He used to recall the party at which he first met Lewis, who arrived very late, unshaven but in a very smart dinner suit. A prominent gap in the upper row of his teeth was distracting. It later emerged that Lewis had been deeply disturbed by impending libel actions and was spending much of his evening time with lawyers and publishers. The gap in his teeth, incidentally, turned out to have been a recent feature of his face and had nothing to do with the libel actions.

Honeyman was puzzled by an apparent contradiction in Wyndham Lewis in that he seemed, on the one hand, so anxious to avoid attention and, on the other, to guarantee that everyone would turn to look at him, on account of his large felt hat which was reminiscent of the great Cunninghame Graham, flamboyant author and Scottish political leader who was sometimes known as Don Roberto.

He found the sculptors Henry Moore and Barbara Hepworth the most shy of people, their gentleness of speech, with its trace of Yorkshire accent, balanced by a quiet confidence in the growing appreciation of their work, which gave them the reward they were due.

He found Hepworth's artist husband Ben Nicholson a tougher

proposition, too intense and not always co-operative in the struggle to find clients. Nevertheless he rejoiced in the honours and distinctions which came his way, declaring that his work reflected his exquisite taste, even if Nicholson had swung the pendulum too far away from Honeyman's centre of balance.

Having come close to people like Edward Wadsworth and Graham Sutherland, he wrote of the latter: "Having bought one of his etchings in the dim past, I have followed his career with more than casual interest and have found pleasure in the evidence that he continues to behave like a man. I could not say that of all the artists I have met."

Honeyman could look around the walls of his home at Harrow-on-the-Hill and find that, from the early loves of Duncan Grant, Vanessa Bell, Hunter, Peploe, Cadell and Fergusson, he was now approaching the same mixture of art that you would find on his bookshelves. It now included people like Ivon Hitchens, Wyndham Lewis, Paul Maze and Matthew Smith. In his later life he would lament that nothing comparable to the stir and fullness of those days had been happening in the years between.

Some regrets remained with him. He loved dear old Frances Hodgkins, for example, but failed to carry an enthusiasm for her drawings and watercolours into her essays in oils. He also failed to persuade colleague Duncan Macdonald to take on an exhibition of John Piper, a man he much admired and to whom he lent pictures for an evening of art discussion, an event easily pin-pointed in time as the night the newsreels were showing Neville Chamberlain coming off the plane from Munich, declaring there would be no war.

With private viewings and evening parties at the gallery, Tom Honeyman was enjoying his view from the bridge, assessing the celebrities and being reminded of first nights at the theatre, where you could often see better acting in the stalls than on stage. The wide range of human beings who passed through the gallery would always include the council of Glasgow Fine Art Institute during their annual visit to London. They would go south with a fixed determination to get what they wanted on loan for their annual exhibition.

XV

MEETING THE STAGE PEOPLE

MUCH as the Honeymans were revelling in the comfort of their lives at Harrow-on-the-Hill, it was becoming apparent that for the convenience of schooling the family, travelling and other interests, they would need to move nearer the heart of London once again. They looked no further than their former haunts in Hampstead and had the good luck to find a desirable residence in exactly the same street as before. They had lost a garden but gained more spacious accommodation.

Tom Honeyman was intrigued by the rather frail old gentleman who lived directly across the street and with whom he would exchange a morning greeting. It was not long before he came to realise that his new neighbour was none other than Sigmund Freud, the founder of psychoanalysis. The very fact of Freud's presence rekindled in Tom Honeyman a lost interest in psychology, a subject on which he had gone rusty. It seemed sensible to brush up on it, especially in view of the trends in art criticism and aesthetics, as revealed in the writings of Herbert Read.

Other neighbours included de Laszlo, the fashionable portrait painter, whose studio looked imposing from the outside though Honeyman was not to make his acquaintance. He was much more interested in the younger artists like Ivon Hitchens, who was also living and working not far away.

As a doctor who had forsaken his calling in order to be an art dealer, Tom Honeyman was also showing a lot of interest in what might have been another career: the theatre.

Round the corner from their new home in Hampstead was the Embassy Theatre, which Ronald Adams and others had made valiant efforts to use as a try-out venue for West End productions.

In an attempt to bring something fresh and more adult to the theatrical scene, Honeyman became involved in a couple of adventures at the Arts Theatre with James Bridie's *Colonel Wotherspoon* and a play called *The Lake*. The latter was of special interest to him since it was the brainchild of his brother Murray, who was not only making his way as a producer but was dabbling in writing for the theatre as well.

The Lake was based on a Glasgow family and arose from the fact that Murray had attended a wedding and was back at the same home for a funeral a week later. Aspects of the tragedy struck him as being worthy of a play. Murray could handle the structure of the production well enough but collaborated with Dorothy Massingham when it came to the dialogue.

Tom thought *The Lake* had possibilities, a view not encouraged by theatrical managements, so he took over as head of a syndicate under the name of T. J. Mellish. With the distinguished Tyrone Guthrie as producer, the play was staged at the Arts Theatre, starring Marie Ney, and was then taken up by the Westminster Theatre, where it ran for several months. If it wasn't exactly a West End smash hit, it did gain enough notice, especially from that doyen of critics, James Agate, to tempt an American impresario to acquire the rights.

Tom and his syndicate were enthused with visions of cinema rights and fortunes in store as the play headed for America, with the leading role played by Katherine Hepburn no less. Unfortunately Miss Hepburn was not a success in the part, prompting the mischievous Dorothy Parker to write that "Miss Hepburn covered the gamut of emotions from A to B!"

This devastating criticism, to be found quoted in Alexander Woollcotts' *While Rome Burns,* killed all prospects of an American run. The play was revived by repertory companies down the years but for Tom Honeyman and partners it was a return to more familiar ground, but without regrets at having ventured so daringly into another territory. Tom still had much fun presenting Bridie's *Colonel Wotherspoon* though it was not one of the playwright's better efforts.

Then came a memorable year at the Old Vic Theatre, which had been going through one of its lean periods. Tyrone Guthrie sent out alarm signals about the situation, gave Honeyman's brother Murray the job of directing a revival and drew together a team which was led by Charles Laughton and Flora Robson, supported by Roger Livesey, Ursula Jeans, Morland Graham, Leon Quartermaine, Athene Seyler, Marius Goring and a young man called James Mason.

Tom was drawn into this Old Vic revival, met the formidable Lilian Baylis, the legendary theatrical manager who had acquired the Sadler's Wells, and was a little depressed when she told him: "We do love having your son here." Brother Murray had certainly kept his youthful appearance, though Tom didn't realise the gap in looks was so marked.

He had better vibrations in his encounters with Charles Laughton, who became a considerable collector of pictures, with a large-scale Renoir as his *pièce de résistance.*

As a persistent play-goer, Tom was in the minority of people who felt enthusiastic about Laughton's *Macbeth.* On a more personal level, he had the pleasure of getting to know the actor through those visits to the Lefevre. At those meetings he found himself treated to some entertaining demonstrations on the art of theatre, leading to his conclusion that Charles Laughton was the most brilliant natural actor he had ever seen.

Some time later, in that same private room at the Lefevre, he treated Laughton to a painting by a Scottish artist, at a price of course. And that turned out to be Honeyman's final act as an art dealer.

XVI

AND SO TO PARIS

BACK IN 1929 Tom Honeyman had paid his first meaningful visit to Paris, as an essential exercise in his conversion from being a practising doctor in Glasgow to being an art dealer in a wider world. It was a chance to get to grips with what he called "the art racket" in Paris and to be put through his paces by the colourful Etienne Bignou, who was very much involved in that scene as well as being a director of the Lefevre Gallery.

As part of his education he attended his first auction sale at the Hotel Drouot. Despite his fascination with what was going on around him, Tom found the room so crowded, the temperature so uncomfortably high and the preceding lunch so substantial that he dozed off at one stage, only to be jogged awake by a sudden burst of applause.

The large panels by the French artist Edouard Vuillard had been bought for the state. It was one of his first discoveries that, unlike in Britain where state purchase often had to compete with high bids, the interest of the French government in adding to the national collection was generally met with preference. It also seemed that many French artists with international reputations were willing to give selected examples of their work to the public galleries for a nominal sum or even as a gift.

Tom Honeyman was also interested to find, again unlike

in Britain, that the buyer in France, not the seller, paid the auctioneer's commission in addition to the tax and other charges.

There were also certain guarantees to the buyer, like the authenticity of the painting, though subsequent experience taught him not to rely too seriously on that. The assurance of genuine purchase was supposed to last for thirty years. The auctioneer in France turned out to be an officer of the law, with a legal training and generally becoming a man of deep knowledge and taste.

Honeyman was intrigued by the procedure of the French auction room. As in London, the bidder raised his catalogue or nodded his head. The price was very quietly advanced by the gentleman in the rostrum and repeated in a loud voice by an attendant, the *crieur,* who moved freely in front of the audience. Finally the attendant would repeat *"Rien à gauche, rien à droite,"* and down came the hammer.

At the table in front of the auctioneer sat two experts, one of whom on this occasion was Etienne Bignou, both looking pleased with themselves, presumably because their estimate of prices likely to be realised had been supported by events. The French "expert" was the equivalent of the London scholar or connoisseur who would be consulted by the auctioneer before he produced the catalogue. Both in London and Paris, of course, the experts could be wrong.

At the end of that first sale Bignou rushed Honeyman here and there to meet a wide range of significant figures on the French art scene, including Greta Ring, the scholar-dealer who later produced a fine book on 15th century French painting as well as being the person who first brought to light the infamous case of the Van Gogh forgeries.

Being the charming rogue he was, Etienne Bignou was in turn introducing Honeyman with a marked lack of consistency. He was variously explained to French journalists as a writer, a member of parliament, an actor, an agent for a millionaire collector, a famous English surgeon and a professor at Glasgow University!

In his own pursuit of how to become an expert, however, Honeyman found Bignou's knowledge and experience quite invaluable. There was so much to learn even though he did have some knowledge of the biographical data from Delacroix to Dufy. He would find in the next few years that it was more important to get to know the people and the paintings than to follow the mixed bag of literature.

Once again, he found that some people in the art world relied a good deal more on emphatic presentation than on cogent reasoning. To be convincing as an art dealer you had to have a good memory, not so much to relate facts as to retell what the fashionable critics, scholars and connoisseurs had to say.

Still coming to terms with his new-found profession, Tom was delighted to be back on a continent whose famous people had influenced his medical opinions. It was a Frenchman, Dr Legrain (he was superintendent of the asylum where Utrillo was treated) who first aroused his interest in the scientific aspects of the alcohol problem.

And it was at a congress on alcoholism in Lausanne in 1921 that he met another of his heroes, Professor Auguste Forel, whose brilliant work in psychology had been rather overshadowed by the man who would become his neighbour in London, Sigmund Freud. A charming and witty man, it was Forel who cottoned on to Tom's surname and said they should get together since, as a sideline, he had produced a body of work on *The Life and Habits of the Bee*.

Through it all, of course, there was the presence of Etienne Bignou, with whom he would be colleagues for ten years and friends for ever thereafter. He regarded Bignou as an enigma with more variations than any man he had ever known.

As a charming and disarming liar, he was so accomplished in

that gentle art that when he did have occasion to tell the truth, it was difficult to believe him. Tom Honeyman would sometimes philosophise about the subject and differentiate between the offensive lie, which was hurtful, the defensive lie, which sought a way out of an embarrassment, the romantic lie, which decorated fact till it became fiction, and the constructive lie, regarded as necessary to create an appropriate atmosphere!

Bignou would even on occasion resort to disguise to put competitors off his scent. Like others in the international art trade, however, he acknowledged that Joseph Duveen was in a class of his own as an art dealer. He was the Englishman, first Baron of Millbank, who gifted a gallery to the British Museum for the purpose of housing the Elgin Marbles.

Fortunately the paths of those two men seldom crossed, since Duveen specialised in the Old Masters, with only the occasional sensational adventure with the English portraitists. Duveen lived long enough to know he had made a mistake in detaching himself from 19th century French painting. But despite his mistakes the United States had good reason to be eternally grateful to the English lord for his persuasive influence in directing so many European treasures to permanent residence across the Atlantic.

Bignou and Duveen had at least one thing in common. To each of them art dealing was an irresistible way of living. It was the manoeuvring and excitement of the game which controlled thought and action. Their extravagances differed only in degree and would often make their associates squirm with anxiety.

Bignou's premises at Rue la Boetie were small but elegant and were not open to the public. He tended to be the finder of pictures, not the seller. Tom Honeyman would recall his first visit to the secret office downstairs, where the distinguished artist and designer Raoul Dufy had been responsible for some unique ideas in decoration. Flags of the nations were incorporated to reflect the international nature of French art, including the Scottish Standard, which marked not only the association with the Reids of Glasgow but was an acknowledgement of the Auld Alliance. On the question of Scotland, Bignou was more sentimental than any Scot.

It was in this setting, mainly at cocktail time, that Honeyman met artists and collectors who were united in their interest in French art. He found Raoul Dufy a delightful man who, at the time of their 1929 encounter, was suffering the early symptoms of arthritis which would later have such a crippling effect. Like Renoir, however, he adapted himself to the infirmity in quite a heroic manner. True to form, Bignou embarrassed Honeyman by telling Dufy that he was a brilliant specialist who could give him good advice on his condition.

As a visitor from London, Honeyman was very much a fringe player on the Paris scene, simply flying in to inspect and discuss pictures at Rue la Boetie, visiting other dealers and snatching an occasional interlude at the Louvre or some current exhibition.

Sometimes the Paris visit would amount to a long weekend, with the intention of enjoying the city beyond business. But even then he would be taken to Paul Rosenberg's or the Bernheim Jeune Galleries where it was very likely he would be introduced to someone he longed to meet.

That was where he had his one and only encounter with Picasso. In London he had already met Matisse, whose visits there were infrequent enough, though he could be persuaded to come on special occasions. Similarly he had met Pierre Bonnard and Georges Braque who would turn up at the Lefevre Gallery for exhibitions featuring their work. He also had the rare privilege of meeting Vuillard when Bignou took him to the château of the Hessel family, with whom he seemed to make his home. He found him a distinguished-looking old man, gentle and reserved and doing little more than exchanging courtesies before withdrawing to his quarters.

XVII

A VISIT TO VOLLARD

IF THERE WAS one name in art dealing which fascinated Tom Honeyman more than that of Duveen, it was Ambroise Vollard, pre-eminent among all those who had ever become interwoven in the history of French painting in the 19th and 20th centuries. Honeyman thought that if his activities could be traced they would throw much light on the process of finding, buying and selling pictures and on the impelling motives which elevated or depressed collectors.

Vollard was indeed a famous name and Honeyman's first meeting with him was memorable. Whereas he may have dreamed of following in the tradition of Duveen, without being able to reach his financial heights, he only had to meet Vollard to snap out of any romantic fantasies about batting in that league.

Through reproductions, he had seen the Cézanne portrait (the one of the shirt front anecdote), the Renoir portrait in the fancy dress of a matador, and the Picasso Cubist (1909).

Though Vollard was something of a recluse with long periods when you could see neither him nor his pictures, Tom's friend Bignou had gained the old man's confidence. It was always the ambition at Lefevre to acquire a picture from the Vollard Collection, knowing there would be little difficulty in placing it in another good collection and at a good profit. The imprimatur of

Vollard was likely to establish confidence with both collectors and critics.

But it was only rarely that Vollard was willing to conclude a substantial deal. He did not live extravagantly. When Tom first met him his chief passion was publishing, in which he was spending large sums on books which were beautifully printed and illustrated, only to find there was little or no market for them. So when funds ran low he could be persuaded to part with some of his treasures; and there were always people ready and eager to see what he had.

On Tom Honeyman's first visit he was accompanied by McNeill Reid, Duncan Macdonald and the inevitable Bignou. His particular brief was to show a special interest in the man's books and to indicate how they might be received in Britain.

In the event, he sat very quietly and could hardly take his eyes off Vollard. He was a large man, by no means handsome, with a scruffy beard, his left eye hidden by a drooping eyelid and his bald head covered by a black skullcap. He shuffled about the room, and now and again would break into a slow smile in response to an observation by Bignou, who did most of the talking.

They appeared to be in the dining-room, with a grubby white cloth covering a large table in the middle. Behind was the Renoir portrait, flanked by a couple of Degas paintings and in the corner there was a powerful looking door which suggested the entrance to a strongroom. In the course of the afternoon Vollard would disappear through this door, eventually to reappear with various paintings for inspection. Every time he disappeared his visitors went into a huddle. On a previous visit Bignou had discussed some pictures wanted by Lefevre but Vollard now seemed unwilling to produce them. But finally he did—and there was much calculating on paper as the mysterious comings and goings would continue.

The others having returned to London, Honeyman went back with Bignou next day when more pictures were produced. He was then shown proofs of a few books which Vollard was anxious to publish. Bignou left, with instructions that Honeyman should take his time over the manuscripts and find his own way back to Rue la Boetie. This seemed to suit Vollard, who disappeared into another room.

Left alone for an hour, Honeyman noticed that Vollard had forgotten to lock the strongroom and was later to confess that he had taken the chance of glancing inside! There were treasures galore in that private den. Wondering if he had been forgotten, he looked into the adjoining room to find Vollard lying fast asleep in the armchair. Honeyman would later reflect, not for the first time, that he had failed to appreciate fully the opportunity that had come his way. What a privilege it had been to view history in the making, through the men and women who had made it. Allowing for the fact that it may not all have been gospel, he regarded Vollard's autobiography as a story without equal in the realm of French art and artists.

One of his treasured possessions was a photograph of himself with Vollard and the great American collector, Dr Albert Barnes, on the occasion of the latter's visit to Paris in 1936 to receive the Legion of Honour. Tom and Cath Honeyman were among the guests at the celebration and after the presentation, Honeyman realised that Bignou was on tenterhooks as to what Dr Barnes would say. Diplomacy was not his strong point and Bignou's fears were fully justified. Replying in high-school French, he thanked the government for the honour but said he should have had it sixteen years earlier! He was probably right, even if he chose the wrong moment to say it.

Honeyman managed to divert himself from the embarrassment by studying one guest in particular. Indeed he could hardly take his eyes off Paul Ambroise Valery, the famous French writer, and reckoned they wouldn't believe him back home when he told them he had dinner in the company of such a man.

The paintings which did arrive at the Lefevre Gallery from Vollard's collection often represented a great deal of money. Invariably they had been lying around in his cupboards for so long that they needed cleaning but their general condition was excellent and the cleaning process tended to be a surface one. Bignou had much faith in a Monsieur Linet for restoration and Honeyman took a very sensible interest in his methods, an attention which would prove invaluable in later years.

At least two of the Cézannes which came from Vollard were among the canvases which the master had discarded after slashing them in one of his fits of fury. One of them, a portrait, still showed signs of the reconstruction, even after three attempts by different experts. The other one, a landscape, went to Glasgow Art Gallery and was so expertly restored at the second attempt that it was almost impossible to detect the original lesion.

Among other pictures acquired from Vollard was a series of Derain paintings of London which Vollard had commissioned from the artist. The partners at Lefevre were divided in their opinion of the paintings. McNeill Reid took one for his private collection and when Honeyman left the firm he took his own favourite, "The Pool of London" which cost him £45, and managed to keep it until 1952 when it found its permanent home in the Tate Gallery.

He refused a tempting offer from the United States so that it could go to the Tate for £1500. When Derain was asked shortly before he died what he thought of that price, he said: "You could knock me down with a feather. The picture took me an hour to paint and I sold it with nine others for £100 in 1906."

Vollard went to America in 1936, accompanied by Bignou, who shepherded him with great attention. There he was lionised, interviewed and pursued with invitations to the point of bewilderment. He had a certain reputation with young women which evidently preceded him across the Atlantic and there were reports of various experiences in restaurants and elevators!

Altogether his American trip was a major event, with faultless public utterances, especially when paying tribute to their own collectors. His visit to the Barnes Foundation in Philadelphia was a thrill for himself as well as for the group which followed him round to hear his comments. Of the Barnes Collection, he said in a broadcast: "With the authority which my age permits me to assume, I assure you that there does not exist, and will never exist in the world, another collection of masterpieces of the two greatest painters of the 19th century, Cézanne and Renoir, comparable to the one assembled by Dr Barnes."

In another interview he said it was Cézanne who made him a collector. Tom was interested to hear that his father was a lawyer who wanted him to become a doctor, but he could not stand the sight of blood and followed his father's profession instead. That took him to study in Paris where he began to haunt bookstalls on the banks of the Seine and there he would pick up a bargain from tattered portfolios. It had been the sight of Père Tanguy in his art shop in the Rue Clauzel which settled Vollard's future.

The law seemed dreary and dry by comparison to the vitality which came out of a painters' canvases. Unlike deeds and law books, they breathed. So he made up his mind to surround himself forever thereafter with works of art.

The changing fortunes of American collecting were often discussed in the light of what Vollard had to say about the paintings which had passed through his hands. Before the 1929 slump the price of pictures had reached astronomical heights, Gainsboroughs selling for $300,000 and early Italian paintings with attractive names, but wrapped up in uncertainty, gaining $500,000 without difficulty.

To live up to their reputations the wealthy found it essential to get into the game of landing the greatest works at the highest prices. But the game was now thought to be finished. Some of the paintings found their way into public galleries while Italy,

France and Britain were keeping a firmer grip on their irreplaceable treasures. The days of easy selling at big prices were over. It was true that the fashion was swinging away from English portraits, Dutch interiors and early Italian "cock-eyed saints with golden backgrounds".

The old rich had been soaked and nobody could expect to have the luck of a Chester Dale or an Albert C. Barnes, who were in on the new fashion for French painting when prices were low. In the Barnes Foundation alone there were more Cézannes and Renoirs than Honeyman had ever seen together. Walls were covered with masterpieces at a cost of what the old collectors had paid for one or two pictures.

Honeyman found it difficult when asked to compare Vollard and Duveen, who had each achieved fame as the leading art dealers in the world, at least outwith the famous firms whose names tended to conceal the identity of active directors.

Comparison was so difficult that the Scot would leave his questioner with the fanciful reply: "I can imagine the moths having a good time at Vollard's. There was a candle there. But in the Duveen palaces I could think only of spiders and webs. Duveen was a master but his peculiar technique had any number of imitators."

Honeyman felt he himself had been doomed to follow the Duveen pattern. In later life he was to find a measure of satisfaction back in Glasgow, where he had his own private office in a basement, after leaving Glasgow Art Gallery. Thanks to some waggish friends, a legend would grow around that basement pad. To gain admittance to Honeyman's place, it was said, you had to knock twice on the window, ask for Mollie and say that Joe had sent you! It amused him later to realise that Lord Duveen had started life with the name of Joe.

XVIII

MANHATTAN MOMENTS

ETIENNE BIGNOU had opened a gallery in New York, on East 57th Street, which was the Bond Street of Manhattan. That became Tom Honeyman's headquarters when in North America, not that he was actively concerned with the business of the gallery but it was a useful base from which he could arrange exhibitions in Montreal, Ottawa or Toronto with paintings from London, Paris and New York.

On his first visit to Manhattan he was asked by Frank Moffat, who not only specialised in interior decoration but knew everything that was going on around town, if the name Ella Logan meant anything to him. Moffat was surprised when he said it didn't. "Well, she says she knows you," said Moffat. "You were her family doctor in Glasgow and helped her into this dark and dismal world."

The fact that the lady in question was appearing at an exclusive nightclub in New York seemed like a cue for further investigation. When Ella came looking for her Glasgow doctor, Tom was confronted by a most glamorous and radiant creature. Though he could hardly have claimed an interest in her babyhood, he did realise that she was a member of the Logan theatrical family whose real name was Short and included at a later stage the well-known Scots comedian Jimmy Logan, who would become his neighbour one day.

Ella Logan was a big name in America, yet unspoiled and charming in every way, even if she did perform that night a swing-time version of "Loch Lomond" which reminded him of his hostility to anything which mutilated the old Scots songs.

But if that offended his ear it was nothing to what happened later when Frank Moffat decided to take him to a nightclub in Harlem and Ella Logan decided to go with them. The purpose of this was to let Tom hear a "Highland Orchestra", which turned out to be a bunch of noisy musicians dressed up in kilts, white spats and flaming red tunics. Ella's arrival created a stir of autograph-hunters and a welcome diversion from the noise of the Highland Orchestra. The star of the night had definitely been the lass from Hunter Street, just off the Glasgow Gallowgate.

Back at business, Tom knew that Alexander Reid had done a lot of business in Canada many years earlier but was surprised to find an amazing array of spurious works of art and some indifferent, if genuine, examples of the great names for which far too much had been paid.

Fortunately, French painting had not suffered so badly but Honeyman still found himself battling to restore a lost confidence. He was, however, greatly impressed by the attempts to promote the fine arts in Montreal. In the same city he was initiated into the mysteries of both American football and ice hockey where, as at home in British football, everyone seemed to know precisely what should be done—except the players.

Tom Honeyman spent five years of the 1930s on those North America visits, moving from a shaky start to better business with a new breed of collectors who brought a more informed judgement to their buying than did their predecessors. Only the outbreak of the Second World War, he felt, interrupted them from adding substantially to their collections of 19th and 20th century French painting.

Back home, even though the Reid and Lefevre Gallery in

Glasgow had disappeared, the firm nurtured a hope that a new generation of art lovers might arise in the city.

They made two noble efforts to find those people but failed. In 1934 and 1937 they put on splendid exhibitions at the McLellan Galleries, the first with a title of "Renoir, Cézanne and their Contemporaries". It included eleven top-rate Cézannes, the Corot figure "The Bordeaux Girl", three Courbets, a Degas portrait, a Delacroix, two Gauguins, two Van Goghs (one was the famous "Peasant"), a Manet, a Monet, two Pissarros, eight Renoirs (including "Rose et Bleu"), a Seurat, a Sisley and two Toulouse-Lautrecs.

There was a grand total of 37 masterpieces and Honeyman reckoned Glasgow sadly missed a fine opportunity. Through the Hamilton trustees, he tried hard to leave behind the Van Gogh "Peasant" and the Renoir "Rose et Bleu", each of which could have been bought for £10,000, whereas their value soon rocketed to unthinkable levels. Within a week of the same exhibition opening in London, the Van Gogh was snapped up by the Chester Beatty Collection.

The 1937 exhibition, "French Art of the 19th and 20th Centuries", totalled 68 exhibits and included Bonnard, Boudin, Braque, Cézanne, Courbet, Corot, Daumier, Dufy, Gauguin, Matisse, Modigliani, Monet, Picasso, Pissarro, Renoir, Sisley, Utrillo and Vuillard.

As Honeyman said, what more could anyone want? The Cézanne "House of Zola" went to the Burrell Collection and the Pissarro "Bords de Seine" to the National Gallery in Edinburgh. Once again, Honeyman tried to interest the Glasgow Gallery in some paintings, many of them priced at a few hundred pounds, without the slightest hint of a nibble.

The day when he could come closer to that situation was not long delayed.

XIX

HOMEWARD BOUND

DESPITE his long-standing connection with Duncan Macdonald and his fascination with the colourful Etienne Bignou, Tom Honeyman was running into difficulty with both men. Ever loyal to those around him, however, he did not elaborate too far on their differences but I gather that ethical standards had something to do with it.

By the autumn of 1938 he had decided to leave the Lefevre Gallery, though he agreed to stay on until April 1939. He had nothing particularly in mind but, in the absence of anything else in the art world, there could always be a refresher course and a return to medicine.

When his decision to leave became known, there was a variety of suggestions. A well-known art firm invited him to join them in either New York or London. Tyrone Guthrie came back with an earlier suggestion that he should take over as administrative director at the Old Vic.

Neither suggestion appealed and in those final months Honeyman busied himself with meeting people who had come down from Scotland for the Winter Exhibition at the Royal Academy of Arts. This comprehensive display of Scottish art brought a strong contingent from Edinburgh, including eminent officials from the National Gallery and Royal Scottish Museum. Significantly, the

Glasgow Art Gallery was not represented at all, a situation raised with Honeyman by the new Lord Provost of Glasgow, Patrick Dollan, who was frequently in London and would call in to see him at King Street.

They would also meet at the famous Café Royal, where they would be joined by some of the much-publicised left-wing MPs from Clydeside. The Café Royal was then the haunt of celebrities who dropped in for after-theatre supper and Tom would take pleasure in pointing them out to his Scottish friends. The MPs were then involved in trying to have placed in Westminster a Benno Schotz bronze of Keir Hardie, a founder of the Labour Party and its very first candidate for parliament.

On one of those London visits Lord Provost Dollan came round to discussing with Honeyman the vacancy for the head of Glasgow Art Galleries and Museums. His views were of interest back home and, if he was to be in Glasgow soon, some of Dollan's newspaper friends (he himself ran the Scottish end of the *Daily Herald*) would like to hear them.

Tom was going north for Christmas and New Year, and went for lunch at the Merchants Club as the guest of James Willock, editor of the *Evening Times* and a close friend of the Lord Provost, who wanted to know what he thought the Corporation should do about the job at Kelvingrove. Honeyman did not hesitate to recommend that they should go for Philip Hendy, then the top man at Leeds who was not too happy with his lot. They should invite him to Glasgow but not before they did something about the totally inadequate salary.

The post, as advertised on 1st April 1939, was for a Director of Art Galleries and Museums at a salary of £800, rising to £1200 per annum by increments every two years, with free house and coal. Honeyman was also consulted by a prominent patron of the arts, J. R. Richmond, chairman of the governors of Glasgow School of Art, an influential man who warned the Corporation that, if they did not make a good appointment this time, he personally would lead the criticism.

Honeyman repeated his recommendation of Philip Hendy of Leeds, who then called to see him during a visit to London. Having heard rumours that his name was being linked with the Glasgow vacancy, he had given it serious consideration. But it now seemed that his troubles in Leeds were being sorted out and he would not therefore be a candidate.

Meanwhile, behind the scenes, there were people rooting for Honeyman himself to be offered the job, not least the man who became Sir John Richmond, and W. O. Hutchison, Director of Glasgow School of Art, who would later be President of the Royal Scottish Academy.

That was when Tom Honeyman, who was soon to leave the Lefevre, began to give the Glasgow job his serious consideration. While a salary of £800 in the 1930s seemed a substantial sum to most people, there was discussion in the Honeyman home that the breadwinner had been earning upwards of £4000 a year in London.

There would likely be a chance to augment the income with outside lecturing, broadcasting and journalism and, with a certain cushion of capital, a decent collection of paintings and a good deal of faith, he might have to regard this as an opportunity to do something for his native city. Perhaps altruism was not dead after all.

So in went Tom Honeyman's application along with twenty-one others, including some who would later become top names in the galleries of Britain. Intriguingly, one of the applicants was C. M. Grieve, better known as Hugh MacDiarmid, the famous Scots poet with whom Honeyman had served in Salonika during the First World War. Given MacDiarmid's flair for controversy, Honeyman concluded that, while poetry in Scotland might have suffered, the art scene would have been dramatically stirred up by such a dynamic personality.

As far as Honeyman was concerned, a degree in medicine hardly seemed the ideal preparation to run a major civic enterprise. Though his interest in art and artists dated back to 1909, when he started his medical studies, he had no direct experience in this kind of administration. Yet the job did appeal to him. One of the ironies of the situation was that Philip Hendy of Leeds had a last-minute change of mind—and would now be competing with the man who had strongly recommended him for the job.

There was much speculation around the City Chambers of Glasgow and the forthcoming appointment was of particular interest to Miss Isabel Mackintosh, a Springburn girl who joined the Town Clerk's office in 1930 but had been secretary to the Art Galleries director, James Eggleton, since 1935. Eggleton's deputy, a distinctive character called John Fleming, became interim boss and thought he was going to get the job.

The arrival of Philip Hendy for interview sent a buzz of anticipation around the corridors of local power. He was tall and good-looking and stirred an excitement among the young ladies. More seriously, he seemed to be the front runner. However, Isabel Mackintosh met an acquaintance from the legal department who told her there was a man called Honeyman who was also being quoted. When she raised this possibility with John Fleming he was furious.

But the information was sound and Tom Honeyman did indeed land the job, an appointment which was confirmed in June 1939. Local gossip was to the effect that he had influence in the right quarters but the fact that he was a dealer did not go down well with the staff. As far as gallery people were concerned, art dealers were the pits.

Honeyman took up office in August 1939, immediately before the outbreak of the Second World War in September. On that Sunday morning when Chamberlain made the fateful announcement the Honeyman household goods were on their way north by road while they themselves were at a church service which was cut short because the German bombers were supposed to be on their way to Clydeside. It turned out to be a false alarm.

Several weeks before he took up his post, however, Dr Honeyman had gone north to introduce himself to the staff, first of all encountering John Fleming who, whatever his disappointment at not becoming the director, had been reconciled to the situation, especially when it became clear that the Corporation had been looking for an art man.

Honeyman understood the position perfectly and came to regard him as a bit of a character, happy to be seen in that light and not beyond playing up his own legend if the occasion arose. Fleming was devoted to "the Building", which was his name for Glasgow Art Gallery, and his devotion dated back to "Paton's time", a reference to his first boss whose tenure of office went back to the previous century.

Fleming's regard for Paton amounted to hero-worship, which would become an irritation when Honeyman came up with some new idea, only to be told that it had been tried in Paton's time and didn't work. Not that Fleming was being an obstructionist; indeed he seemed to go out of his way to help the "new boy". Honeyman readily acknowledged that Glasgow Art Gallery had enjoyed a high reputation in Paton's time. In fact it was James Paton who, in 1891, had bought Whistler's "Carlyle" and caused at least as big a furore as Honeyman would so sixty years later when he flirted with Salvador Dali.

John Fleming was most helpful in introducing the new director to his staff, giving him a thoroughly entertaining day as he put him right on the cranks and culture vultures who made life interesting—and gave him the low-down on all branches of Corporation activity, from Lord Provost, magistrates and officials to the trade unions, the work-shy and the twisters. All of this, Honeyman noted, was conveyed with a smile which lit up his face and cancelled the menace of his deformed nose. He also had a slight stammer which did nothing to deter him in his racy guide to touring parties.

Even before Dr Honeyman took over, there was something John Fleming wanted him to do. The Gallery had received a bequest and because of a certain urgency, he had had to take action on his own. They had been allowed to choose a selection of pictures from the collection of Mr W. Y. Chrystal and Fleming had already made a choice, though he was not at all confident that he had chosen well.

Honeyman had never heard of Mr Chrystal, who turned out to have been a partner in a well-known Glasgow chemical manufacturing company. His beautiful home was out by the banks of Loch Lomond, at Auchendrennan, which later became a youth hostel and summer school, and that was the destination of Honeyman and Fleming as the new boss went to check on the wisdom of the choice.

Fleming had taken as his guide the purchase price from the valuation schedule. But Honeyman could bring his considerable knowledge of French art to bear on the problem and suggested several changes to the original selection. These were gladly accepted and the only people annoyed by the intervention were the auctioneers, who were instructed to sell the remainder. The values rose sufficiently for the new boss to conclude that he had been of service to Glasgow Corporation even before he joined the payroll.

He reckoned the ten paintings acquired from the Chrystal bequest had come from a very mixed bunch and that Glasgow had landed the cream of an improving taste—two Daubigny, two Monticelli, two Fantin-Latour, a Corot and a Ziem.

On the way back from Loch Lomond Dr Honeyman asked Fleming if he knew anything about the house he would be getting when he took up the post. "I'm in it," laughed Fleming, who went on to explain that their committee convener, Tom Kerr, had told him that a new house was being planned alongside the Palace of Art in Bellahouston Park, built for the Empire Exhibition of 1938.

The fact was that the Honeymans were still staying in a small hotel five months later, with their furniture in store. Eventually, when the Honeymans found a house for themselves in Kensington Gate, the Corporation approved the purchase at £1200, with some more for decoration. Honeyman was learning quickly about the workings of a local authority. Whereas he had been told that the council had consulted with Glasgow University and that the new man would be offered a lecturing appointment to augment his income, the truth was something different.

He called to see the Principal, Sir Hector Hetherington, who put him wise to a number of things, including the fact that any idea of an approach by the Corporation to the university could be dismissed as eyewash. As it happened, Sir Hector was keen to see some kind of lectureship established, perhaps in the history of art, but that could be discussed later.

Honeyman felt comfortable with the proximity of the Art Gallery to his old university. From the window of the Principal's office he could see the masts and funnels of the ships down on the River Clyde, as well as the Art Gallery down below, separated only by the Kelvin.

From the window of his own new office he could look up to the university, in more ways than one. He could listen once more as the great bell chimed out from the tower, even if that same bell, striking out the quarters, used to torture him during examinations.

Tom Honeyman settled into his new job, learning to cope with town councillors who were, apart from the odd case of congenital idiocy, a fairly supportive bunch. Among the early frustrations, he found it hard to reconcile the needs of his department with "party policy". A more light-hearted discovery was the fact that the department came under the general description of "Parks, Burial Grounds and Art Galleries and Museums". The city chamberlain couldn't see the joke!

The first priority would surely be to create the kind of atmosphere which would prove that a museum was not a mausoleum but there was clearly an uphill struggle if he was to build a brave new art world from within the Corporation structure. The convener of his committee, Tom Kerr, was later to be Lord Provost of Glasgow, a keep-fit fanatic who must also have been the first civic head to install a piano in his official room so that he could entertain his visitors to the songs of Scotland.

Just as he took up the new job Dr Honeyman attended the International Congress of the History of Art, in London, where he was tackled by a formidable bearded gentleman who wanted to speak about Glasgow. This was the distinguished architectural historian Henry-Russell Hitchcock from America, who said he had rushed up one night and down the next just to have another look at the Greek Thomson churches and terraces of the city.

He wanted to say he thought Glasgow had the perfect situation and reckoned no town in Europe had so many natural features for planning—three rivers and seven hills, all of which he could name. When Honeyman suggested Glasgow had lamentably wasted its inheritance, Hitchcock explained how it could all be won back in three generations if the city was so inclined.

At the beginning of his new adventure, Honeyman had this man's words to think about and he would repeat them whenever the opportunity arose, as an attempt to stir action in the city.

He did not, however, get off to the best of starts. His own first practical effort concerned the River Kelvin, which flowed down to the Clyde through Kelvingrove Park, between Glasgow University and the Art Gallery. At the International Exhibitions of 1901 and 1911 it had provided a most picturesque setting and during his own student days it was the pleasant river which enhanced a walk through the park. But now it was covered by an ugly scum, created by the waste products from paper-mills further up the river. His personal campaign to have this pollution cleaned up was met, however, with a cold indifference. In the corridors of the municipal chambers he was quietly told to mind his own business. He had to realise that he was a Corporation official, not expected to behave like this. It was an early lesson he had to learn.

The pawky mischief in Honeyman threatened to come to the surface when he subsequently staged an open-air exhibition of sculpture in Kelvingrove Park beside the river. His suggestion to display a poster saying "Scum and see the sculpture" was not well received!

But if others had had their doubts about the new director, Isabel Mackintosh (she later became Isabel McLean of Carnwath) was soon beginning to take her own independent view, from the vantage point of being his secretary.

"I was interested to watch him at work," she said. "I got on well with him and soon realised that he was absolutely right for the job. He knew about business—and nobody knows more about paintings than dealers. After all, they have to put their money where their mouths are."

When Dr Honeyman arrived there had been a recent history of bad blood running between the Art Gallery staff and the local newspapers. And with that atmosphere not what it should be, Isabel Mackintosh was soon aware of her new boss's skill in what came to be known as public relations. She concluded that he was a very clever man, determined that the newspapers would have to become his friends.

He would invite journalists to hear about his plans and Isabel Mackintosh was instructed to keep a notebook recording what was going on elsewhere in the art world. The reasoning was that, if they came looking for a story on a quiet day and there was nothing to tell them about Kelvingrove, they could at least be sent away with ideas for something else, perhaps the latest on-goings of Dali or Picasso.

Isabel Mackintosh was deeply impressed by his bright ideas and his determination to reach the man and woman in the street. She would listen with fascination to the stories of people he had met and paintings he had seen—and she quietly wanted to show that she was as good a secretary as he had known in the allegedly smarter environs of London.

XX

FRICTION AT KELVINGROVE

TOM HONEYMAN set about the task of assessing the calibre of his staff and their reaction to his arrival. Many a new boss likes to bring in his own people, guaranteeing a loyalty which may not be found among those already there. But he would make do with the inheritance, at least until he had sorted out who was who.

Some were clearly going to work with him in harmony; others would wait and see, while a few gave the impression that he might be an interloper. An invaluable asset from the very start was the presence of Isabel Mackintosh as his efficient secretary. In her own quiet way she was capable of summing up a situation and the people concerned with penetration and humour. Apart from her ability to decipher his illegible writing, she had the tact to drop him a gentle hint which would amount to a useful piece of guidance. From her own point of view she realised the place could do with a boost and was right behind her new boss as he prepared to meet that challenge.

Dr Honeyman was making some pretty blunt assessments. Whereas one third of the staff could be counted upon in every respect and another third could be chaffed or provoked into a good day's work, the truth was that the remaining third were complete passengers. It did not take him long to detect a lack of discipline throughout the whole department and he had to get to the bottom of it.

The general debility was due in the first place to the Corporation's failure to understand the importance of the Art Gallery and Museum to the life of Glasgow. The responsible committee was the Cinderella of them all, with very few councillors regarding their attendance as anything more than a pleasant interruption of more important matters.

There had been some good men appointed as curators of departments and Dr Honeyman found they had put up some excellent suggestions. But nothing had been done and by the time he arrived their enthusiasm had vanished. There was also a sense of insecurity, with attendants and cleaners divided into two camps. The old hands were hostile to a number who had arrived in recent years, many having been given jobs through the influence of the convener of the committee, Tom Kerr, a kindly man who no doubt went out of his way to help those needing work. There were at least eighteen in this category and John Fleming told him that a feud had developed between the Kerrites and the anti-Kerrites.

Honeyman didn't want to fall out with the convener who had been so keen to bring him back to Glasgow but he did have to take steps to establish his own authority. After a confrontation at a council meeting he was advised by a well-intentioned member of the Labour group: "You'll have to learn that, as an official, you are not supposed to argue with members at committee meetings. You are there to answer questions or give advice when you are asked." From this and other experiences he became increasingly aware that he was not being very successful as a local government official.

For many years Dr Honeyman had known that Glasgow Art Gallery and Museum had not been playing a significant part in the life of the city. It would be his job to put that right, to turn it into a place of familiarity to the general public, most of whom would know very little about art.

This would become Honeyman's mission and, to that end, he realised his role had to be that of a showman. It would not be difficult for a man with a keen sense of publicity who was not devoid of that vanity which drives a great deal of human achievement. But if he was to be the showman for the city's art treasures he had to discover in the first instance what there was to show.

An even more pressing need, however, was the distribution of the treasures to places of safety because of the war emergency. Whereas the National Galleries had plenty of money to undertake this task—they converted a disused coalmine in Wales—Glasgow would have to do with less. Honeyman set about assessing the important possessions and looking behind the scenes at the storage accommodation. It proved a depressing experience, leaving him critical of a previous regime.

Or perhaps the root of the problem lay in a lethargic Corporation, some of whose members he regarded as "intellectually disreputable". He would need to see dossiers, only to find there wasn't a dossier in the place. Apart from a catalogue published in 1936, he could find no files on the history of any of the paintings or records of exhibitions or collections.

There was a well-kept register of the source of every item, when it was presented to the gallery or bought or loaned. But no more than that. Nor was there any method of storing pictures. Without help from the gilder in charge of the store, who relied on his memory, it was often hard to find a particular picture. They were piled in deep rows against the wall, often ten or more to a row, which meant a lot of clumsy moving to get at what you wanted. Honeyman ordered the building of racks and, with the help of Isabel Mackintosh, devised a card-index system which pinpointed the exact position of each painting.

The museum stores were in an even worse state than the pictures, lacking any system whatsoever; and the staff accommodation and amenities were also inadequate. Believing that the Art Gallery at Kelvingrove had been fifty years out of date when it was built, Tom Honeyman tackled the problem as best he could, considering the fact there was a war in progress.

In the course of rummaging round the stores and trying to make best use of space, he came across some old favourites among the paintings, long since consigned to the basement. War or no war, he decided they must try to create special exhibitions and find new ways of bringing them to the public's attention. How better to start than with pictures which people would find easy to look at, even if they were not to the taste of those who thought they knew something about art? With all the items already there, an exhibition like that would not be costly to organise. And with the scattering of Old Masters to places of safety because of the war, there was plenty of wall space; so Honeyman set out on his first exhibition, which he called "Narrative Paintings". These pictures would tell their own story and bring some understanding to people who may have thought that art was not for them.

The exhibition was opened by the President of the Royal Scottish Academy, Sir George Pirie, ran from March till September 1940 and told something about the standard of taste of those who were buying for the gallery—or gifting their pictures—in the early part of the century.

There were names like Sir David Wilkie, William McTaggart, Sam Bough and Sir W. Q. Orchardson, as well as examples of the Glasgow School before they abandoned the picture which tells a story.

There was Josef Israëls' "The Frugal Meal", Sir John Millais' "The Ornithologist", Ford Madox Brown's "Wycliffe on Trial", John Pettie's "Two Strings to her Bow", Albert J. Moore's "Reading Aloud" (Honeyman found it in the Council Chambers), Briton Riviere's "The Last of the Crew", Robert Gibb's "Alma—Forward the 42nd" and W. Q. Orchardson's "Peveril of the Peak".

His interest in modern art was apparently not a recommendation and the idea of going back to the Victorians was treated with suspicion. He claimed that his own motives were quite simple: he had to feel his way in planning exhibitions and to test the public's response. Though he was in demand as a speaker he knew that the invitation was quite often to fill a syllabus rather than to hear what he had to say! Many a speaker knows the feeling.

Dr Honeyman therefore set out instead to bring the audience into the gallery. At first there wasn't much encouragement from John Fleming, who adhered to his traditional line that "We tried lectures in old Paton's time—but it didn't work. Besides, there's a blackout and it's not worth opening the place up in the evening." Nevertheless, Honeyman forged ahead with afternoon lectures and found to his delight that they were crowded out.

The objective was to talk about art as well as displaying it. And just as he had discovered at university that the class is half the lecture, he was also learning that an audience is half the speech. He was trying to apply to the Glasgow situation the approach to art appreciation which he had seen elsewhere, especially at the Barnes Foundation in America.

His own education in art appreciation had begun with distinguished writers like Roger Fry and Clive Bell, dating back to the celebrated exhibition of the post-Impressionists at the Grafton Galleries in London in 1910. The man behind that exhibition had been Roger Fry, who was also credited with having first coined the phrase "post-Impressionist".

Fry clearly made a big impression on Honeyman, who recalled that to sit in Fry's company in front of a newly-discovered Renoir and hear him say in his deep voice: "It's swell!" was an unforgettable experience. Fry gave Honeyman a convenient definition of Romantic and Classical Art: "Romantic art produces its effect by relying on the association of ideas which it sets up in the mind of the spectator. Classical art creates its emotional effect through its own formal and pictorial organisation."

News of Honeyman's lectures reached even to the City Chambers and magistrates and councillors began to appear. On one occasion, when distinguished visitors were having tea in the director's room afterwards, convener Tom Kerr broke away from a group and said to Honeyman: "I was just telling them, doctor, what I told them long ago. You are the man who will bring art to the midden-heid!"

This compliment, which survived as a family joke for many years, at least acknowledged that he was reaching the so-called man-in-the-street.

XXI

FACING THE PHILISTINES

TOM HONEYMAN was disappointed he had not been accepted by Glasgow School of Art in general. Nevertheless, he did have good friends on the staff, not least the director, Douglas Percy Bliss, who he had known since the Lefevre days in London when Bliss was art critic of *The Scotsman*. He was also very friendly with Benno Schotz, who became head of the department of sculpture as well as Queen's Sculptor in Ordinary for Scotland.

Benno dated back to Tom's days as a doctor in Glasgow and advanced the drive to bring people to the Art Gallery with a highly successful series of lecture-demonstrations. He would model the head of someone taken at random from the audience and keep up a witty running commentary on the art of sculpture. It was tremendous fun, stripping away any notion of solemnity in these matters and proving a total fascination to the public.

The same kind of service was provided by Hugh Crawford (he later went off to be head of the Art School in Aberdeen) who would start with a blank canvas and give a step-by-step demonstration of how a portrait in oils acquired the vitality which made it a work of art.

Through all of this, however, the hostility of the Art School staff persisted. Honeyman's interest in people like Jankel Adler and

Josef Herman, at the time when the Poles were "invading" Glasgow, did not go down well.

In fact he was taken to task for writing a foreword to Herman's one-man show in this country and told it was his duty, as director of the Gallery, not to become mixed up with young painters "who didn't know what they were talking about." It was an attitude which would find louder echo in the years to come when Honeyman had the audacity to secure the Dali painting which caused such an uproar.

While pulling in the people, Honeyman was still spending an inordinate amount of time on public speaking but whether he was addressing a Women's Guild, a Burns Supper or a St Andrew's Night, he invariably managed to combine his skill and humour as an orator with the message that you couldn't live a full life if you had no place for the arts.

He was under some attack for publicising himself and there was no doubt that he enjoyed the public spotlight and regarded himself as "honoured" and "flattered" more often than was justified. But he did have the saving grace of humour, through which he acknowledged that, if ever he became puffed up by his own conceit, there would always be friends to bring him back to earth. Whatever the vanities, Tom Honeyman never scrimped with the energy he gave to his work. As Director of the Art Gallery and Museum he had to reach beyond painting and sculpture, to areas outwith his own range, as in the case of the outstanding collection of arms and armour which was bequeathed by Robert Lyon Scott, head of the old-established Greenock family business, Scotts of Greenock, shipbuilders and engineers.

To help accommodate the Scott Collection, he rearranged the Museum Section, clearing the Glasgow Room by removing its contents to the People's Palace, the branch museum at Glasgow Green.

If the truth be known, Dr Honeyman didn't think much of

branch museums unless they had a specific character of their own. Too often, he thought, they were just a collection of nondescript items, surplus to those of the central institution and merely on loan to brighten things up.

He regarded the contents of the People's Palace as an odd mixture. It certainly had the Sir Thomas Lipton Collection which reflected the remarkable career of that famous Glasgow merchant and sportsman. Most of it was to do with his yachting trophies and there were fascinating stories attached to most of them.

There was also a fine collection of regimental uniforms, badges and accoutrements associated with the history of Glasgow's military achievements. The curator, Captain Phillipe Durand, was an authority on the subject and much of the collection was his own property. But his enthusiasm was regarded as something of an embarrassment, inasmuch as his personal hobby had become mixed up with a civic collection.

The dilemma was eventually cleared up and Honeyman managed to establish what was called the Old Glasgow Museum. He still clung to his view, however, that the museum concentrating on "The History of Glasgow" should have a more central location and he had the frustration of knowing that this opportunity had arisen and was then lost. More accurately, he thought, it was rejected without proper consideration.

The idea had been planted in his head by Gray Buchanan, a businessman with headquarters in London, though he spent much of his time in Rothesay and had strong connections with Glasgow, especially through Bonar Law, the city iron merchant who worked for Buchanan's company before entering politics and becoming Prime Minister in 1922.

It was in Rothesay one evening that Buchanan said to Honeyman: "You must get hold of the Glasgow Royal Exchange building. It is a museum piece and I have good reason to believe that a big commercial firm has an eye on it." He explained that the old

Exchange method of doing business had faded out and that the building itself, with its central site, could be of civic importance.

Together they planned how to make use of the Royal Exchange if the city managed to acquire it. With that fine island position in Exchange Square, it had an architectural importance as a period piece dating back to the tobacco lords and the 18th century.

It was something to be preserved and Honeyman's idea was that it could house "The History of Glasgow" and provide gallery space for regular exhibitions, with lunch-hour concerts and so on. Gray Buchanan's main concern was that the building should be saved from the speculators and that the amenities in the area should be kept. They had further visions that Exchange Square might become a centre for trading in antiques, rare books, paintings and sculptures, giving Glasgow a kind of Bond Street, or Rue la Boetie, or 57th Street, New York.

Honeyman promoted the idea with a newspaper article and tried to stir enthusiasm. Perhaps he tried too hard, for it came to nothing. It did come into the civic realm but he had to face the galling fact that the libraries committee had its eye on the splendid building as a means of accommodating the Stirling Reference Library. His art gallery committee didn't stand a chance.

The possibility of making it the Old Glasgow Museum was certainly raised as an alternative. But the news was that the art gallery committee had been consulted and that the Director—that was Tom Honeyman, of course—was against the idea! It was supposed to be unsuitable for the purpose.

He eventually discovered the source of this misleading information who, when confronted, said: "Oh, I remember now. It wasn't you who said it. It was somebody else. Anyway it doesn't matter very much. Besides, the library committee has more pull with the Corporation."

No wonder Dr Honeyman was frequently struck dumb by the

workings of local government and the philistine attitudes of those who allegedly guided it.

He remained convinced that the wrong decision had been made. He had nothing against a central reference library as a necessary public service but the Royal Exchange was a Glasgow landmark which, he felt, could be better operated as an architectural feature of the city's history, as well as being a down-town centre for art exhibitions.

Twenty-five years after his death one can imagine, from the distance of the celestial places, that a wry smile broke over Tom Honeyman's face when the Stirling Library moved out of Exchange Square and that splendid building did indeed take on the role of an art gallery.

XXII

THE MAN FROM THE GLASGOW EMPIRE

AFTER that period of the Phoney War when nothing much happened, the dreaded blitz came to Glasgow in due course and the Art Gallery did not escape. On one of those bombing raids, a landmine came careering out of the night sky and exploded on the banks of the River Kelvin. There was a tremendous blast and when the dawn broke Tom Honeyman surveyed the shambles and realised his worst nightmare.

The only parts to escape were those corners most remote from the riverside, where they had placed the Scott Collection of armour. Some of the gallery towers had moved slightly and, with a few freak exceptions, the windows, roof lights and display cases had been reduced to glass fragments. In fact fifty tons of broken glass was removed from the building, for which they received ten shillings a ton by way of salvage.

In Honeyman's view, there was just one blessing from the blitz. He had always regarded the Sculpture Hall, the central feature of the Art Gallery, as an eyesore with a lot of bad sculpture and plaster casts dotted around like men on a chessboard. When they salvaged the good works, they certainly were not enough to fill the space and it was decided to use the area for changing displays. There was quite a number of very large marble ladies who had originally come out of Italy, relics of the days when Glasgow merchants did the Grand Tour and came back with Eves, satyrs and nymphs to decorate their grand conservatories.

They may have looked not too bad in the large mansions of Kelvinside, Dowanhill or Maxwell Park but the next generation had no use for them and they found a home in the Art Gallery. Tom Honeyman thought he knew an even better home and, with the co-operation of the Director of Parks, had them placed in the large glasshouse known as the Kibble Palace at the Botanic Gardens in Great Western Road. This was met with general approval, though not from his friend Professor John Walton. As Professor of Botany, Walton had a special affection for the Botanic Gardens and felt they had spoiled the overall vegetation climate of the Kibble Palace and turned it into a cheap imitation of Palm Court presentation.

The friendship remained, however, with some good-humoured exchanges, underlining another of Tom Honeyman's connections with the significant figures of the past. For John Walton was the son of E. A. Walton, one of the founders of the Glasgow School. Edward Arthur Walton was a good friend of Whistler and became his neighbour when he moved to live in Chelsea in 1894. When Whistler received word that Glasgow was giving him an honorary degree he immediately contacted E. A. Walton to find out about the procedure, what he should wear at the ceremony and how he should word his letter of acceptance. John Walton provided much information when Tom Honeyman compiled his pamphlet on Whistler in 1951.

In the restoration of the Art Gallery after the German blitz, Honeyman began to speculate on what should be done about the ethnography room, dealing with individual human societies. The first problem was there was nobody in charge of that department.

But a man for the moment materialised in the shape of Dr Henry Farmer, who created a new approach to the selection and display of the material which survived the blitz and anything else he could find in store. Dr Farmer needs some explanation—and is a classic illustration of the versatility to be found in so many people of that era.

He was basically a musician, best known as conductor of the orchestra at the famous old Glasgow Empire. From 1914 until 1947, in fact, he occupied the rostrum at that memorable variety theatre and knew the great artistes of the day. He spoke crisply, as if to match his short, dark moustache, and seemed rather anxious to hide his scholarly pursuits. Dr Honeyman became especially curious when he learned that, whenever the experts gathered to discuss Arabic music, they would end up by saying: "We had better ask Farmer about that."

So what led a man whose main occupation was to keep contact with the great music hall stars of the period to become an Orientalist of the very highest standing? With his interest in Scottish music, he had also written the first complete treatment of that subject, entitled *The History of Music in Scotland*.

Apparently it all started when a London publisher, who had issued two of Farmer's books on military music, persuaded him to do a translation from the French *La Musique Arabe*. This led to more appeals for information and when Farmer found so much confusion among the so-called authorities he decided to learn Arabic so that he could read the old treatises in their original form and come to his own conclusions.

This remarkable man had gained an MA in 1924, a PhD in 1926 and a DLitt in 1941, all from Glasgow University, and was also given a Doctorate of Music from Edinburgh. The ever-enthusiastic Honeyman had to find out more about the Jekyll and Hyde life of the man and was given this explanation: "Except for a couple of hours at a Monday morning rehearsal, my livelihood is made from 6pm till 11pm, which means that the morning and afternoon can be devoted to my avocations."

So Dr Honeyman engaged Farmer to arrange the first exhibition held by the Art Gallery after the blitz. Opened by Lord Provost Patrick Dollan on 21st May 1941, it was called "Instruments of Music", the first complete show of its kind to be held in Britain. It was an ambitious and risky venture, with more than a dozen lecture-recitals throughout the summer, but was hailed as having made a major contribution to the history of music. One important sequel, again through Dr Farmer, was that the museum was able to acquire the famous Glen Collection of Instruments for little more than a nominal figure.

But to return to the restoration of the ethnography department, it was the talented Farmer who came to the rescue and devoted himself to more than two years of the most painstaking work. You would find him in the Gallery at the back of eight every morning, before anyone else had appeared, and he would have to be dragged away for lunch, disappearing only when it was time to head for the Empire Theatre to conduct the orchestra for the rest of the evening. The damaged showcases had to be reglazed and adapted and a chance now arose to get rid of the funereal black paint which had hidden some beautiful light mahogany.

Dr Farmer transformed the whole place and designed a large wall map with a colour key to indicate the distribution of races in the different areas of primitive and civilised peoples. Once again, Farmer had been given free access to the stores and came up with valuable material which had not seen the light of day since the building was opened in 1901. This included a box of rare Persian tile fragments, showing a beautiful sense of design, which seemed to have been received in the 1880s.

Dr Farmer had done all this as a labour of love but Honeyman couldn't rest until the Corporation gave him some kind of honorarium. After a bit of bickering at the council, the princely sum of £200 was handed over as a token of his two years' work. With much good humour Farmer later calculated that the rate of pay was less than the twopence an hour paid to the boy who helped him! But as a sign of different times, this charming and scholarly man never did measure his work in terms of money.

As people adapted to the wartime experience, the problems of food rationing meant there was no dining out. The positive side was that people would meet in each other's houses for snacks, coffees and conversation—and new friendships were formed. Tom and Cath Honeyman would find themselves frequently at the home of Sir William Robieson, editor of the *Glasgow Herald*, whose guests made up a formidable range of the interesting people around Glasgow at the time.

Meanwhile, in those early dark days of the Second World War, just before France surrendered to the Germans, Honeyman received an urgent message: Could Glasgow accept custody of several cases of pictures? These would include Raoul Dufy's entire collection. Honeyman agreed and took delivery of seven cases of paintings, which were hidden for the rest of the war in a branch museum at Tollcross Park. It was not till the fighting was over that he realised he had broken the law by not declaring that these paintings were regarded as "enemy property".

They were eventually returned to Dufy, having survived not only the risks of war but, according to Tom Honeyman, innumerable temptations! Dufy made plain his gratitude to Glasgow and promised to repay the generous hospitality by donating an important work to the city. Sadly he died before he could carry out his promise though Louis Carré, who succeeded Etienne Bignou as the artist's agent, did his best. There was some consolation in the fact that Mr and Mrs A. J. MacNeill Reid gifted to the Glasgow Gallery in 1960 a splendid example of Dufy's work.

After that concentration of bombing of the city early in 1941, there were fears that the Art Gallery would be out of commission for at least a year. But with remarkable energy and cheerfulness—and a great deal of help from the city engineer—the place was reopened in a matter of weeks.

XXIII

ADDRESS BY CHURCHILL

THE FIRST five years of Dr Honeyman's tenure at Glasgow Art Gallery and Museum, covering most of the Second World War, were by no means his worst. The strains and anxieties of the war produced in the public a kind of spiritual hunger which had to be satisfied.

From the outbreak in 1939 until after the fighting had ended there were fifty special exhibitions, that is, ones organised by outside bodies and circulated around the country, as opposed to those arranged from within. Some of the titles indicated co-operation with government information services, like "British War Artists", "RAF in Action", "BBC at War", "Battle for Freedom", "Vegetables for Victory" and "The Stalingrad Sword". In the aftermath of the war this even extended to "Princess Elizabeth's Wedding Dress". Most of those depended on photography to convey information and lend support to propaganda but painting and sculpture were not neglected and nor were the efforts of the Allies.

Tom Honeyman's own favourite was "The Spirit of France" exhibition, to which he devoted himself personally. Glasgow had built up a strong Friends of France organisation and the spirit of the Auld Alliance was much emphasised. Lord Inverclyde took a keen interest in the movement but the main driving force was Etienne Vacher, manager of the Central Hotel in Glasgow, where so many VIPs were entertained as they passed through, to and from the United States. Monsieur Vacher was well placed to keep in touch with all the movements, anxious to advance the cause of his native land.

Among those who took the Glasgow route was General de Gaulle, the French leader, whose aloof and rather arrogant attitude was fully confirmed when Honeyman met him. "The Spirit of France" ran throughout June 1943, with a busy programme of lectures and musical recitals. The subjects included "Cézanne" by Sir Kenneth Clark, "Impressionism" by Stanley Cursiter, "French painting—its background of ideas" by James Laver, "Painting since Cézanne" and "French paintings in Scotland" by Dr Honeyman himself, "Quartets of Ravel and Debussy" by the Scottish Chamber Music Players, led by J. Mouland Begbie, "Cesar Franck and Debussy" by Wight Henderson and Bessie Spence, and "Concert of French Music" with the BBC Scottish Orchestra conducted by Ian Whyte.

Activities were not limited to within the building and Dr Honeyman accepted invitations which would give him the chance, in his own words, "to show off elsewhere". Some of his masters at the Corporation were concerned once again that he was taking too much limelight on himself. But he was confident in his role of showman for the city and confessed that he would sometimes risk getting permission after the event!

In that same year, 1943, he became only the second recipient of the St Mungo Prize, awarded every three years to the citizen who had done most to promote the amenities, welfare and prosperity of Glasgow. The idea came from Alex Somerville, a quiet little man who manufactured shoes and painted in watercolours as a hobby. Nobody paid much attention to him but his idea has survived down the years. In addition to a gold medal, Tom Honeyman received £1000, a sizeable sum in those days.

The first winner of the St Mungo Prize had been Sir Patrick

Dollan, widely regarded as the most successful Lord Provost the city had seen this century.

Tom Honeyman treasured a particular menu card from the Central Hotel at the height of the French crisis in 1940. It was signed by Pat and Agnes Dollan and New Zealand's High Commissioner, W. J. Jordan, and his wife Winifred. The prospect of an early German invasion was being discussed and the up-to-date news of government plans was brought to the table by Jordan, who was privy to the consultations with Commonwealth countries. They were sworn to secrecy around the dinner table, where the tension was all the higher since Patrick Dollan knew he was on the enemy hit-list. Dunkirk was not far off.

As the consultation proceeded, Dollan told Honeyman he had arranged a box at the Empire Theatre to entertain their distinguished guests. If Honeyman would take the ladies to the theatre, he and Jordan would join them later. The Empire was packed as the audience, out to enjoy itself in the face of impending catastrophe, gave a great Glasgow welcome to George Formby, with his ukelele. Honeyman and the three ladies shrank back into the shadows of the box, hardly in the mood to accept that all was well with the world. Dollan and Jordan joined them at the end of the evening, trying to put on a brave face in the light of what they knew.

Dollan was ever active in the cause of Glasgow and Tom Honeyman found himself drawn into many a dinner party when a VIP was passing through the city. On one such occasion he met Jan Masaryk, the Czechoslovakian statesman, not long before his mysterious death in Prague.

One of the most significant occasions in Glasgow's history was when Winston Churchill brought President Roosevelt's personal agent, Harry Hopkins, to the city for vital talks.

Churchill had toured Scotland with the American, seeking some sign that his country was going to join Britain in the fight against Hitler. So far there had been no such sign. Glasgow gave them a tumultuous reception, as civic dignitaries and eminent citizens turned up at the City Chambers to hear an address by Churchill. The Prime Minister gave a masterly summary of the war at home and abroad but Hopkins, in a non-committal mood, merely boasted of his Scottish ancestry.

A dinner party given in Glasgow that evening has been described in three different books—the autobiographical *A Letter from Grosvenor Square* by American Ambassador John Winant, Harry Hopkins' own *White House Papers* and the *Memoirs* of Tom Johnston. Honeyman claimed that Tom Johnston's account was the most accurate. Under pressure from Churchill, he had succeeded in getting Harry Hopkins to say something, making mention of his granny who came from Auchterarder.

At a dramatic point in his short speech, Hopkins looked straight at Winston Churchill and quoted from the Bible that passage from the book of Ruth which begins: "Whither thou goest I will go. . . ." Tom Johnston wrote: "That was all. He sat down in dead silence. Churchill's eyes welled up with tears. Here was the first news that the United States was throwing its weight on the Allied side."

XXIV

REACHING THE PEOPLE

THOUGH the name of Tom Honeyman would become dramatically identified with those of Sir William Burrell and Salvador Dali, his significance to Glasgow lay largely in the fact that he revolutionised the city's attitude to its artistic treasures.

In his pursuit of the man-in-the-street, he was out to destroy any notion of élitism. He sympathised with Charles Carter, Director of Aberdeen Art Gallery, who once said he had known museums and art galleries where officials seemed to regard the collection as their own property, to be maintained principally for themselves and a few specialists.

Honeyman realised that some of the exhibitions he and others had put on in Glasgow, London and Edinburgh during and after the war had been freely described as "stunts". The idea that the general public might form queues outside was seen as some kind of vulgarity to be discouraged; surely it was quality of visitor, not quantity, that a well-run gallery should pursue. Honeyman preferred the notion that there might be some quality concealed in the quantity.

He would sometimes say how much he envied the city librarian, whose customers had at least learned to read. At an art gallery they arrived with an intelligent interest but more or less abysmal ignorance. To remedy this situation the answer lay surely in the schools, an idea he picked up in the United States. There must be trained teachers and a proper piece of organisation so he went straight to the Director of Education in Glasgow, Dr R. M. Allardyce. The director listened to the proposition but gave a flat "nothing doing!" on the basis that the curriculum was already too crowded.

Then something happened to Honeyman's advantage. In the wartime emergency, school holidays were cancelled. Suddenly Dr Allardyce's department was glad to find something for the children to do. So back he went to address a headmasters' conference and to point out that Glasgow had this art gallery facility with untapped possibilities. Surely it was a place for the young. At first the response was slow but in no time at all it was overwhelming. Teachers could relax with a cup of tea as gallery staff conducted the youngsters among the array of treasures.

Soon Dr Honeyman was having his dreams realised in the formation of a Schools Museum Service, of which a teacher from Bellahouston Academy, Sam Thompson, was chosen as the man in charge. The service was extended to include features like Saturday morning art classes, run by the elegant Jean Irwin, whose popularity in this pursuit brought a massive demand from parents.

Thus Glasgow gained its Schools Museum Service which was still thriving half a century after it was launched in 1941.

In the Art Gallery itself, most of the top-level irreplaceable pictures had been removed because of the risk of bomb damage. Enough harm had been done already. Two layers of the roof glass had been thoroughly smashed and many of the flying splinters had broken the glass on the paintings.

The greatest damage was inflicted on a large painting which became well known to Glaswegians towards the end of the century. Because of its size, Sir John Lavery's historical document on the opening of the 1888 Exhibition by Queen Victoria had been left on the stairway. After the bombing, it was found in shreds, apparently beyond repair.

However, in the faint hope that something might be achieved in the future, they rolled up the tattered canvas to see if some pictorial plastic surgeon might one day attempt the impossible. The fact that that was truly achieved can be seen in the magnificent restoration of Lavery's painting as you descend from the circle of Glasgow Royal Concert Hall and marvel not only at the painting itself but at the work which salvaged it.

Shortly afterwards, Dr Honeyman was discussing with Sir Kenneth Clark, Director of the National Gallery, his belief that they should be cleaning and restoring their most famous pictures now, since they were already hidden from public view because of the war.

Sir Kenneth agreed and immediately recommended that Helmut Ruhemann should come to Glasgow for a two-year engagement. Honeyman remembered Ruhemann from his days in London and knew he was an expert on the scientific methods of restoring pictures. He had been well known as chief picture restorer at the Kaiser Frederich Museum in Berlin in the late 1920s, arriving in England in 1933, when he became associated with the Courtauld Institute. Trained as an artist, he was also an expert on the technical methods used by the Old Masters.

As Ruhemann began work in a makeshift studio on the balcony of Glasgow Art Gallery, his presence attracted a predictable amount of criticism from those who did not believe in cleaning pictures. Honeyman faced up to his critics but grew restless at what he regarded as some of the nonsense being spoken.

In his defence, he would summon the evidence of Arthur Laes of the Brussels Museum of Fine Art, who arrived in this country during the war still dressed in his dinner jacket, having been attending the opening of an exhibition in Holland as the Germans poured in.

In Glasgow he had been delighted to see what they had done with the cleaning of a painting by Paul Bril, the Flemish landscape artist. He later wrote of the outstanding success in resurrecting the work, dated 1602, "which had formerly been hidden under a coat of brown varnish and which can now be seen in all its pristine freshness; this picture, which is more than three centuries old, is in a perfect state of preservation."

To see Ruhemann at work was for Honeyman a pleasure and a reassurance. His initial examination was followed by a restraint which kept retouching to the minimum.

Ruhemann divided his time between the Art Gallery and private work. He cleaned some of the university pictures, including their famous Chardins which were in the Paris exhibition of 1937. On that occasion Honeyman was teased by the French authorities for the dirty condition of the paintings, a responsibility he passed on to the university. But they got even. In the cleaning process, Ruhemann revealed a date on one of the Chardins which put the French experts twenty years out in their catalogue entries.

Of course Ruhemann could not be kept in Scotland indefinitely and Tom Honeyman knew that you really needed to train your own people. The fates played into his hands. A colleague from his medical days phoned him to say he had a patient who might be of some use to him. A graduate of Glasgow School of Art, this patient had been temporarily under the weather and was not quite sure about the career to follow.

That was how he met Harry McLean, who brought the benefit of his art training and soon began to build himself a reputation. Before Harry had reached full mastery of his craft, however, Honeyman was faced with a decision about the greatest picture in the collection, "Christ and the Adulteress" by Giorgione.

This was always going to be a highly controversial matter since the practice of cleaning and restoring works of art had long attracted prejudice and conflict. Before recommending that the

Giorgione should be cleaned, Dr Honeyman consulted a range of leading authorities and was so encouraged by their support that he set the process in motion.

There was only one place with the necessary equipment for the job and that was the National Gallery in London. The full report, with X-ray photographs, microchemical analysis and so on are all in portfolios in the gallery archives. The picture landed back in the hands of Helmut Ruhemann, who was clearly the man for the job.

But that did not stop the critics. Michael Ayrton was much against it, as revealed in a couple of BBC programmes. Of the result, he said: "Cleaning has caused the blue robe of the central figure to advance from its proper tonal place so that it seems nearer to the eye than the shadowed arm and knee of the armoured man in front of it."

Honeyman agreed that, at a distance of three or four feet from the picture, that was correct. But at the proper viewing distance for a picture of its size this was not so. When the dirty brown varnish was removed, not only were the colours restored but the space relationship of different passages appeared to regain the original values which had been lost. Personally, he was delighted with the result.

With his ever-inquiring mind, he was curious about the neglect of a Scot called William Buchanan, who was mentioned in all the diaries and records at the beginning of the 19th century. He was a graduate of Glasgow University, became a lawyer in Edinburgh then an art dealer in London (rather like his own pattern) and was responsible for importing some of the great masterpieces in art.

Buchanan's name kept cropping up—and it appeared once again when he read about a major case of art forgery, involving the celebrated bust of "Flora", which had been supposedly a genuine Leonardo da Vinci. In fact this "Leonardo" bust, he discovered, was made in 1846 by Richard Lucas, to the special order of William

Buchanan, who supplied the sculptor with a painting "in the style of Leonardo", to serve as a model. Neither Lucas nor Buchanan was to be described as a forger and the work was never offered by them for sale as a genuine piece. It was not until experts began to proclaim it as a Leonardo that it became a forgery.

Some of the finest paintings in the National Gallery apparently passed through Buchanan's hands and Honeyman believed that Scotland should know a lot more about him. A start could be made at his burial place in the Glasgow Necropolis, where he went in 1864 at the age of eighty-seven. Towards that end, he encouraged a London-Scottish friend, Colin Clark, to embark on an autobiographical study, the fate of which crops up in a later chapter.

In March 1942 Glasgow Corporation gave its approval to Tom Honeyman's latest bright idea: the Glasgow Art Gallery and Museum Association, which soon became known as GAGMA. Having aroused some misunderstanding and suspicion, he explained the purposes: to ensure good attendance at lectures, exhibition openings and so on through the creation of a mailing list; to provide a new form of publicity; to create a fund for producing up-to-date literature; to form a link between existing organisations and to persuade them to make better use of the civic collection and to cultivate private collectors—with the obvious end in view!

Dr Honeyman set the minimum subscription at one shilling to encourage the young, and a later life membership of five guineas. GAGMA was under way in 1944 and the founder would surely have been delighted to know that the calendar of events was still going strong more than fifty years later.

A membership ranging upwards of 2200 (almost 1000 of them life members) continued that basic support of the galleries and museums, which included a voluntary guiding service of 160 people, available at Kelvingrove, the Museum of Transport, the Burrell Collection, Pollok House and the Gallery of Modern Art.

There were private views, lectures and excursions, financial backing for the young people's art competition and funding of recitals and maintenance of the Kelvingrove organ. In the 1990s GAGMA had a turnover of more than £70,000 and administered funds of more than double that.

The format for GAGMA was taken from Honeyman's friend Martin Baldwin, for many years director of the Toronto Art Gallery. The first issue of the illustrated magazine appeared in 1946 under the name of *Glasgow Art Review* and Tom Honeyman was delighted that the front cover displayed the portrait of F. H. Newbery, famous director of Glasgow School of Art, who exerted a great influence on the artists of his own generation. The background of the portrait silhouetted the School designed by Charles Rennie Mackintosh. The name of the magazine was later changed to the *Scottish Art Review* when it was discovered that the Glasgow School of painters, which flourished towards the end of the 19th century, had issued a magazine under the previous name.

When Tom Honeyman eventually bowed out, his farewell coincided with the centenary celebration, in print, of Archibald McLellan, the real founder of Glasgow's civic art collection. This was done in a well-illustrated historical essay by Elspeth Gallie, curator in charge of the Glasgow Art Museum.

Archibald McLellan (1797-1854) was the man who set the pattern for art collecting and general patronage of the arts which became such a feature of Glasgow life in the 19th century. A coachbuilder by occupation, he was a prominent and highly enlightened citizen who advocated that the university as well as the city should be involved in furthering an appreciation of the arts.

In his will he provided for his art collection to go to the city and for a Chair of Art to be established at Glasgow University. Sadly he died insolvent and the city ended up buying his paintings for £15,000. He did, however, set the scene for the collectors who would follow.

XXV

FROM McINNES TO CARGILL

THE OUTGOING NATURE of his personality and a certain knack of getting to know people of significance were a decided advantage when Tom Honeyman came to encounter the great art collectors of his day.

Making the acquaintance of such people was important for a man in his position, not only for the pleasure of their company but for the hope that they might eventually leave their treasures to his beloved Glasgow.

Honeyman would give you the frank opinion that very few of those great collectors had much in the way of artistic taste. But what did that matter as long as they had a well-developed instinct, the knack of finding good advisers—and plenty of money?

He would mull over the motives of that strange body of people, suspecting they were after some kind of immortality, and he reckoned it was on the basis that the collection outlives the collector and provides a monument to a public-spirited citizen.

In examining collecting, which seemed to come from a primitive urge, he would look around his own house at 3 Kensington Gate, Glasgow, and question why he himself had acquired his own modest gathering. It might have been less modest if he had held on to a few treasures, like Derain's "Pool of London", which he bought for £45, passed on to the Tate Gallery for £1500 and would soon be testing his philosophical attitudes when it was valued at £60,000.

Similarly, his Pissarro painting of "The Marne at Chennevieres", which he bought for £542, had always been seen as the country cottage of the future. Instead it went to the National Gallery of Scotland in Edinburgh, a necessity at the time to pay for daughter Margaret's wedding. That picture was soon worth a small fortune and to those outwith the immediate art world it seems strange that he would part with such a treasure for a purpose which most fathers have to meet from savings. It tells us something about an art scene where paintings can become currency. Anyway, it was all part of life's own tapestry and Tom Honeyman claimed he had no regrets. As an art dealer, it had been his job to encourage people to buy; and that gave him a keen insight into the motivating impulses of human beings.

The kind of collector who became important to Honeyman was William McInnes, a man he came to know about the time he switched from medicine to art in the late 1920s. McInnes was a bachelor who lived modestly and without ostentation in a flat in the Pollokshields district of Glasgow. He was a partner in the shipping firm of Gow Harrison of Gordon Street, Glasgow, the head of which, Dr Leonard Gow, was an art collector with some notable pictures, including Old Masters and examples of 19th century French (Manet, Degas and Renoir). He also collected Chinese porcelain and some of his treasures found their way into the Burrell Collection.

This enthusiasm obviously rubbed off on William McInnes, who had occupied his leisure hours in painting and music, having played the church organ in his younger days.

Honeyman first met him through Scottish artist Leslie Hunter and used to see him almost daily before the move to London as an art dealer. They were part of a small group which used to meet for morning coffee in the Bon-Bon, a little café within Glasgow Central Station.

McInnes was just one of a number of shipping people involved in art collecting. The Scott Collection of armour had come from the Scott family of Greenock. There was Sir William Burrell and of course the Gow and McInnes connection.

It was that common admiration of Leslie Hunter, one of the Scottish Colourists, which helped to bind Honeyman and McInnes in friendship. Indeed it was when the former arrived back to take up his Glasgow post in 1939 that McInnes presented the Matisse "Head of a Young Girl" to Glasgow. In his letter to the Lord Provost he said he was doing it as a mark of his approval of Honeyman's appointment. When he died in 1944 his entire collection became part of the civic collection and added greatly to the gallery displaying French art.

As Honeyman used to point out, McInnes was comfortably off but could not be regarded as a wealthy man. When he bought a picture it was because it meant something to him and that was not related to price. His main object was to acquire works of art which could be enjoyed by himself and his friends. McInnes also took the view that the finest and most original work of an artist was often not to be found in the so-called important productions.

The measure of what McInnes did for Glasgow Art Gallery can be seen in the names he added to the catalogue: Bonnard, Braque, Cézanne, Van Gogh, Jongkind, Matisse, Picasso, Renoir and Seurat. The Braque and Matisse are regarded as outstanding.

Honeyman regarded the McInnes Collection as an invaluable introduction to a school of painting around which controversy raged for many years. It included several "minor" works which were gems. The Van Gogh was of the Paris period, the Monet and Sisley landscapes contained the whole purpose and achievement of Impressionism.

The three Renoirs (portrait, still-life and landscape) were an excellent guide to more famous paintings and the "blue period" Picasso brought great delight. Honeyman summed up McInnes's collection as an exciting range of paintings, drawings and prints which were a fine memorial to a true lover of the arts, a public-spirited gentleman.

He began to encounter a wealthier class of collector, some becoming well known through the saleroom, others working quietly through an agent. His main interest was that the ultimate owners of those collections should be the general public.

It was not always understood how the great industrialists of the West of Scotland had come to fill their houses with 19th century French and Dutch paintings. Honeyman knew a little of collections like those of Coats, Brechin and Burrell but he got to know about David Cargill only when he joined Reid and Lefevre.

On his first visit to the Cargill home near Lanark he was amazed at the quality and importance of what he saw. He had heard that Cargill had Cézanne, Renoir, Van Gogh, Seurat, Courbet, Toulouse-Lautrec, Gauguin and others, and was familiar with some of Cargill's pictures from catalogues which he had swotted up as part of his training. But he had no idea they were in Scotland.

Cargill was a burly but kindly man with a gentle voice who spoke in short sentences. Every comment was to the point. The Cargill family had been associated with the founding of the great Burmah Oil Company and there were other business interests in the Far East, where David had spent part of his early life. Despite the reticence and occasional eccentricity you would find in such people, they were usually anxious to share their pleasure with others.

Among those privileged with a visit to David Cargill's home in Lanark was the well-known theatrical impresario, C. B. Cochran. On his return to Glasgow with Honeyman that evening, Cochran gave a vivid impression of his day, which indicated how much it had meant to him. Apart from the paintings, the two elderly serving maids had reminded him of Rembrandt or Hals.

In time, the Cargill trustees allowed Tom Honeyman to choose three pictures for the French section of Glasgow Art Gallery—an important Corot painting, "Mademoiselle de Foudras", a large Courbet, "Flowers in a Basket", and a well-known Seurat, "Boy Sitting on the Grass". The others went mainly to America, with the proceeds used to augment the Cargill Fund, which backed Scottish charities and stimulated interest in the arts.

However, there was not just one Cargill but two—David's half-brother William, who lived at Bridge of Weir. And as a measure of this unusual gentleman, the disposal of his own collection following his death in 1962 became the art event of the year and raised over a million, including £105,000 for a Degas.

William was smaller than David, a shy and reserved bachelor who remained devoted to his mother, a sweet old lady and last of her breed, who went shopping in Sauchiehall Street in a horse-drawn brougham, before the family moved out to Bridge of Weir.

William was a talented tennis player and golfer—he reached the final of the amateur championship—but when his mother died he withdrew into a spartan way of life which crossed the border of eccentricity.

When Tom Honeyman returned to the Glasgow job in 1939 and faced the emergency of war, he set about organising exhibitions and finding out where he could borrow from private collections.

He had known of the magnificent paintings at Bridge of Weir, though a difference of opinion with old Alexander Reid had taken William Cargill away from Reid and Lefevre. Nevertheless he was invited to Carruth, William Cargill's home at Bridge of Weir, where most of the paintings acquired in the 1930s were still in their packing cases, hidden in wardrobes or tucked under beds.

On one occasion Dr Honeyman would take with him two members of his staff, including the restorer Harry McLean who not only found a career when he arrived at Glasgow Art Gallery but his future wife as well. She was none other than the boss's secretary, Isabel Mackintosh, who was also in that small group which arrived at Bridge of Weir to face a scene of considerable fascination.

For the rest of her life Isabel has carried the memory of William Cargill, a Dickens-like character, polite and anxious that you were all right but a very nervous man, she soon deduced, not used to women, except the old-fashioned housekeeper who had been there from his mother's time and bossed him around.

Isabel soon realised that he was totally thrown off guard by the unexpected appearance of another woman and the minor crisis seemed to centre on the fact that they would now be one scone short for afternoon tea. In a bizarre scene, the housekeeper ordered him to get out one of the big limousines and drive into the village for an extra scone!

Apparently William would drive her to one church on a Sunday while he went on to another. Her sermon would last longer than his so you would find him dutifully waiting to chauffeur her home in the Rolls!

Isabel also came to the conclusion that he was rather a sick man and realised that Dr Honeyman was giving him advice as a medical man as well as advising on his collection. Harry McLean weighed in with guidance on what needed to be done with those treasures under the beds.

Tom Honeyman was given the freedom to sort out the Cargill Collection, tidy it up and hang the paintings. William in turn was glad of the gallery resources in cleaning, recording and photographing his possessions.

So he came to rely a great deal on Kelvingrove and Tom Honeyman was naturally hoping that he would emulate McInnes and leave at least some of his works to Glasgow.

Two factors killed off that hope. The first was the Corporation's decision, after Honeyman retired, to elevate the museum side at the expense of the art side ("They don't seem to think much of their art collection," was Cargill's comment). The other factor referred to the Burrell Collection. He said: "Look at what they have done—or not done—with Burrell's magnificent gift!" No more needed to be said.

Another provider for Glasgow Art Gallery, of course, was the Hamilton Trust, founded in 1927 with £60,000 from within a family which included its chairman, George Primrose, for twenty years the commercial editor of the *Glasgow Herald*.

Honeyman agreed that some notable additions had been made to the gallery but felt the trustees had also missed many fine opportunities. While they had often benefited from his advice, he felt they could have listened to him more often and done Glasgow a power of good.

Honeyman felt they had all missed the boat with artists like Picasso, Braque and many others, who had changed so profoundly the nature, purpose and condition of pictorial art. All this emphasis on art collectors leads us, of course, to the most significant name of all as far as Glasgow is concerned: Sir William Burrell.

XXVI

A PHONE-CALL FROM BURRELL

A PHONE-CALL to Dr Honeyman's home one December evening in 1943 sparked off the single most dramatic happening in the artistic life of Glasgow. The caller was Sir William Burrell, the wealthy shipowner who no longer lived in his native city but was to be found in the splendour of Hutton Castle at Chirnside, not far from Berwick-upon-Tweed.

His call was a matter of great secrecy, he emphasised, but he wanted Dr Honeyman to travel as soon as possible to see him at the castle. All her boss could say to explain his absence to Isabel Mackintosh was "There's something I can't tell you about; it's apparently so secret. But I have to go on this journey."

Even his wife didn't know what was going on. Cath Honeyman phoned the secretary to see if she knew where her husband had gone that day. She couldn't find anything in his diary at home. He wasn't driving in those wartime days so Isabel thought he must be going by train, in which case he would have taken a rail voucher from the office. But none had been taken.

By whatever means, Tom Honeyman was on his way to Hutton Castle with no inkling of what might be in store. But he didn't have long to wait to be put out of his agony.

In plain language, Sir William and Lady Burrell had decided to give their entire collection of 8000 items to the city of Glasgow. In addition, there would be a sum of £450,000 to provide a gallery for its display.

A man seldom stuck for words, Tom Honeyman found himself in such a state of excitement that any coherent response seemed to desert him. By any standard, it was a most stunning piece of news, one which he tried to absorb on the journey back to Glasgow, as he turned over in his mind the incredible story of William Burrell.

Here was the son of a Glasgow shipping agent who started work in his father's office at the age of fifteen and eventually grew into a ship-owner of great means, quietly building up over the years this amazing collection of ancient and Oriental art, European textiles, metalwork, glass, woodwork, stone, ivory, pottery and of course hundreds of paintings.

In the course of a busy life in shipping, Burrell had done it all himself, while managing with a rare talent to protect his privacy.

People in the art world knew what he was up to but it remains an astonishing fact that, even when he died as recently as 1958 at the age of ninety-seven, his name meant little to the general public in his native Scotland.

Tom Honeyman had first met Sir William in 1929, by which time he had already moved across to the east coast. He still had a Greek Thomson house in Great Western Terrace, Glasgow, with a panelled hall and staircase which were designed by Sir Robert Lorimer. But if business didn't keep him overnight in the city, he would catch the four o'clock train for Berwick and complete the nine mile journey to Hutton Castle, beautifully situated near the Tweed.

Occasionally, between lunch and train time, he would call at Reid's gallery in West George Street, to which Dr Honeyman had recently diverted himself as an art dealer. The firm was, of course, in the process of moving to London so there was less and less chance that the Glasgow gallery would have anything to gain his attention.

But Sir William would always look at anything by Joseph Crawhall, one of the members of the Glasgow School (the Burrell Collection has no fewer than 132 Crawhalls). Honeyman could remember an early encounter with Sir William who quizzed him about this and that before giving some illuminating views on art and art dealing and finally buying a Crawhall drawing after a bit of bargaining. Honeyman was still congratulating himself on the transaction with Burrell when a telegram arrived from Edinburgh, cancelling the purchase. Sir William had decided he had plenty of Crawhalls. But he wished Honeyman all the best nevertheless!

When he appeared at Reid's, the budding art dealer would try to detain him long enough to stir a reminiscent mood. It was well known that Burrell was among the very first people to appreciate 19th century French art, though he always gave Alexander Reid full credit for having introduced him to the best examples of it. Strong characters like Reid and Burrell would not have agreed on everything but on certain members of the Glasgow School and the French Impressionists, they shared a high enthusiasm.

Burrell used to recall a memorable supper party given by Alexander Reid when he moved to new premises at St Vincent Street. Leading members of the Glasgow School present that night included Guthrie, Lavery, Hornel, Walton, Henry, Stevenson and Kennedy.

"I was the only non-artist invited," Sir William used to say. "It was a very merry evening."

By the time Honeyman met him, Sir William had become less interested in painting, feeling that the picture side of his collection was more or less complete.

In his art dealing days, he had become involved in a painting which eventually landed with Burrell. It was Cézanne's "Château de Médan" or "House of Zola", which had once belonged to Gauguin but which Honeyman had bought in New York in exchange for Toulouse-Lautrec's "L'Accroche-coeur". He had hoped it would find a home in the National Gallery but their interest was not sufficiently strong and Burrell landed the Cézanne for £3800.

Considering the times in which Burrell lived, Honeyman reckoned his collection of French paintings would have been even more notable if Sir William had been less of a bargain hunter and more courageous, less prejudiced and more aware of what was happening to art and artists.

He would illustrate this by showing what Burrell had paid for his paintings: "The Empress Eugénie on the Beach, Trouville" by Boudin was bought in 1923 for £250; "Portrait of Duranty" by Degas, also bought in 1923, for £1900; "The Rehearsal" by Degas, bought in 1926 for £6500; "Jockeys in the Rain" by Degas, bought in 1937 for £3885 (this came from the Gow Collection); "Self Portrait" by Rembrandt came in 1948 for £12,500 and "Portrait" by Franz Hals was bought in 1946 for £14,500. The Rembrandt and Hals came late in Burrell's life so the £14,500 seems to have been the most he ever paid.

A great deal of care, therefore, went into his purchases. Catalogues were scrutinised and his amazing memory made it easy for him to identify works which might have eluded him on an earlier occasion.

Until advancing years made it impossible to visit London or Paris, Sir William was a regular attender at the big exhibitions arranged by leading art dealers and at previews of auction sales.

Tom Honeyman would make the point that he couldn't recall a single case where his name was associated with a dramatic purchase at an extravagant price. On the contrary, there were several instances where his wide knowledge bought him an important item at a bargain price. There was, for example, the case of a restored Romanesque portal which the Hearst Collection bought for £5000. Burrell marked time and, when that collection was finally dispersed, Sir William got it for £550.

So Burrell built up his famous collection and long before he chose Glasgow for his spectacular gift, many of the treasures were on loan to cities throughout the country. The tapestries were on show in a number of cathedrals but, for reasons of safety and preservation, there were strict limits on the number of special exhibitions. Against that, Sir William and Lady Burrell seemed to find great pleasure in sharing their works.

Tom Honeyman had heard Sir William give an account of the history of his pictures, tapestries and sculptures and found it a fascinating experience as well as a valuable education. Honeyman regretted, however, that Burrell had resisted all suggestions to have prepared a factual record of his unequalled experience as a collector.

If only someone had been allowed to write his story! But Sir William remained paranoid about his privacy. Whereas journalists would have been queuing up to get the story of his life as a collector, he resisted all approaches—and that was the end of that. Such was his obsession with privacy that he even refused all attempts to have him sit for a portrait or a sculpture.

In view of the gift to Glasgow, Honeyman was already envisaging a place in the Burrell Collection for the man himself. But it was not to be.

"The collection, not the collector, is the important thing," was Burrell's response, a refreshing enough thought in an age of rampant publicity. But imagine the extra dimension of interest which would have been added if the power behind this amazing feat had revealed even a little about himself and the instinct which drove him to such heights.

But far from gaining a portrait of the great man, the public finds it hard enough to judge him even from a picture. Apart from a very early studio portrait, one of the rare photographs was taken when he received the Freedom of Glasgow. For the record, Sir William was a tall, slender and distinguished-looking man with a long, narrow face, white hair and short moustache and he spoke with a pronounced burr and nasal twang. Isabel Mackintosh remembered him as "a grand-looking man who always seemed to be barking at people."

In the modern world his business activities would have been open much more to scrutiny but those who were privileged to witness him in action within Glasgow shipping circles used to vouch for the fact that his foresight and enterprise belonged to the realms of romance.

But he didn't confine himself to his own business interests. For such a private man, it is surprising to find that he did serve for seven years as a town councillor in Glasgow, as well as being Consul for Austria and Hungary before the First World War, a trustee of the Tate Gallery in London and of the National Gallery in Scotland.

He also came to the assistance of Glasgow's oldest house, Provand's Lordship, which was in danger of being demolished at the turn of the century. Most of its period furniture was to come from a "Burrell Fund".

The concealing of himself was all the more regrettable since Sir William had a delightfully amusing way of lighting up a conversation with reminiscences which usually had a historical significance. He was also capable of turning a story against himself, as Dr Honeyman discovered one day when the two men were walking round the Kelvingrove Gallery.

Sir William was recalling some pictures he had given to the gallery in 1923, when he had stipulated that they were all to be hung together. On one occasion he had wandered into the building and was moving about, unrecognised, when he asked the attendant to tell him about those Burrell pictures.

Apparently the attendant said: "Ach, I don't know much about them. We've got to keep them together; that's the condition. But we'll likely scatter them when the old buffer dies."

After his early contact with Burrell at Reid's gallery in Glasgow,

Honeyman strengthened the rapport during the collector's visits to the Lefevre in London. It is sometimes difficult to envisage the worldwide travelling of the well-to-do in a bygone day but it was not uncommon for Sir William and Lady Burrell to be off on some cruising holiday in the West Indies and dropping in for a few days in London on the way through. On those occasions they would seek out Honeyman from the Lefevre Gallery and take him to Christie's or Sotheby's to discuss some lot which was due up for sale.

Sir William would jot things down on odd pieces of paper and Honeyman would encounter his impish sense of humour. One day he asked Honeyman if he could decipher a line of writing which had defeated him. It was in the middle of an important memorandum which looked like Stock Exchange prices. Honeyman could make out only the words "Get your hair cut!" Sir William remembered with a chuckle that that was indeed the message—and reminded himself never to get domestic instructions mixed up with business!

XXVII

HOUSING THE COLLECTION

DR HONEYMAN journeyed home from Hutton Castle that day, casting it all over in his mind and marvelling at the good fortune which had come Glasgow's way. It never failed to astound him that one man had studied, assessed and acquired this massive collection and that, at the end of it all, he had not squandered his accumulated treasures.

Now that Sir William Burrell was into his eighties, there had been speculation as to what would happen to his great collection. The possibility of Edinburgh or London had been discussed but there was a hint that he had developed a bias against these cities. Something which displeased him greatly was the wartime removal of beautiful railings around Hutton Castle (this was a common order at the time, to help with the scarcity of materials) and the decision had been made by a government department based in Edinburgh. On such slender whims are decisions sometimes reached!

A more positive reason for choosing the destination of the Burrell Collection was to emerge when he revealed that a major factor had been the great knowledge of art and serious effort being shown in his native city by Dr Tom Honeyman.

Whatever the reason, the Burrell Collection would now belong to Glasgow and Honeyman couldn't wait to get back to tell Baillie Burnett, the convener of the Art Gallery committee.

Together they went to break the news to Lord Provost James Welsh. And Isabel Mackintosh remembers the moment when Honeyman returned to his own office, bursting to give her the news: "We've got the Burrell Collection!"

In the days and weeks to follow, there were many exchanges of letters and phone-calls, in which Sir William was putting Tom Honeyman under the hazardous obligation of seeing that there would be no fuss or publicity. A further telegram in January 1944 asked for an immediate meeting between Sir William's solicitor, Mr Logan, and the town clerk, Mr Kerr, so that the matter would be either "on or off" with Glasgow by the end of the month.

Dr Honeyman attended that meeting and was gratified to hear Mr Logan repeat that Sir William's decision for Glasgow had been swayed by the successful work being done at the Art Gallery. His regard for Honeyman dated back for some time and had been revealed in the reference provided when Dr Tom applied for the job in 1939.

The fact that it took forty years from that initial move in 1943 until the Burrell Collection finally went on show in its own home in 1983 became the subject of much argument, bickering and controversial discussion. But in fairness to the authorities, it had much to do with the conditions which Burrell attached to his gift. That in turn was all to do with the siting of the proposed gallery which had to be somewhere in the vicinity of Killearn and no less than sixteen miles from the Glasgow Royal Exchange, in the heart of the city.

This condition was because of the delicacy of the tapestries and the damage which could be inflicted by the industrial smog so prevalent in Glasgow in those days.

A number of legal points had to be considered. For example, it might not be possible to provide a site within the narrow limits laid down, especially in view of the uncertainty of post-war planning. Honeyman himself had doubts about the conditions, seeking to loosen them to allow more power to Sir William's trustees in the future, when conditions might have changed.

But exchanges with Sir William merely stirred within him a mixture of annoyance and exasperation and Tom Honeyman came to the conclusion that the man had made himself captive to an obsession. The menace of fog seemed to haunt him.

Anxious to overcome the hurdle, Tom Honeyman looked into modern methods of air-conditioning and, with this in mind, Sir James French of the well-known Glasgow firm of Barr and Stroud prepared an elaborate scheme covering every possibility of providing a gallery within the city which would be safe. But Burrell wouldn't even look at it. (Long after Honeyman had retired, he was appalled to find the Corporation calling for a report on air-conditioning, evidently unaware that there was a splendid one in existence.)

Glasgow Corporation delegated the affairs of the Burrell Collection to a special committee, leaving the Art Gallery and Museum Committee to handle the in-gathering of the various items scattered among galleries, museums and cathedrals around the country.

The administration of funds lay with the city treasurer and Honeyman felt that art and even the Burrell Collection were sometimes regarded as minor matters. He once heard a former holder of the office being asked when the Corporation was going to get a move on with Burrell. He was surprised to hear the reply: "Damn the Burrell Collection! I wish we had never seen it."

The work of gathering, registering, cataloguing, photographing and storing the collection became too much for the immediate control of Honeyman and the Corporation created a new appointment, a Keeper of the Burrell Collection. The man appointed, with Sir William's enthusiastic approval, was Andrew Hannah, who did a fine job, not least in organising the first large-scale exhibition of the works, which was held in the McLellan Galleries in the summer of 1949. The main purpose of this exhibition was to give

Glasgow people the chance to see this famous collection which was now their own property.

Tom Honeyman suggested they might leave out the tapestries but, despite his fear of fog, Sir William felt they would be the main attraction. He was willing to have them displayed during the ten days of the Glasgow Fair, when industry would be at a standstill and the city free of smoke. Honeyman had to point out that the expense of all this could not be justified for a show which ran for less than three months.

Both Honeyman and Andrew Hannah naturally wanted to include the tapestries if possible and, after a pleasant meal and after-dinner chat, Sir William relented. This was major progress, considering he had once insisted the tapestries would not be shown in Glasgow at all.

That exhibition in the McLellan Galleries caused widespread interest and brought a query from Philip James of the Arts Council about the possibility of an even greater selection going to Burlington House in London. Since those London shows were international events, Tom Honeyman was keen on the idea, if only for the publicity value. Sir William seemed favourable at first but then put too many conditions in the way.

Philip James tried again in 1950 and Honeyman satisfied himself on the atmospheric conditions. But Sir William was still against it—and that was when the hint of an anti-London bias arose. Similarly, he laid down that under no circumstances was Glasgow to lend any item from the Burrell Collection to be shown in Edinburgh!

Then came something of a different nature which seemed to answer the whole problem of where to site the Burrell. A press release from the Corporation announced in its headline: GIFT OF DOUGLASTON ESTATE TO THE CORPORATION OF GLASGOW. The story ran: "At a meeting of the special committee on the Burrell Collection it was intimated that Mrs Therese Connell was prepared to offer the estate of Douglaston, Milngavie, as a gift to the city of Glasgow, subject to her retaining a life interest in it.

"The offer follows on conversations between Sir William Burrell and Mrs Connell and it is a condition of the gift that a site on the estate will be used for the gallery to accommodate the Burrell Collection. Sir William has expressed his delight at the gift and his complete agreement to the use of the estate for the purpose of the Burrell Collection. The agreement between Sir William and the Corporation will be modified accordingly."

Dr Honeyman pondered the fact that, in rethinking his site conditions, Sir William had at one stage looked at Mugdock Castle at Milngavie as a possibility, finally rejecting it with a return to his original agreement "which must be rigidly adhered to".

But if Mugdock Castle was too near Glasgow, what was so acceptable about Douglaston, which was even nearer? The Art Gallery committee had met Sir William at Douglaston and convener Jack Kelly was ready with a persuasive speech in the hope that the matter could be resolved.

But to his surprise and delight, Sir William concluded the proceedings almost before they had started by saying: "All right, I approve. And I'm hungry. When do we have lunch?" Many had not realised that their benefactor was indeed a master of the quick change from irresistible obstruction to willing co-operation. All now seemed set fair, with the Parks Department taking over the care of the grounds and everyone weighing in with suggestions about the best situation for the gallery to house the Burrell Collection. At last there was a solution. Or was there?

Suddenly it all fell apart when the government announced that it was planning to establish a new coal-mine by the Douglaston estate! This was too much for Sir William. The Corporation had already spent £36,000 on the matter but Mrs Connell's gift was promptly returned. With a little less haste, the whole scheme might have been salvaged, since the coal-mine plan was suspended.

Sir William found it difficult to understand Honeyman's point that the trustees should have some freedom, in case circumstances changed. Douglaston proved that circumstances could indeed change.

Anyway, the great benefactor died in 1958, aged ninety-seven, and the controversy rumbled on for quarter of a century after that before the Burrell Collection was finally housed and opened. Tom Honeyman favoured a complex which would include a new art gallery, a museum of shipbuilding and engineering, a new concert hall or opera house, a civic theatre—and the Burrell.

In the event, the site ultimately settled on was at Pollok Park, on the South Side of Glasgow, thanks to the generosity of Mrs Maxwell Macdonald and family, and the Burrell Collection was given a splendid home within those picturesque grounds in 1983.

Such was the spreading fame of the collection that it soon put Glasgow at the forefront of international attention, attracting a regular flow of visitors from all over the world. More than anything else, it was the Burrell Collection which diverted some of Edinburgh's limelight to its industrial neighbour in the west and spurred the momentum which brought it the title of European City of Culture in 1990.

No more than one third of the items can be shown at any given time but it allows for a rotating display, which includes the reconstruction of Sir William and Lady Burrell's private quarters at Hutton Castle. So the story gained its happy ending, albeit after long years of wrangling and public accusations of Glasgow dragging its heels over such a magnificent gift.

There is a footnote to the story of Sir William Burrell which intrigues, harking back to that obsession with privacy. He certainly grew up in a tabloid-free age when many a powerful personality was able to hide a skeleton or two in the cupboard. But why did a man of such genius, not to mention charm, have to protect himself so fiercely when he so enjoyed sharing the wonder of his treasures?

The question arises because Sir William's name creeps into the latest re-examination of the scandalous case of Oscar Slater, the German Jew who served nineteen years in Peterhead Prison for a murder he did not commit.

Slater was originally sentenced to death in 1908 for allegedly killing a well-heeled Glasgow spinster, Miss Marion Gilchrist of West Princes Street. The hanging was commuted to life in prison, from which he was eventually freed after his case was fought by Sir Arthur Conan Doyle, the writer who used his detective powers to prove a case of mistaken identity.

Miss Gilchrist's maid, Nellie, kept referring to a man known as AB, as she knew him by his initials. AB was investigated but his name then disappeared mysteriously from police records. When the full records were opened up after seventy-five years, they revealed an obvious person to fit the initials—Alexander Birrell, who was Miss Gilchrist's nephew.

But Birrell had changed his name from Burrell and Alexander was evidently a cousin of Sir William. Further investigation shows that Sir William was an influential member of Glasgow Police Committee and the suspicion of modern sleuths is that he took steps to protect his family name.

XXVIII

THE SCOTTISH COLOURISTS

IF THE BURRELL COLLECTION raised the artistic profile of Glasgow in the last quarter of the 20th century, claiming much credit for the accolade of European City of Culture in 1990, there were two other phenomena which fortified the foundation.

In the 1880s, a group of young artists and sculptors, who had mostly reached their twenties, rebelled against the traditions of the Royal Scottish Academy and established a tradition of their own, in which they adopted a more realistic approach to subject matter.

This remarkable coincidence of talent formed themselves into the "Glasgow School", becoming more popularly known as the "Glasgow Boys".

Picking up from William McTaggart (1835-1910), the crofter's boy from Kintyre who became the great landscape painter of his day, they were led by people like Glasgow's own W. Y. Macgregor and sparked off a whole new interest in art in the city. Their influence was quite staggering.

Those young rebels eventually became people like Sir John Lavery (1856-1941) who survived long enough to paint Shirley Temple. Another leading light became Sir James Guthrie (1859-1930), who studied law but switched to art and became one of Britain's leading portrait painters. A century after their heyday the work of these artists was in high demand.

The Glasgow Boys were followed by a second phenomenon, roughly half a generation later, about whom Tom Honeyman wrote an appreciative account and gave them the descriptive name of the "Three Scottish Colourists".

The Glasgow Boys were at the peak of their influence on the Scottish art scene as the three young men were starting out. They were Samuel John Peploe, born in Edinburgh in 1871, Leslie Hunter, born in Rothesay in 1877 and Francis Cadell, born in Edinburgh in 1883. Again influenced by McTaggart and the Glasgow School, they were more concerned with colour than line, introducing a boldness of approach which was seen as the artistic response to a feeling that there was a lack of colour in Scottish life.

Whether Honeyman was right to number them as "three" Scottish Colourists is open to challenge—and indeed that challenge came from a leading Scots art consultant, William Hardie, who runs his own gallery in Blythswood Square, Glasgow, and has gained a name as an art historian.

A keen admirer of Honeyman, he failed to understand why he had not included J. D. Fergusson, the Perthshire artist who clearly belonged to the same bracket, as well as being of precisely the same generation. Honeyman did not dispute Fergusson's place in that group—he was in fact one of his greatest admirers—but he sought to justify his decision by saying that, when he first coined the phrase, the painter was living abroad. It was an explanation which did not exactly wash. Fergusson had certainly made his home in Paris before and after the First World War but he returned to live in Clouston Street, in the Maryhill district of Glasgow.

For that matter, both Peploe and Cadell had lived in Paris, while Leslie Hunter had emigrated with his family to California, returned to Paris but planned to settle as a professional artist in San Francisco, where he came to know people like novelist Jack London. By an appalling misfortune, the eve of his first one-man show coincided with the devastating earthquake and fire which destroyed the city. His work perished in the disaster but he returned in that year of 1906 to work as an illustrator in Glasgow.

When Tom Honeyman came to write about them as the "Three Scottish Colourists", the one element they had in common, apart from their art, was that they were all dead. All three had passed away in the 1930s, still in the prime of life, whereas Fergusson lived on until 1961, when he was eighty-seven.

William Hardie is among those who believe the real reason Honeyman put Fergusson on the fringe of the group was through a desire to avoid confrontation with the artist's life partner, the famous dancer and choreographer, Margaret Morris. And if that were the motive, he earned widespread understanding if not support! For Ms Morris was a formidable lady, keen to promote her partner's name and reputation to the point of his own embarrassment. Fergusson himself was a charming and popular man.

Dr Honeyman's secretary, Isabel Mackintosh, confirmed the difficulty with Ms Morris. She recalled going to the flat in Clouston Street to talk over a forthcoming catalogue and having to resist the lady's attempts to put Fergusson's name in ever-larger print, to the exclusion if necessary of other essential material. Uneasily from the background, the more modestly charming artist would be calling for moderation.

He became well known for his portraits of the female nude and had new ideas about dance and rhythm, tying in with the special talents of Margaret Morris. Back in Glasgow in 1939, they cut quite a dash, an attractive couple, good physical specimens who were highly acceptable on the city's social scene.

After Fergusson's death, Lord Macfarlane of Bearsden became a trustee of his work and had 160 of his paintings stored in Sauchiehall Street, near his own office in Newton Place, awaiting a suitable destination. When the artist's home town of Perth provided the setting of a splendid art gallery, Fergusson's collection was handed over as a major part of its artistic assets.

Since Tom Honeyman's day, William Hardie has been at the forefront of establishing J. D. Fergusson within the same bracket as the famous "three", to the point that there is now a more general acceptance of the "Four Scottish Colourists".

Tom Honeyman and William Hardie, who were separated in age by fifty years, could air their differences in good open discussion. Son of the managing director of Scottish Oils and Shell Mex, Hardie had gone from Glasgow Academy to Glasgow University to study modern languages. But the arrival in the city of the famous Dali painting of Christ inspired him towards an essay competition, which he won. Veering towards a career in art, he remembered the help and encouragement of the older man.

William Hardie became deputy director of Dundee Art Gallery and was delighted to renew the acquaintance when he came visiting in connection with a touring exhibition of the "Three Scottish Colourists".

Dr Honeyman was looking for someone to write the catalogue and the eager young Hardie was not slow to offer his services. What he wrote didn't exactly meet with approval but Honeyman had the sense to recognise the positive spirit in his own mould and may have acknowledged some truth in the young man's approach.

At the distance of time, we imagine that groups like the Colourists would have been in regular touch but it was not always so. Cadell and Peploe would occasionally meet up while painting in the Hebrides but there is a letter from Cadell in 1936, the year before he died, in which he says he hasn't seen Fergusson since 1909.

Together, however, they gave art in Scotland another boost and helped pave the way towards that time when Glasgow could lay claim to a cultural heritage with justification and pride.

XXIX

GREEN LIGHT FOR TOURISM

WITH the Normandy landings of 1944 and the prospect of victory in the Second World War now in sight, much thought was already being given to the kind of life we would face when it was all over. If Scotland had a visionary on the political scene at the time it was Tom Johnston, the Secretary of State and one of the ablest men ever to hold that post.

Johnston was a Kirkintilloch man who became a journalist early in life, founded the socialist weekly called *Forward* and served as Labour MP for Dundee and West Stirling before taking on the Scottish Secretary role in 1941. With the idea of home rule always behind his thinking, Tom Johnston was anxious that Scotland should become economically independent, and towards the stability of that goal he had already set up The Scottish Council (Development and Industry) to attract new industry to his native land.

That body was headed by Sir Steven Bilsland—and it was Sir Steven who came on the phone one July evening of 1944, just as Tom Honeyman was leaving for home. Tom Johnston had something else in mind and could he come round to Bilsland's office right away. Johnston wanted to find out the prospects of a tourist industry in Scotland once this war was over and Honeyman was being asked to lead that investigation. It was a challenge he wanted to accept, with reservations only about the encroachment on what was left of his leisure time.

There was the other matter of being a local government official, requiring his council's permission to take on a role of this kind. In the event, that clearance was granted only by a casting vote but he made immediate contact with Sir David Milne at the Scottish Office, who underlined the importance of the remit and said he wanted a report as quickly as possible.

For the next two years the shape of a possible tourist industry became a major part of Tom Honeyman's life. He and his committee set about collecting evidence and, with a sense of urgency, produced interim reports, along with the advice: "Don't wait for a final report. Get a move on and set up a Scottish Tourist Board."

This was done, with Tom Johnston himself as chairman, a sure sign of the importance he placed on tourism for the future of Scotland. Given Johnston's political prowess, he surprised many people by retiring from parliament at the end of the war, but Tom Honeyman detected the method in his madness. With that passion for Scotland's future, he had three main thoughts for development—hydro-electricity, tourism and reafforestation. He was also keen on action which would be as free as possible of government interference.

As a member of the Cabinet, he would be subject to government policy. But as chairman of these three post-war undertakings he could practise what Honeyman called the "Daft Jock technique". In other words, if he thought action was necessary, he would give orders accordingly. If it was subsequently shown to be against the law, he would shrug in innocence and say "Too bad—it has been done!" So he came out of parliament to gain greater freedom.

The founder members of the Scottish Tourist Board included Sir Alexander B. King, the Scottish cinema magnate, J. Ure Primrose, Lord Provost of Perth, Sandy Trotter, editor of the *Scottish Daily Express*, Provost Robert Wotherspoon of Inverness, Bill Ferris of

Edinburgh University Court, and Bill Stevens of Edinburgh Chamber of Commerce and former Queen's Park footballer.

Honeyman reckoned that Tom Johnston's one mistake over tourism was to insist on financial independence. Holding cinema premieres, football matches and the like on behalf of Scottish tourism was not the way to finance an industry.

From Tom Johnston's initiative, however, Scotland's tourist industry was established, proper funding became available and Tom Honeyman's main concern was to see that it was not squandered. Personally, he was critical of what he regarded as the futile efforts of a number of "Come to Britain" campaigns. He would point to the fact that, in New York alone, the agencies concentrating on the one idea of selling Britain, and all occupying expensive premises, ranged from the British Information Service, the British Travel Association, Thomas Cook, British Railways, British Overseas Airways Corporation, and Cunard and other shipping lines.

He favoured the idea of persuading Scottish businessmen promoting their own interests overseas to work for our tourism as a sideline. He was also an early advocate of keeping Scotland tidy, believing that the pollution of our rivers and the menace of a litter-strewn landscape were a serious threat to the beauty of our countryside.

But a major new industry was under way and the man whose business was art had helped to give it shape and colour and to set the scene for a prosperity which could benefit all corners of the land.

XXX

BRIDIE'S BRIGHT IDEA

THE ARTS COUNCIL began life under a name which Dr Honeyman much preferred—the Council for the Encouragement of Music and the Arts, abbreviated to the initials CEMA, which he felt sounded active and friendly. The first chairman of its Scottish committee was Osborne Mavor, who became better known as playwright James Bridie, and Tom Honeyman was invited to join him.

The association of the two men went back, of course, to their student days at Glasgow University and had continued through the 1920s when they were both medical figures in the West End of the city. When Honeyman moved to that side of Glasgow, Dr Mavor became a near neighbour, just round the corner in Woodlands Terrace, travelling to the other side of the Clyde where he was on the visiting staff of the Victoria Infirmary.

Mavor—or Bridie, as he should now become known—had a large head, broad brow and bright eyes which, with his round glasses, helped him assume an owlish expression. Indeed he used to caricature himself in Christmas cards. He had more of a grin than a smile and Honeyman reckoned his voice was something he never quite knew how to use. His brilliantly witty remarks were often lost because he addressed them to his waistcoat. When speaking in public he would cause the front rows to titter when there should really have been a louder roar of a laugh.

The two men would drop into each other's houses unannounced, when Honeyman would find Bridie, pad on knee, engaged in the writing of his next play while his wife, Rona, sat across the fireside darning socks. In such mundane domestic settings were major dramas created.

So James Bridie led the way by publicly fostering the arts in Scotland, building a team which also included Dr Ernest Bullock, Professor of Music at Glasgow, Sir William McKechnie, HM Inspector of Schools, Dr J. R. Peddie of the Carnegie Trust and Sir George Pirie, president of the Royal Scottish Academy.

But it wasn't long before the Scots became frustrated with London domination, in which the voice of Scotland would be heard with courteous attention before they passed on to next business, as if the interruption had been an unfortunate waste of time. However, Bridie kept on fighting for greater autonomy for the Scottish committee of CEMA and eventually gained it.

But as for art, Honeyman felt it didn't operate to Glasgow's advantage. Whereas they had previously been given major exhibitions, like the Van Gogh or the Picasso, which were organised in the south, those events disappeared with greater independence. When the Edinburgh Festival came along in 1947 there was a resumption of co-operation from London but that did nothing for Glasgow, which was Honeyman's main concern.

Nevertheless he acknowledged that the arts in Scotland would be in a worse state without the council; and there was the consolation, at a later stage, that the Director in Scotland was none other than Ronald Mavor, son of James Bridie, who had qualified in medicine.

But if Bridie had a major part to play in establishing the Arts Council in Scotland, he had an even more significant role in creating the Citizens' Theatre.

It was in 1943 that he called together a few likely people to examine the chances of restarting a repertory theatre in Glasgow, similar to what had happened before the First World War. Bridie's little group agreed that the time was opportune for another attempt. As soon as the post-war conditions would allow, they must try to get a theatre of their own this time. What most of them had in mind was a civic theatre, eventually involving the Corporation. One or two favoured independence.

Bridie didn't think they could rely on immediate help from the city but that they could approach the Town Council with a proposition once they had shown some success. In the meantime, if they could persuade a few private citizens to put up money, the Arts Council would do the rest. The timing of the venture was perfect.

It was launched with the greatest of goodwill and the sum of money Bridie thought would be required was certainly forthcoming. Of course it is never enough and Honeyman felt the first big mistake was in failing to launch a major appeal and give it the kind of spectacular launch it deserved.

The finances allowed the venture to start at the modest Athenaeum Theatre in Buchanan Street, which was the only place available. It was a neat little theatre but the backstage facilities were totally inadequate; it had always been associated with amateur productions and there were those who felt it had been a mistake to start operating there at all. With that kind of setting, it was claimed, the public would not realise the professional nature of the Citizens'.

Bridie spent much time trying to find a suitable name for the venture, rejecting them all as hackneyed and deciding on the Glasgow Citizens' Theatre as a temporary measure only. But, in the absence of further inspiration, that is how it remains more than fifty years later.

When they left the Athenaeum, a colourful character in local theatrical circles, Harry McKelvie, offered his Princess Theatre on a ten-year lease at the thoroughly reasonable sum of £1000 per year. Harry was a keen admirer of Bridie and went as far as to pay the first year's rent himself. The theatre could not be sold because, according to a trust deed, the property would eventually pass to the Victoria Infirmary. In the event, a gentleman called Sir Fred Stewart coughed up, in hard cash, the £10,000 required to meet the guarantee.

Apart from Bridie and Honeyman, the original team at the Citizens' included R. W. Greig, a prominent Glasgow wood merchant who spent much of his time furthering the interests of the Scottish Orchestra; Norman Duthie, a leading city accountant; an entertaining character called Paul Vincent Carroll, who made his name as a playwright with *Shadow and Substance* in New York; that master of show business George Singleton, who created the Cosmo Cinema for continental films in Glasgow; and John Boyd, Professor of Mercantile Law, who acted as legal adviser and had been part of that Mavor-Elliot vintage period at Glasgow University.

The first managing director of the Citizens' was Guy McCrone, who became well known as a novelist and was actually a cousin of James Bridie. McCrone was persuaded to suspend his writing career until the theatrical venture was off the ground and he and his wife Sylvia did some fine work in handling the early crises and seeing the project into being.

If Tom Honeyman had a particular part to play, it was in creating the Citizens' Theatre Society, a kind of supporters' club which would hopefully form the basis of an audience. At first, Bridie was against this idea, on the grounds that it would stamp them as amateurs, whereas it was necessary to convince the public they were professionals, ready to compete with the commercial theatre.

Tom Honeyman argued that the difference from people like the Howard and Wyndham group already existed, in that the Citizens' was a non profit-making organisation and it didn't have a theatre of its own. If the society did no more than provide a mailing list, he thought it would serve a useful purpose.

He was not claiming originality for the idea of a theatre society. To find out how it worked elsewhere, he consulted Tyrone Guthrie and Lewis Casson, both of whom had experience of the theatre in Glasgow. Sir Tyrone had more of less begun his distinguished career with the Scottish National Players and had been prominent in taking Bridie's plays south.

Lewis Casson, who gained a knighthood, as well as an LL.D from Glasgow University, was then director of drama at CEMA. Both men favoured the idea of a theatre society and advised them to go ahead. A packed and enthusiastic inaugural meeting persuaded James Bridie that it was a good idea after all and he happily became its first president, with Tom Honeyman as chairman and Gordon Laing, a local accountant, as secretary.

Three thousand people signed up in the first flush of enthusiasm and large crowds turned out to hear people like Dame Sybil Thorndike, Ivor Brown and J. B. Priestley. When it came to supporting the theatre, however, it has to be said that the society members behaved in much the same way as the general public. If the plays were too heavy, too classical or experimental they didn't come. Only when the shows were of a lighter variety could they be sure of capacity houses. It would be wrong, however, to suggest failure since the members frequently came to the rescue when funding was required.

From the outset, Glasgow Corporation adopted a friendly attitude towards the Citizens' and appreciated the fact that it had established itself as the main focus of drama in the city. When the lease of the Princess Theatre ran out, the city acquired it, spent a good deal of money and guaranteed that the Citizens' would have a home for the future.

Thus the Lord Provost and city treasurer became *ex-officio* members of the board, a logical follow-up to what James Bridie had said twenty-five years earlier, that "it is our intention that the Citizens' Theatre should become the Glasgow civic theatre, as permanent and as much a public concern as the art galleries."

Tom Honeyman was succeeded as chairman of the board by Michael Goldberg, an outstanding citizen of Glasgow who combined the talents of playwright with the business experience of running the family department store in Candleriggs with his brother Ephraim.

Under his chairmanship they complemented the work of the Citizens' by starting the smaller, more intimate Close Theatre, which became the base of some highly imaginative experimental plays, stirring up a great deal of interest, not to mention controversy.

The artistic direction of the Citizens' came under the influence of the highly talented Giles Havergal who, along with Robert David MacDonald and Philip Prowse, raised the profile until it became one of the foremost theatres in Britain, admired and respected throughout Europe.

XXXI

CITIZENS' IN FULL SWING

TOM HONEYMAN looked back on twenty-one years on the board of the Citizens' Theatre and felt glad to have been in at the foundation of such a splendid institution, marvelling for the rest of his life at what an array of memorable friendships it had produced.

Not least of these was the one formed with Patricia and John Casson and their family. Rather belatedly, John Casson followed the theatrical tradition of his famous parents, Sir Lewis Casson and Dame Sybil Thorndike, but went on to add his own chapter to the history of theatre in Scotland. In a strange way, he also followed his father to Glasgow, where Sir Lewis had directed a number of plays at the start of the First World War. As a student, Tom Honeyman remembered in particular his performance as John Tanner in *Man and Superman*.

But young John Casson started life in a very different manner. Scorning the theatre where his parents were making such a name, he was off instead to the Navy and by 1932 was extending that career by learning to fly at Leuchars in Scotland.

As a naval pilot in 1940 he led a dive-bombing attack on the dreaded German battle cruiser *Scharnhorst*. Of the fifteen planes involved in the raid, only seven returned—and John's was not one of them. Shot down, he managed to pull off a forced landing but spent the next five years as a prisoner of the Germans.

He was home in time for VE Day in May 1945 and as a regular in the Navy was stationed in Ayrshire later that year. Concluding he was now unlikely to gain further promotion, he decided on a career change and phoned Matthew Forsyth, Director of the Citizens' Theatre in Glasgow to ask: "If I leave the Navy, will you give me a job?" Forsyth offered him £9 a week as assistant stage manager and small-part actor, Casson promptly accepted and was driven in an Admiralty car to the stage door of the theatre in the Gorbals, literally delivered to the threshold of a new career.

His wife and three children would follow at a later date but John Casson was now applying himself to a profession in which he may have had good connections but no personal experience, except in the German prison camp where they redesigned a hut and put on shows like *Macbeth*. One of his fellow prisoners was a chap called Rupert Davies, who was so good that Casson insisted he should seek out a stage career when the war was over. He was soon making a name for himself as Maigret in the popular television detective series.

John Casson had, of course, grown up in one of the great theatrical households in the land and some of it was bound to rub off. At first, however, he was under the command of the stage manager, 25-year-old Gracie Dodds, duly learning his craft while remembering that, not so long ago, he had commanded more than a thousand men in the heat of the Second World War.

Soon he was being introduced to the great James Bridie himself, a man he came to worship and to regard as the greatest influence on his life outwith his parents. But it was Tom Honeyman, close associate of Bridie in founding the theatre, who threw a party for the Cassons when Patricia and the children came to live in Glasgow and from then on, there was a friendship which lasted for the rest of their lives.

In his late eighties—and still living in the charming surroundings of the Chelsea where he grew up—John Casson remembered the new season at the Citizens', opening in August 1946 when he played a few small parts as well as fulfilling the function of assistant stage manager.

But his wartime role of commanding large numbers of men soon began to show up in the theatre and Matthew Forsyth appointed him as his deputy director, entrusting him with *Gaslight* as his first professional production, which he took on tour to the Gateway Theatre in Edinburgh.

The Cassons had no sooner settled into a house just off Great Western Road, Glasgow, than Forsyth invited John for lunch and to break the news that he was taking up an offer from the London Academy of Music and Drama—and had recommended him to be his successor as Director of the Citizens' Theatre.

The appointment was confirmed and he opened that season of 1947-48 with James Bridie's new play, *John Knox,* which had that distinctive Scotsman, John Laurie, in the lead, with a cast of thirty and seventeen scene changes. He was off to a resounding start as a director, with *The Observer* declaring that "It was John Casson's evening."

With touring companies performing at the Citizens', John would have the visiting actors back to his West End home for supper and on one such occasion he was entertaining the memorable Michael MacLiammoir and Hilton Edwards when a furious row broke out between the two. The owner of the property lived in the adjoining flat and the trouble reached such proportions that the Cassons were given notice to quit.

So they moved across town to the South Side, taking over a splendid flat on Queen's Drive, right at its junction with Victoria Road and overlooking Queen's Park. John Casson did not have a car in those days so his new home was all the more convenient for the Citizens'. He just caught a tram-car at the top of Victoria

Road and headed down towards the Gorbals, a short ride away.

Once a play was under way, John would nip out for a quick dram at a pub across the street. He still remembers the night a pint-sized nyuch sidled up with the information that he didn't like the colour of his waistcoat. Humouring the little runt had no effect and John Casson soon realised that three others were closing in, fingering the ties behind which the old razor-slashers used to conceal their weapons.

Anticipating a death scene more dramatic than was being enacted across in the theatre, he was saved by a voice from behind the bar which roared: "Hey, leave him alone. That's Mr Casson from the Citizens'!" The sudden change of heart tells us much about the Glasgow character. Sinister scowls turned to warm greetings and hand-shaking and an insistence that the colourful Englishmen join them for "a wee hauf"!

Tom Honeyman continued to take a personal interest in the Cassons and suggested they might like some pictures with which to decorate their Queen's Drive flat. He unearthed a selection of paintings not currently on show at Glasgow Art Gallery and went out personally to hang them. The Cassons and Honeymans sat down to dinner and further cemented their friendship.

As Bridie's health deteriorated, Dr Honeyman took over as chairman and John Casson saw him more and more at close quarters.

"He was very much aware of money and at board meetings was always trying to prevent extravagant ideas," he recalled. "He had a wicked wit but you had to be careful in return because, with his religious scruples, he could be quite touchy. Cath Honeyman was much quieter. At first she may have seemed rather forbidding but you soon found that she was an absolutely gorgeous lady. We adored her. She was gentle, with a very Scottish sense of humour. There was a side of Dr Honeyman which had never grown up and Cath rather treated him like a naughty boy."

Tom Honeyman went ecstatic about one particular show which Casson put on around Christmas. It was *The Tintock Cup*, which needed to be slashed mercilessly at the last minute but ran for fifteen weeks and made a profit of £7000, allowing money for other productions. The people around John Casson at the Citizens' at the time included names like Stanley Baxter, Douglas Campbell and Andrew Keir.

He gave an early opportunity to up-and-coming actors like Fulton Mackay and James Gilbert, and he had the highest admiration for Duncan Macrae, regarding him nevertheless as a difficult man to work with, a former schoolteacher who liked to argue for his own way on stage.

Towards the end of 1950, when John Casson was earning £20 a week at the Citizens', he received an offer to be a major theatrical producer in Australia. The money, quite spectacular at the time, was £50 a week. He went to break the news to James Bridie, who said: "Don't be a bloody fool. You don't really want to go to Australia, do you? Look, I'm writing a new play which will go on in London—and you will be the director."

The lure of London was certainly a telling point with Casson, who promptly agreed to the proposition. Three weeks later, in January 1951, Bridie was dead. So there would be no London production and John Casson went back to tell Tom Honeyman that he planned to accept the Australian offer.

Honeyman was naturally disappointed about losing his director but showed a lot of understanding and was responsible for the farewell occasion, when he made the parting speech. So John remained until the end of the season, in July 1951, when he and Patricia and their family set off for Down Under to further the theatrical experience from their base in Melbourne.

That was where the Honeymans would meet up with them again in 1963, when they were introduced to a wide range of new acquaintances. At the end of his Australian contract, John Casson was giving a lunchtime talk on the subject of applying certain theatrical principles to business. Next day he had a call from the boss of PA Consultants offering him the job of teaching people how to put themselves across to the public. It was a career change which was to last for the next fifteen years, delaying his return to Britain until 1969.

As far as the Honeymans were concerned, those theatrical years in Glasgow opened up their home as a base for many a distinguished visitor. Appointing himself as butler to their guests, the ebullient Tom could boast of having served breakfast in bed to Dame Sybil Thorndike, Dame Edith Evans, Dame Flora Robson and Dame Rebecca West. But they weren't all dames. He could add people like Joyce Grenfell to the list!

XXXII

VISITING THE TROOPS

IT IS HARD for post-war generations to grasp how much was happening during that biggest of all world conflicts, not least when it was drawing to its close. After D-Day, the Allied forces were driving on towards victory in Europe. The Desert War had already been won by Montgomery and his men but there were still British forces in the Middle East, for whom time was hanging heavily now that their part of the fighting was over.

The Advisory Council for Education in HM Forces, seeking to prepare the troops for a return to civilian life, was sending out an array of people to begin the re-acclimatisation process.

Tom Honeyman's invitation was to give the lads "a shot of culture", the mission on which he set out from Glasgow on a flight to Cairo in December 1944. He found the Egyptian capital seething with Scots, including people like James Fergusson, the man who would later be knighted as Keeper of the Records.

After years in the sandy wastes of the Middle East, it was a pleasure for the soldiers simply to meet somebody from home and to hear at first hand what was happening in the old familiar places. As one officer wrote to Honeyman the morning after hearing him speak: "Could you tell them to send out more people to talk to us, people like Bridie, Linklater, Compton Mackenzie, Grieve and some of the younger men? We would like to know what has been happening in Scotland since 1939. Like sleepers in the fairy-tale, we will have to waken when peace comes, to recoup as best we can the lost years."

So Tom Honeyman entertained the troops as best he could and travelled on through desert towns and villages, camping overnight in places until recently unknown but which had now made headline news around the world.

When the war was finally over, Honeyman received an invitation to visit art galleries in the United States, with the offer of a substantial grant from the Rockefeller Foundation to meet expenses. It was something he had had in mind anyway but he would need to seek leave of absence from his employers, the Corporation of Glasgow. The councillors seemed to have some difficulty with the matter, wondering if this was not the sort of offer which should be made to a worthy councillor!

In the end they let him go and Tom Honeyman went off with his customary enthusiasm, determined to absorb as much as he could. He made the most of a fascinating trip, returning with not only a wealth of new experience but with a wealth of literature and a report which he was ready to put before his masters.

Arranging an evening at the Art Gallery, at which councillors and officials could see and hear about the fruits of his American visit, Tom Honeyman felt he could have saved himself the trouble. Very few turned up and he was left with the impression that he had misjudged the situation.

He was later to write: "I think it was at this time I sensed my star, Corporation-wise, was in the descendent. My journalist friends must have been overdoing the personal build-up and I was beginning to topple."

One of the great bonuses of his American visit was renewing his acquaintance with Dr Albert C. Barnes of Philadelphia, whose Barnes Foundation represented a phenomenal collection of paintings and whose experiments in art and education were controversial at the time. Barnes had been a distinguished pharmacologist whose fortune was largely the result of one invention.

It was an antiseptic called Argyrol, a silver nitrate preparation with many uses and on sale around the world.

Honeyman's former colleague at the Lefevre Gallery, Etienne Bignou, had created a fantastic picture of the formidable Dr Barnes, so much so that he was to be approached with caution. When he first met him he had turned out to be a man of distinguished looks, smoking a cigar and talking in a forthright and fascinating manner about his acquisitions.

His observations struck Honeyman as the most original he had ever heard, and in his home surroundings what an array of pictures he had to discuss. On the wall before them was the most amazing group of Cézanne, Renoir and others of the French School he had seen.

There was an immediate rapport with the Scot because in his own student days Dr Barnes had come in contact with one of Honeyman's own teachers, Professor Ralph Stockman, who was for many years in the medical faculty at Glasgow University. Barnes could give a highly entertaining account of his one and only visit to Glasgow. He intended to come again but this extraordinary man was killed in a car crash in 1951.

Tom Honeyman had learned to take people as he found them and he had assessed Dr Barnes as a totally original human being, well worth listening to, though perhaps with some qualities which could hardly be classed as admirable.

Sir Kenneth Clark of the National Gallery took a more blunt view of both Dr Barnes and Scotland's own Sir William Burrell. He regarded the pair of them as monsters, once writing: "Dr Barnes and Sir William Burrell, two of the greatest collectors I have ever known, would tell with relish hair-raising stories of how they had watched at the bedside of dying widows or paid monthly calls on poor clergymen, in order to get their teeth into some delicate morsel."

Honeyman had not sensed anything Frankenstein about them though he did not think either of them knew much about the art of living.

XXXIII

THE RUMPUS OVER DALI

IT HARDLY NEEDS STATING that Salvador Dali became one of the most controversial artists of the 20th century. Born in 1904, the flamboyant Spaniard moved to Paris in 1928 and was soon a leading figure of the Surrealist movement. By 1940 he had settled in the United States, later becoming a Catholic and devoting his art more and more to paintings of religious symbolism.

Dali was no stranger to Tom Honeyman, who was closely associated with the large-scale London Exhibition at the New Burlington Gallery in 1936. This was the historic occasion on which the artist perpetrated a Houdini-like stunt by dressing up in a diver's suit, attempting to speak from within—and coming very close to being asphyxiated!

Emilio Coia, the Scottish artist, was standing just a few feet away from this unexpected drama and later put it on record that he took no part in the rescue attempts! In fact he was drawn into the emergency at the last minute, helping to unstrap Dali when he seemed in real danger of dying.

Salvador Dali was already an enigma to the general public and Tom Honeyman treasured his original sketch from the invitation card to that exhibition. It was a variation on the theme that the mind and body could be analysed into compartments. Here was the mind pictorially represented as a drawer in the cabinet of the brain. And for the purpose of the exhibition, he was suggesting that the spectator should keep an open mind.

At least that was Honeyman's interpretation but when he asked the artist if that was what was also in his mind, he just shrugged and grinned.

The events of 1936, however, were nothing to the furore which blew up fifteen years later after Dr Honeyman had dropped in to see his friends at the Lefevre Gallery during a visit to London. The place was crowded and the focus of attention was Dali's large painting of Christ on the Cross. Joining in the general curiosity, he found himself strangely moved and felt a little uneasy with his reactions. He was anxious not to be taken in by an artist's trick and it wouldn't console him if other people were being fooled at the same time.

There was no doubt about the effect the picture was having on the stream of spectators and Honeyman felt so disturbed by the experience that he had to get out of the gallery and find some peace in which to gather his thoughts. He wandered along to the National Gallery, feeling that Dali's general colour scheme was faintly reminiscent, and there his vague impression was sharpened. Confronted by "The Virgin of the Rocks" by Leonardo da Vinci, he felt Dali must have been influenced by this. When he later challenged him on the matter, the painter said it was an interesting point, since it was one of the masterpieces which had always stirred him deeply.

But he claimed he was not consciously thinking of Leonardo when he painted his Christ. No, he rather had in mind his fellow Spaniard from another age, Francisco Zurbaran.

Honeyman headed back to the Lefevre Gallery for a second look, still finding it difficult to reconcile the theme with Dali's philosophy of art and his public utterances as he remembered them from their earlier association.

Clearly Honeyman was not up to date with Dali's shift of stance.

He simply thought the painting was out of period, a piece of unashamed romanticism in an age of eclectic classicism, and he was interested in the association of ideas which was being set up in the mind of the spectator.

The arguments began to rage. What was Dali up to? What was his purpose, if any? Was it propaganda, such as they had seen in Italy and America? Was it satirical? Was the peaceful setting and placidity of the lake beneath a pointer to the Prince of Peace—or was it plain sermonising as in the early days of church patronage of the arts?

Somebody reminded him of Beethoven's letter concerning his Mass in B: "My chief object in the composition of this Grand Mass was to awaken, and deeply impress, religious feelings in both the singers and the hearers." Then again, couldn't a picture have an aesthetic value in its own right? And did they need to concern themselves with the man concealed behind the artist?

Whatever the view, there was no doubt that Dali's Christ was an artistic event. But in his mental turmoil Honeyman knew that Glasgow could not purchase "events" at crazy prices. Still, what about the reasonably priced drawing which was also on offer?

He went hot-foot back to Glasgow with nothing much but Dali in his mind, immediately telephoning his convener and friend Jack Kelly, who was also the city treasurer at the time. It didn't take Kelly long to gather that, in talking about the possibility of the drawing, Honeyman was enthusiastic about the painting itself.

To his eternal credit, Jack Kelly had the imagination to think something might be done and that this could be the occasion for Glasgow to risk a courageous act, if it were at all financially possible. At least there would be no harm in having the painting sent up for inspection.

For a number of years Honeyman had been misinformed by the town clerk that only the interest from the 1901 Exhibition Art Fund was available for art purchases. But Jack Kelly was able to confirm with the town chamberlain that capital from the art fund itself could also be drawn upon. This made a difference.

When the picture was rushed to Glasgow, Tom Honeyman was much in demand with the sub-committee appointed to examine and report on the possibility of acquiring the work. He told them all he knew about the artist and his place on the contemporary scene, especially the so-called Advanced School.

He had known Salvador Dali and his work for twenty-five years and understood that he had recently been concerning himself with religious themes. If the city did acquire the painting, it was fairly likely that there would be some strong opposition. He reminded them that in 1891 (the year of his own birth) there had been quite a hullabaloo when Glasgow bought Whistler's "Carlyle". But perhaps it was time to be bold again.

With his art dealer's instinct, Tom Honeyman was also thinking about the fact that the purchase price of the picture would include the copyright of whatever else was produced. Of course that was an unknown quantity but he thought it might well become valuable property and passed on these views to the committee.

Whatever else might be said of council committees and philistine attitudes, Tom Honeyman maintained that, on this occasion at least, and throughout the discussions, the most significant factor of all was the unanimity of the council. Step by step they moved towards the idea of buying the Dali painting, without putting it to the vote on a single occasion.

But while it was one thing for Glasgow to decide it wanted the controversial painting, it would be quite another to land it, in the face of what would surely be massive opposition from the larger and more powerful centres of art around the world. Could Glasgow actually do it?

Whatever Tom Honeyman's judgement had done to put the city in the frame of possible purchasers, subsequent events would underline once again the importance of who you know in this world, to complement what you know.

Of course he knew Dali on a personal basis and was perfectly capable of making persuasive overtures on his own. But other parties were to play a vital part, not least the man called Georges Keller, who was Dali's agent in New York. With his knack of getting to know people, Honeyman had made the acquaintance of Keller as far back as 1929, when they met in Paris. In the years to follow, they would meet up in various parts of the world and indeed Keller once worked for the Bignou Gallery in New York.

So there was a good basis of connection but it was their second meeting, in 1930, which had cemented it. That was when Georges Keller and two friends arrived in Scotland for an overdue holiday. Tom Honeyman was busily engaged on art matters with his partners of the day, McNeill Reid, Duncan Macdonald and Etienne Bignou. But he was not too busy to see that Keller and his friends were looked after, to the point that he arranged a motoring trip around the west of Scotland, complete with hired car and chauffeur, who was under instruction to see that the visitors from France would get a good impression of our scenic land.

They apparently stopped for lunch at Helensburgh and decided that the liquid of the meal would have to be the famous brew of Scotland. What else?

It was, however, their first experience of whisky and when the waiter brought the normal proportion at the bottom of the glass, they protested their need for a decent-sized glassful, no doubt mindful of their own wine glasses at home. The waiter saw no good business reason to dissuade them. The Frenchmen were duly impressed by the potency of the Scottish "wine" and concluded that the Scots must indeed be a sturdy race. Their last vestige of memory concerned the return to the limousine, by which time they were ready for such a comfortable and prolonged sleep that they never did catch up with the wonders of Scotland's scenery.

Georges Keller was unlikely to forget the hospitality of Tom Honeyman and those wild men of Scotland. One cannot always trace with accuracy the motives of human beings but it can be said with certainty that, when it came to Glasgow's interest in Salvador Dali's famous "Christ of St John of the Cross", Georges Keller could not have been more helpful. He built up for the artist the significance of Glasgow's collection and persuaded Dali to complete the negotiations before the painting could be shown in Madrid and Basle, for which there had been an agreement.

If the painting had in fact gone to those cities, Glasgow would have been faced with such opposition as to make the purchase a much weaker possibility. Of course there was wild argument about the merits of the work, but within the range of feeling was a growing appreciation of the massive publicity it would excite.

Other key people included McNeill Reid, head of the Lefevre Gallery, who was naturally well disposed to both the city of Glasgow and to Honeyman, his old colleague in business. He went out of his way to be helpful, not least in being satisfied with a very nominal commission for his services.

Yet another person to whom Glasgow owed a debt was Margaret Sharkey, well known to Honeyman through the Bignou Gallery in New York, where she was highly regarded for her taste and influence as well as her personal charm. Evidently she knew how to handle Salvador Dali. So the influences were running in Glasgow's favour, though the purchase still had to be finalised.

The catalogue price for "Christ of St John of the Cross" was £12,000 but Tom Honeyman negotiated the lowest price that could possibly be accepted by the artist and that was £8200, viewed as an incredible bargain in the light of history but by no means regarded as such at the time. Around the same period, a small picture in an imperfect state, "Christ and the Woman taken in Adultery" by Pieter Brueghel I, was sold at an auction for over £11,000. The art critic of *The Times*, Denys Sutton, commented on that one: "Its price, though high, bears greater relation to its value than the £8200 paid by Glasgow for a painting by Salvador Dali."

Criticism like that goaded Honeyman to reply: "Some years ago a leading gallery in this country paid something like £12,000 for a 'genuine' Old Master. It has now been discovered that the Old Master is still alive and the picture now reposes in a basement as a curio. At least we know who painted Dali's picture. Recently a collector paid an even larger sum for another 'Old Master' which is a triumph of the art of the restorer. The 'hand' of the master is buried in the velvet glove of contemporary pigments. Paint and canvas begin to undergo the perishing process within a short time after the completion of a painting. By that token, we should be able to enjoy 'pure' Dali for a much longer time than some other expensive works."

Of course Tom Honeyman expected criticism but not perhaps to the extent to which he had to respond. Augustus John was among those who deprecated this "wilful extravagance" and deplored such a "mad price" for a work by a living painter.

Again Honeyman came out with all guns firing: "Extraordinary! Why do they not rejoice that for once the artist rather than the collector or dealer or their descendants reaps the benefit from his labour? Salvador Dali is a man with an international reputation. His "news value" is at least as great as that of Matisse or Picasso and he considers this painting of Christ to be his masterpiece."

Stephen Bone of the *Manchester Guardian*, in reporting the distribution of works commissioned by the Arts Council, said: "Will any of them reach Glasgow, a city that has just spent thousands of pounds on a Surrealist Crucifixion by Salvador Dali that no art critic could take seriously? After this sensational extravagance it may possibly be felt that Glasgow Corporation is a little ill-placed for receiving gifts from the taxpayer, but this would be a short-sighted view. Glasgow may soon feel the need of good modern paintings in its galleries."

This angered Honeyman once again. He railed against what he regarded as Stephen Bone's own short-sighted view, since no gallery in the country had acquired through its own limited funds more modern works than Glasgow. In all fairness, he shouldn't have had to defend his record. Within his time, and on his recommendation, Glasgow had acquired by purchase "Blackfriars" by Derain for £150 and a Utrillo for £450. Through the Hamilton Trust it had gained other French paintings by artists such as Cassat, Courbet, Gauguin, Marquet, Monet, Pissarro, Signac and Sisley, none costing more than £4000.

They had bought excellent examples of L. S. Lowry for as little as £42 in 1943 and £135 in 1944. The works of Scottish and English artists at the beginning of their careers were acquired for very little expense. The Arts Council had never favoured Glasgow by adding works to the collection and, while the Contemporary Art Society had given some good works to the city, the fact that they were more distant than their English colleagues meant that the first choice seldom came their way.

Journalist Mamie Baird recorded some of the abuse that came from artists, art students, highbrows and lowbrows, saying it was a waste of money. A dozen better pictures could have been bought. "But then again, the thousands queued and paid a shilling a head," she reported. "They bought prints of pictures and hundreds are being sent all over the world."

Criticism of the Dali picture was not confined to distant parts. With very few exceptions, Glasgow Art School staff and students were against it and even some of Honeyman's friends at Glasgow University thought he had made a grave mistake.

"It will be down in the basement in three years," was one of the prophesies. Others had no objection to a Dali painting since he was, after all, a leader of a particular movement in the history of art. But why didn't they get a typical Surrealist painting instead of this "non-characteristic example"?

For better or worse, Tom Honeyman had acquired his much-publicised "Christ of St John of the Cross", and nearly half a century later it remains a matter of intense public interest, having attracted to Glasgow Art Gallery countless thousands who would otherwise never have seen inside its doors.

XXXIV

A VENTURE OF FAITH

TOM HONEYMAN contemplated his Dali painting and remembered that, when surrealism was at its height in the 1930s, it had seemed to him, retaining some knowledge of psychoanalysis, that quite a number of practitioners were bogus. Their efforts were little more than pictorial illustrations of mental case histories borrowed from medical literature. It could be argued that Picasso did much the same thing in his "morphological" period, inspired by textbooks on anatomy.

Salvador Dali was a detached phenomenon, so detached that his change of front, political as well as pictorial, had lost him friends of his early days. Now his painting of Christ had brought down upon his own head, as well as that of Glasgow, one mighty volume of rage and indignation.

The final purchase of the painting was completed in February 1952 but it was not put on show in the Art Gallery until June, when the storm broke out again. The BBC's *Arts Review* programme on 27 June featured a discussion on the Dali in which all the participants, except distinguished Scots writer Edwin Muir, damned the painting in what Honeyman regarded as the finest collection of sneers ever to come over the air in such a short space of time. Muir simply reserved judgement. An appeal to give the other side of the argument a chance was made in vain.

Tom Honeyman was eventually allowed to discuss the Dali on a BBC programme. But seventeen years later, long after he had retired, he was to discover how touchy a subject it had remained. Having agreed to take part in another BBC discussion, he then received a letter which said: "That proposed interview between you and (the Rev) Campbell MacLean has had to be cancelled. The Director is unwilling to let us use the gallery on the double score of blocking off the Dali section—and that it ought to be one of his staff who does the talking. We may involve you in a studio discussion but we are not at that stage of planning yet."

Honeyman concluded that the regime which succeeded him had probably had enough of Dali and would now like the public to turn its attention to other features. Back in his own day it occurred to him that one way to meet the charge of extravagance was to give the public the chance to contribute to the Art Fund. The net receipts for the first six months of Dali in Glasgow amounted to £3200, not a bad contribution to the purchase price of £8200. By the time Tom Honeyman was due to take part in that cancelled broadcast, Glasgow had reaped four times the purchase price of the painting from sales of reproductions. Miniatures were being sold to religious seminaries all over the world, with many young priests keen to have a reproduction, even though their churches were not at that time in approval of Dali. An approach to the local papal nuncio cleared the way in Scotland. Indeed it had been a shrewd move on Honeyman's part, when the painting was in Glasgow for consideration, to call in the heads of all the churches for their opinions. Surprisingly perhaps, unanimous approval came from Church of Scotland, Roman Catholic, Jewish faith *et al.*

Many people were surprised that the artist had so willingly parted with the royalty rights, especially when he had accepted the minimum price for the work itself. In fact, Dali was delighted to give Glasgow the copyright, mainly because of the control they would exercise. Despite all that, in an imperfect world the pirates have still had a field day.

Having acquired the copyright with the original, Glasgow then had to find someone who would make the prints. The Ganymed Press had already made excellent reproductions of the Matisse, Utrillo and Braque in the Glasgow collection but it was thought they would not be so keen on such a "popular" religious subject. However, they were delighted—and so was Glasgow.

The Ganymed Press was part of the *New Statesman* organisation and in the course of negotiations managing director John Roberts invited Dr Honeyman to that journal's weekly lunch. A distinguished gathering around the table was led by the editor of the *New Statesman*, Kingsley Martin, who had turned it into a powerful organ of socialist opinion. He himself could rub people the wrong way and in the course of their discussion he introduced the subject of the Dali painting with the comment: "I thought it was an odd way to view the Lake District."

Dr Honeyman found himself on the defensive once more and was ready to develop an argument that the failing of current art criticism was that it had become too political and too strongly partisan. In his own particular style, however, Kingsley Martin intervened to change the subject.

Honeyman later read in Martin's autobiography that he blamed himself for failing to be elected to a fellowship at Cambridge. "I had been tactless, conceited, doctrinaire and opinionated," was his own assessment. From his one and only meeting with Kingsley Martin, Dr Honeyman came to the conclusion that nothing had changed. The man simply couldn't help it.

Salvador Dali continued to paint religious subjects, the most notable of which, "The Last Supper", went to the National Gallery in Washington, and another to the New York Metropolitan Museum. But nothing he did thereafter had the popular appeal of his controversial "Christ" in Glasgow.

In the retrospect of his retirement, Dr Honeyman considered what he thought should be done with the painting. He favoured putting it into circulation as often as possible. It was once loaned to an exhibition in Rome and Dali was none too pleased when Glasgow refused to let it go to Venice. If any responsible institution wanted to put on a retrospective Dali exhibition, especially in America, Honeyman's view was that they should have it.

Eventually, he thought, it wouldn't be a bad idea to give it a permanent home in Glasgow Cathedral, whose minister at the time of purchase, the Very Rev Dr Nevile Davidson, once said: "Glasgow Corporation had made a venture of faith in purchasing a picture. . . . I believe posterity will judge that faith to have been justified."

In view of Honeyman's opinion so many years ago, it is interesting that, in the mid 1990s, it did in fact find a home at the St Mungo Museum of Religious Life and Art, just a stone's throw from the Cathedral.

XXXV

THE SLASHING OF 'CHRIST'

FOR ALL THE CONTROVERSY over Dali's painting of Christ, Honeyman did not regard it as the greatest work of art in Glasgow's civic collection. It was certainly a masterpiece of its kind but there were others, in all the schools of painting, which were greater within the pure aim and purpose of pictorial art.

The acquisition had stirred an astonishing variety of emotions, covering every aspect of love and hatred, and he believed it would continue to do so. It had become a tourist attraction.

The critics included his artist friend Emilio Coia, who regarded Dali as "a show-off, always behaving like a crazy man—but a splendid and original artist, though not a Picasso."

As far as the painting was concerned, he added: "I'm sure Dali did it as a commercial proposition. As far as Tom was concerned, it was a good commercial buy for Glasgow. He knew what he was doing as far as creating attention. But the painting is not characteristic of Dali's natural view of art. There is nothing surreal about that concept of Christ on the Cross."

Lord Macfarlane of Bearsden, an authority on art as well as an international businessman, said: "Tom Honeyman knew well the colossal amount of criticism he would attract but it was a marvellous thing he did.

"Personally, I'm all for the painting. Whatever Dali meant by it, there is no doubt it had a profound effect on people. And no matter where I go abroad, people come up and tell me they have been to Glasgow—to see the Dali."

In Dr Honeyman's retirement, his instinct as an art dealer surfaced long enough to say that if Glasgow ever wanted rid of the picture he would be freely at their service. There were plenty of places where they would be delighted to have it.

"I have no regrets," he wrote. "Why should I have? I retain the friendship of all concerned in the production and the purchase, notably that of the artist. He continued to address me in scribbled notes and catalogues with sketches depicting me as the Don Quixote of the museum world, tilting a lance at the Establishment."

On several occasions after the purchase Honeyman tried to persuade Dali to visit the city, but it was always proving impossible to pin him down to a date though he never doubted the warmth of welcome which awaited him. He greatly disliked travelling, refused to fly and thought Glasgow was too much off his beaten track.

When the two men did meet up again in New York, he said: "You come to see me in Spain and I'll come to Glasgow." Out of the blue one day Honeyman received a telegram from Georges Keller saying: "Can you meet me in Barcelona and we'll go together to visit Dali?"

Honeyman kept the appointment and found Dali in top form, preparing pictures for an exhibition in New York and discussing the problems which faced art and science in the reigning international climate. With no-one else around except Keller and Honeyman, Dali had no need to put on an act and it turned out to be a most illuminating and rewarding experience for the visitors.

Honeyman recorded that you didn't often meet a man so well informed on so many subjects. There came back to mind a sentence which seemed to sum up Dali's attitude on the art of painting:

"Art is the imagination having fun with the understanding." When he said something of the kind to Dali, he responded with: "There is so much more to it than that." Then he added with a sigh: "They criticise my interest in religious subjects. I stated my views thirty years ago and I have not changed them."

Honeyman checked later and found that in the 1941 *Secret Life of Salvador Dali*, he had written: "Since 1929 I have ceaselessly studied the processes, the discoveries of the special sciences of the last hundred years. It has not been possible to explore all the corners of these because of their monstrous specialisation. I have understood their meaning as well as the best. One thing is certain: nothing, absolutely nothing in the philosophic, aesthetic, morphological, biological or moral discoveries of our epoch denies religion. On the contrary, the architecture of the temple of the special sciences has all its windows open to Heaven."

During the visit Dali was busy on a large canvas to which he gave the subtitle "Homage to Crick and Watson" and, from his conversation, they gathered he was up-to-date in the knowledge of recent drug discoveries and the phenomena of perception.

One thing which became clear was that Dali was not bothered by the "two cultures". He insisted that art and science were not separate human activities. They were always converging on each other, each of them concerned with Truth—and Truth was another name for Beauty.

As they were conducted here and there through his rambling house, with its nooks and crannies and extraordinary objects, each with a history or a purpose, Tom Honeyman felt he was beginning to grasp a little more of the man's philosophy of art.

Back in Glasgow, that most famous of his creations continued to be a matter of intense public interest, hanging there in a corridor of Kelvingrove, well roped off from the spectators.

It was on an April day in 1961, as the viewers passed slowly along, respectful as ever, that all hell broke loose in the gallery.

Suddenly an attendant saw a man stepping over the rope and pulling a broken brick from his pocket as he lunged at the painting, breaching it and tearing it downwards. The attendant managed to grapple with him and hold his hands but not to prevent the damage. In the commotion, one member of the public fainted.

The attacker was a patient from a mental hospital who evidently had an illusion that he was Christ and that Dali had not given a fair representation of him. He was said to have had two targets in mind that day, the other being a military museum in Sauchiehall Street.

While the slashing of the Dali painting was naturally well publicised, what did not reach the public ear in those less tabloid-conscious days was the fact that, after the picture had been restored, a doorman at Kelvingrove was vigilant enough one day to spot a man who looked very much like the original culprit. He was not wrong. The same man was out of his institution once more—and had returned to the gallery, with whatever purpose in mind. This time they managed to have him removed but not without some angry words at the hospital.

Those dramas took place after Dr Honeyman had retired but he always clung to the hope that Salvador Dali would still visit Glasgow one day, creating another art event which would certainly have given the city a fresh burst of world-wide publicity, with the man himself coming face to face with his famous picture.

Dali outlived Honeyman but his own life came to an end in 1989, when he was eighty-five, and sadly that hope was never fulfilled.

XXXVI

WHY HONEYMAN RESIGNED

IF TOM HONEYMAN caused controversy and excitement over Dali's "Christ of St John of the Cross", his attempts to bring the public through the doors of Glasgow Art Gallery were never more successful than in two exhibitions which took place in that post-war period.

The sight of long queues snaking their way round the building for the Picasso-Matisse Exhibition of 1946 and again for the "Van Gogh" of 1948 were a sure sign that the public imagination had been fired as seldom before.

There had, of course, been widespread publicity from the London showings at the Tate Gallery and now that they had been brought north, with sponsorship from the Arts Council, Glasgow's curiosity was sufficient to bring out the crowds.

Having drawn them into the building, Honeyman wasn't going to let them out without seeing what else there was to savour in the city's famous art show. Always keeping his ear to public opinion, the general impression he was gathering as people passed from Picasso to the Old Masters was: "Ah now, this is what I call art. That modern stuff is just a passing phase."

Picasso could raise as many eyebrows as Dali and the public clearly wasn't quite sure what to make of him. They felt much more at home with the earlier artists, though, when Honeyman inquired as to when they had last been in the gallery, the answer was usually that they hadn't been there for years.

With his showman's instinct, however, he knew the irrelevancies surrounding Picasso and Matisse could be put to good use as the bait to hook a wider audience.

As a light-hearted reflection of public opinion, the *Glasgow Herald's* distinguished columnist Alistair Phillips reported the incident of a man running down the steps of the Art Gallery, escaping from Picasso and Matisse and muttering: "For God's sake, let me out of here. I'm beginning to like them!"

The Van Gogh Exhibition was just as memorable but in this case the visitors were better prepared for what to expect. The surprises were more related to pleasant discoveries. What very few people knew (I suspect many were still unaware till reading this book) was the Van Gogh connection with Glasgow through the remarkable Alexander Reid, who happened to share that flat with the up-and-coming artist when he moved to Paris.

Apart from circulating among the large crowds and sensing the excitement being generated by the exhibition, Tom Honeyman had the added pleasure of welcoming some distinguished visitors from Holland. The most interesting name was that of Engineer Van Gogh, nephew of Vincent and son of the artist's brother Theo, who employed Alexander Reid in Paris. Others from Holland included Dr Sandberg of the Stedelijk Museum in Amsterdam and Dr Hammacher of the Kroller Muller Collection.

The Dutchmen, accompanied by their ladies, were accorded the full treatment of Glasgow hospitality. That this was given the added mantle of royal prestige was due to the fact that Princess Margaret happened to be on a visit to the city and the Dutch guests were invited to the Lord Provost's evening reception given in her honour. They were delighted to find themselves rubbing shoulders with the princess as she danced around the crowded floor.

The Arts Council arranged another party and altogether the visitors from Holland went away with a marvellous impression of Glasgow, which they viewed as far superior to either London or Birmingham. Glasgow was certainly attracting international attention and you would find people like Harold Nicholson writing in *The Spectator*:

"I spent two hours last week in the Glasgow Art Gallery and Museum and was much impressed by the ingenuity and enterprise devoted to rendering this superb collection part of the community. The citizens of Glasgow are encouraged to regard the gallery as a proud personal possession and as a source of enlightenment and pleasure.

"Perhaps the most striking merit of the gallery is that it contains one of the most comprehensive and illuminating collections of French pictures from Delacroix to Matisse that I have ever seen. Any person wishing to understand the development of 19th century French painting would find in this gallery a succinct summary of the whole movement."

The highbrows had sniffed at the Picasso and Matisse and the director was under more fire when he persuaded the Corporation to use the Art Gallery for an exhibition of the famous Stalingrad Sword—and for the public viewing of the Queen's wedding dress in 1947. But the public queued in their thousands to see both.

Whatever Tom Honeyman had done to put Glasgow back on the map of world art, he was always rather mindful of the fact that he had come back to his native city at roughly one quarter of what he used to earn as an art dealer in London. When senior officials' salaries came under review in 1946, he was asked to find out the scale applying in other cities and to state a reasoned case for a fair remuneration for his own job. In his report, he made out a case for "a satisfactory arrangement regarding the repayment of expenses incurred on Corporation business."

In fact no satisfactory arrangement was ever reached. One

evening, however, his convener, Mrs Helen Gault, did phone to say her committee had agreed to raise his salary by £150. This decision would have to be confirmed but she was sure that that was no more than a formality.

A fortnight later Dr Honeyman was on an early morning train journey to Oban to inspect some pictures being offered to the Gallery when he just about choked on an item in the morning paper, which announced that his salary increase had been refused. He arrived home to an atmosphere of depression, furious with a Corporation which could so humiliate its senior employees by publicising the rejection of a salary increase which had not even been asked for.

Unable to contain his anger, Tom Honeyman sat down and wrote his letter of resignation. He and daughter Margaret went off to the Cosmo Cinema to see *The Grapes of Wrath* and found some light relief in deciding that, in his unemployed state, he could always go off to the fruit-picking in California!

Apart from a notice in the *Glasgow Herald* which read like an obituary, the people who sought to intervene with a view to reversing the decision ranged from Stanley Cursiter of the National Gallery in Edinburgh to Sir William Burrell. What made him pause to reconsider, however, was the arrival of the Lord Provost, Sir Hector McNeill (not to be confused with the Scottish Secretary of the same name), accompanied by his predecessor, Dr James Welsh, elder statesman of the Labour Group in the council, who was acting in defiance of his colleagues' attitude to what they regarded as the Art Gallery director's rebellious publicity stunt.

Honeyman made it clear his resignation had nothing to do with the refusal of an increase but with the ham-fisted way of going about it, having little regard for the feelings of the individual and his family. It had also to do with the fact that he had obviously failed to convince the Corporation that the Art Gallery job was, or should be, the biggest job of its kind outside London.

Sir Hector agreed with much of what he had to say and ended with a request that he withdraw his resignation. After some consultation with the family and a conclusion that perhaps he should try again, he did indeed withdraw. He wrote afterwards: "It would be pleasing to record that from then on everything in the garden was lovely and that thereafter we all lived happily together. But it would not be true."

Nor was there unanimous satisfaction on the outside. It inspired some sarcasm from the distinguished Scottish poet, Hugh MacDiarmid, with whom Honeyman had served in the First World War and who was an unsuccessful applicant for the Art Gallery job in 1939. Often ready with some testy comment, MacDiarmid had a swipe at both the Art Gallery boss and his playwright friend Bridie, when he said: "The two most recent disasters to afflict Scotland have been the withdrawal of Honeyman's resignation and the return of James Bridie from America." Bridie had gone off with the intention of writing for the film industry in Hollywood but came back after a short spell in New York.

XXXVII

HIS VISION OF GLASGOW

THE RESIGNATION rumpus over, Dr Honeyman settled back uneasily to the job, caught up in what was known everywhere as "post-war planning". Asked to point the way ahead, he wrote a memorandum which made several far-reaching suggestions. For a start, he thought the Art Galleries and Museums Committee should be renamed the Arts Committee, to administer civic enterprises in the three fine arts—music, drama and painting. For a long time he had been saying that a new art gallery was essential for a proper development. He thought the present building should be adapted as a museum.

He repeated another of his major thoughts—that Glasgow should have a museum devoted to shipbuilding and engineering. For a city which once built the ships of the world (around 80 per cent of them at one stage) it was surely long overdue.

Once again he thought Glasgow should acquire the historic Royal Exchange building, just off George Square, and turn it into a museum devoted to the history of the city, with lunch-hour music and down-town exhibitions.

He also thought they should take over the care and maintenance of historic churchyards, like the Ramshorn, with particular reference to the tombstones of famous citizens like the Foulis brothers who established an academy of art in the 18th century.

He pursued his daydreams with a vision of Glasgow as the city which would show the rest of the world what could be done in giving prominence to the place of the arts in the life of the community. Against his own interest, as events would prove, he was in favour of dividing his job in two—a Museum Director and an Art Gallery Director, operating in separate buildings. One of the chief tasks of the museums man would be to stir that interest in industrialists, engineers and shipbuilders towards that focus on the part they had played in Glasgow's history.

Among his other ambitious schemes, he failed to see why art galleries were open only in daytime while music and drama went on to all hours of the night. He thought the staff must be prepared in future to take on evening work. He was also advocating a publicity officer whose duties would include the preparation of material for broadcasting, especially with thoughts of television in the future.

As Tom Honeyman approached the decade of the 1970s—and towards the end of his life, as it happened—he went on an extended cruise in the Pacific and wrote an account of his fifteen years at Kelvingrove.

"I like living in Glasgow," he said. "I know it has squandered much of its great inheritance. It is at present badly governed and it is the worst publicised city in the kingdom. But in no other place have I found more love, more tolerance, more wit, more brilliance, more mediocrity, more encouragement, more frustration, more sympathy, more envy, more big men in small jobs and small men in big jobs. There may be places where women are more lovely but none where beauty and charm are found so often together. Whatever its present shortcomings as a city, Glasgow has always been hospitable."

Drawing his thoughts together, he was in no doubt that he had enjoyed his fifteen years as head of the Art Gallery but posed the question: "Why then am I left with a sense of failure?" This seemed to grow out of the circumstances of his departure from the job and the changes which the Corporation carried out once he had gone.

Whatever his own shortcomings, he was in no doubt about the rightness of his mission: to put Glasgow back on the map of the art world.

Every now and then you would read reports of the stupidity of city councillors on matters concerning the arts. He recalled that Frank Rutter, art critic of the *Sunday Times* and former curator of the art gallery in Leeds, had drawn his attention to what he wrote about local dignitaries: "Of the Leeds City Council I find it most difficult to speak in parliamentary language. Never before had I come into contact with the kind of men who became councillors and aldermen. With remarkably few exceptions, I was appalled by their grossness, their ignorance and general lack of manners."

For all Honeyman's frustration with bureaucracy, he claimed a rather different experience, saying the committee bogey had not shown itself. But there was the odd notable exception, like the man who finally proved too much for both himself and his doctor.

Evidently, when James Ritchie was appointed convener of the committee, he proudly informed council officer Tom Wilson: "I am now in charge of the f——g culture!" And he was apparently doing his best to adhere to his brief, which was "to keep that bugger Honeyman in his place. He thinks he owns the Art Gallery."

Honeyman went on to paint a vivid pen-picture of this convener: "A small man, he had a way of shooting his head forward when making a point. In repose, he had the disconcerting habit of over-exposing his upper dentures while his tongue rolled around in search of the debris from his previous meal."

More than forty years later, Art Gallery director Julian Spalding, himself embroiled in controversy, felt Dr Honeyman had oversimplified his relationship with the council: "There is often politics involved in that kind of situation and that particular councillor

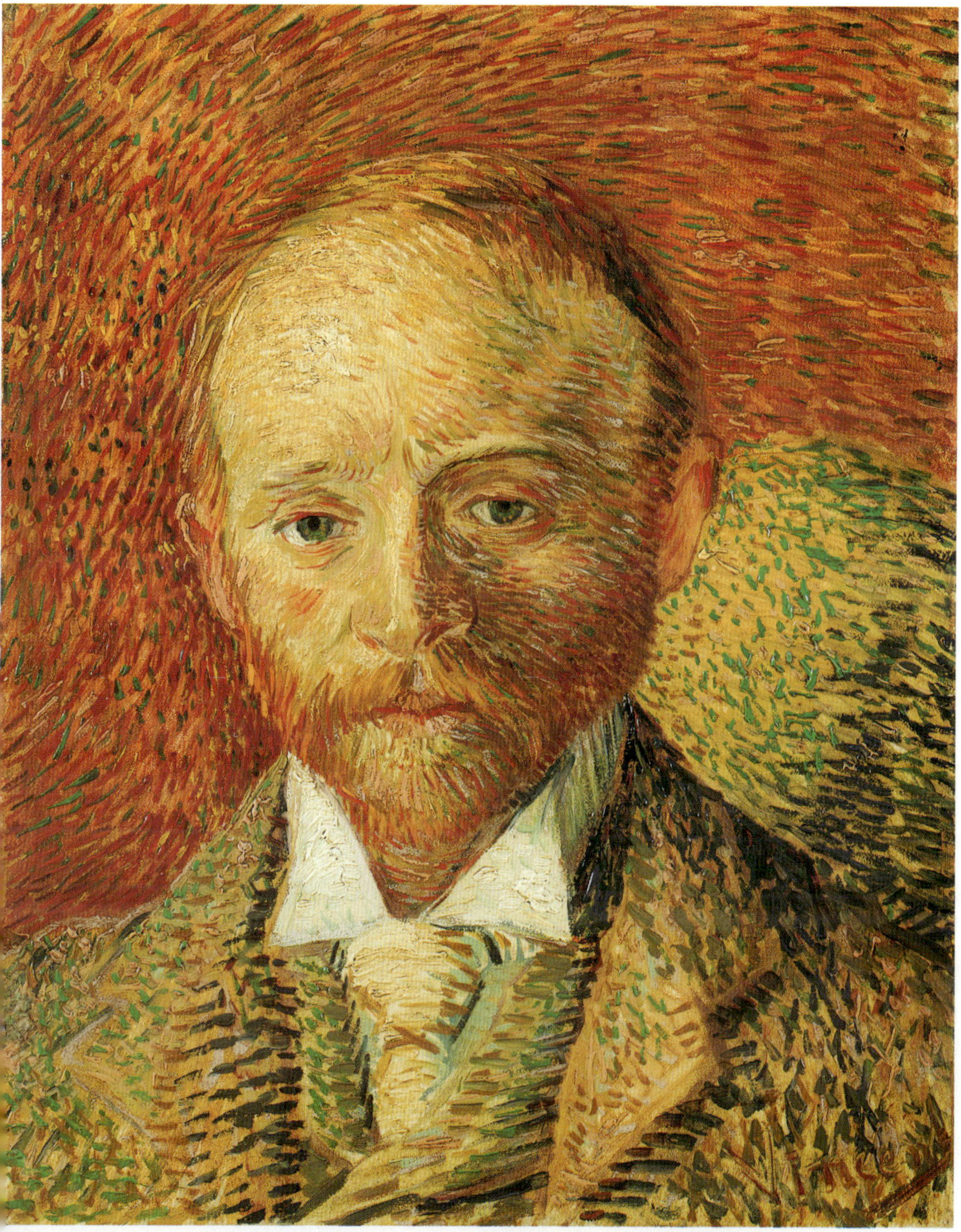

Portrait of Alexander Reid (c. 1887) by Vincent van Gogh
He gave his name to the prestigious art dealers *Reid and Lefevre.*

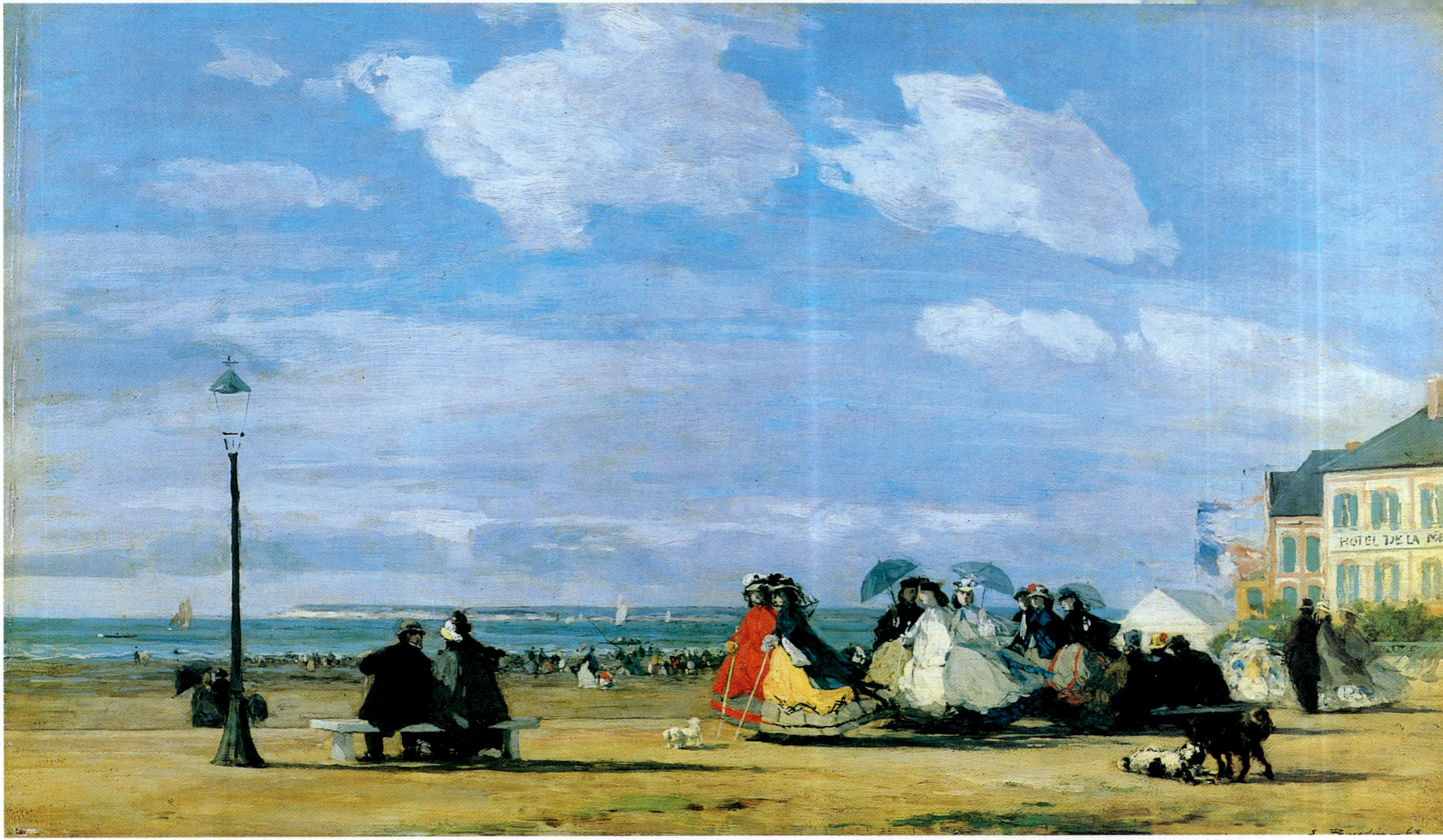

The Empress Eugénie on the Beach at Trouville (1863) by Eugène Boudin
Bought by Sir William Burrell in 1923 for just £250.

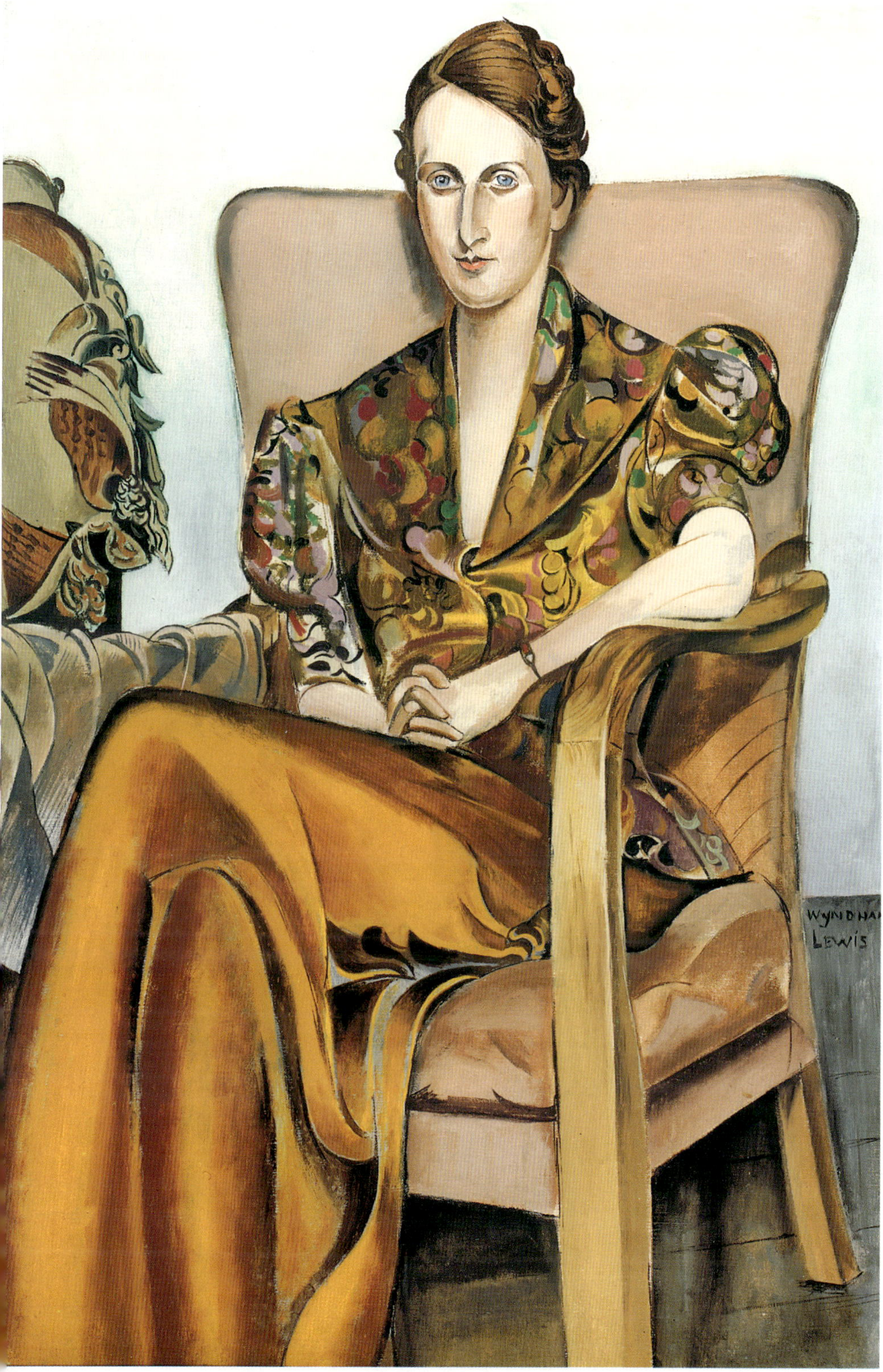

Mrs. T. J. Honeyman (c. 1937) by Wyndham Lewis
Commissioned by Honeyman at a low point in the artist's fortunes.

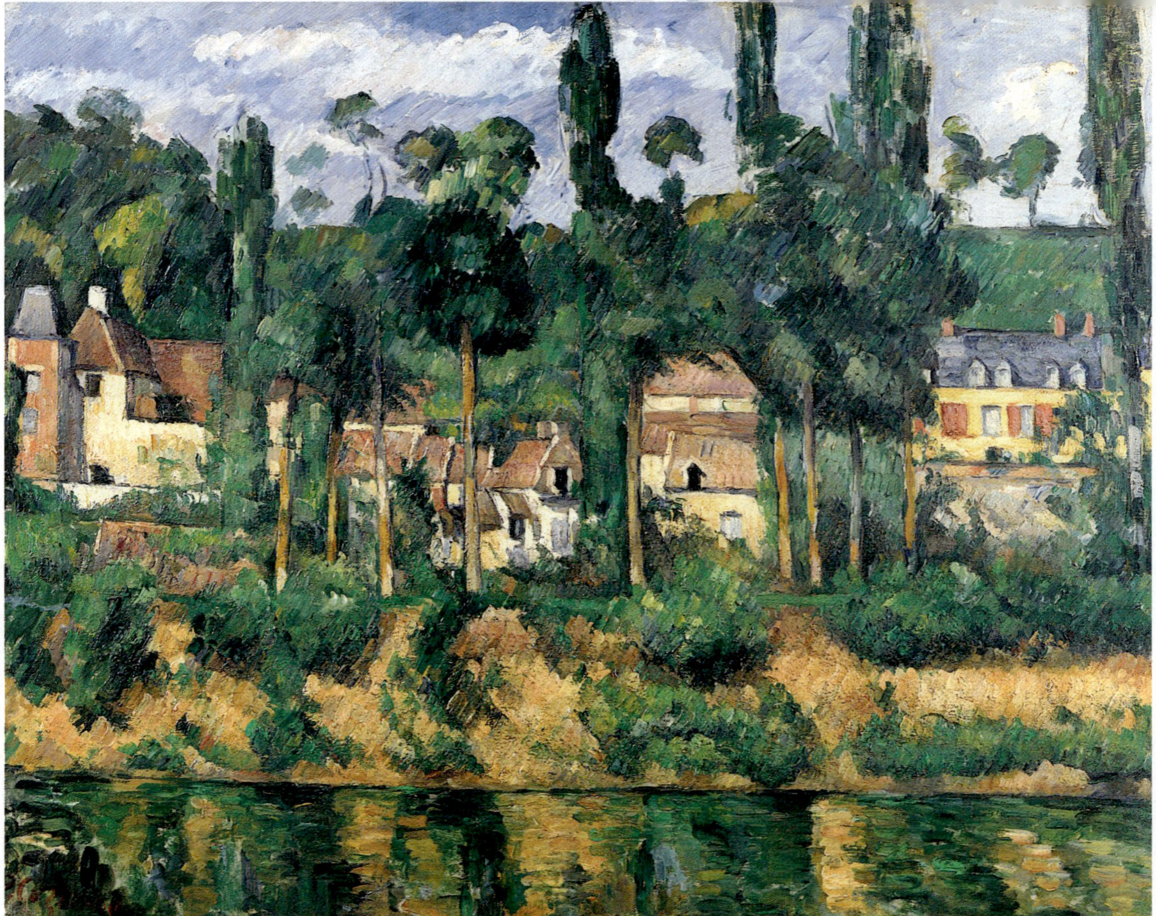

Le Château de Médan (c. 1880) by Paul Cézanne
Sold by Honeyman to Sir William Burrell. The only Cézanne in his collection.

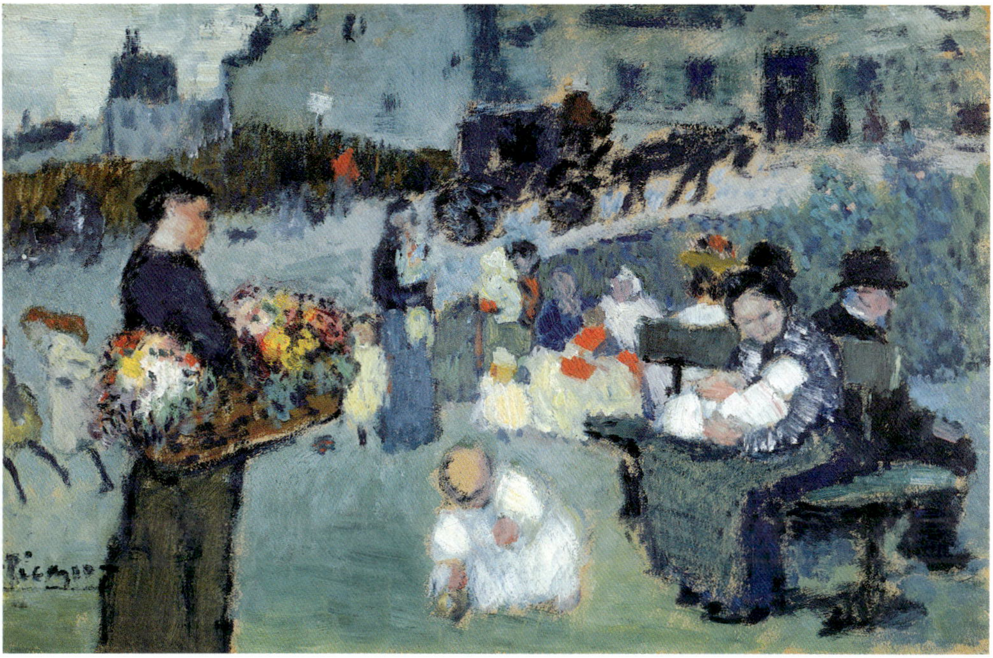

Flower Seller (1901) by Pablo Picasso
Gifted by William McInnes to Glasgow Art Gallery.

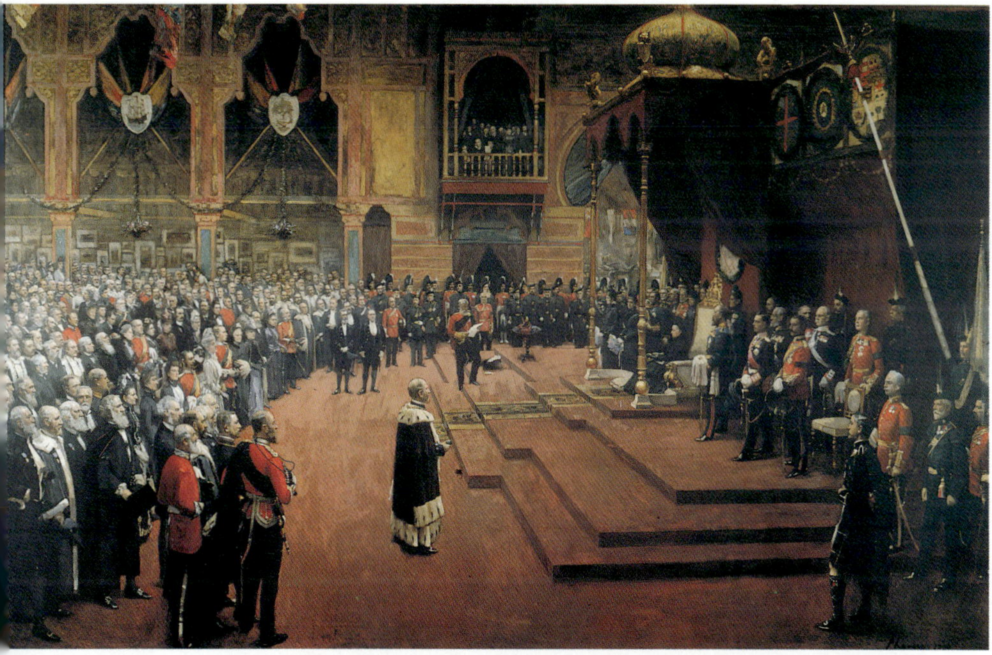

State Visit of Queen Victoria (1888) by Sir John Lavery
Bomb damage left the painting in shreds, but it was later painstakingly restored.

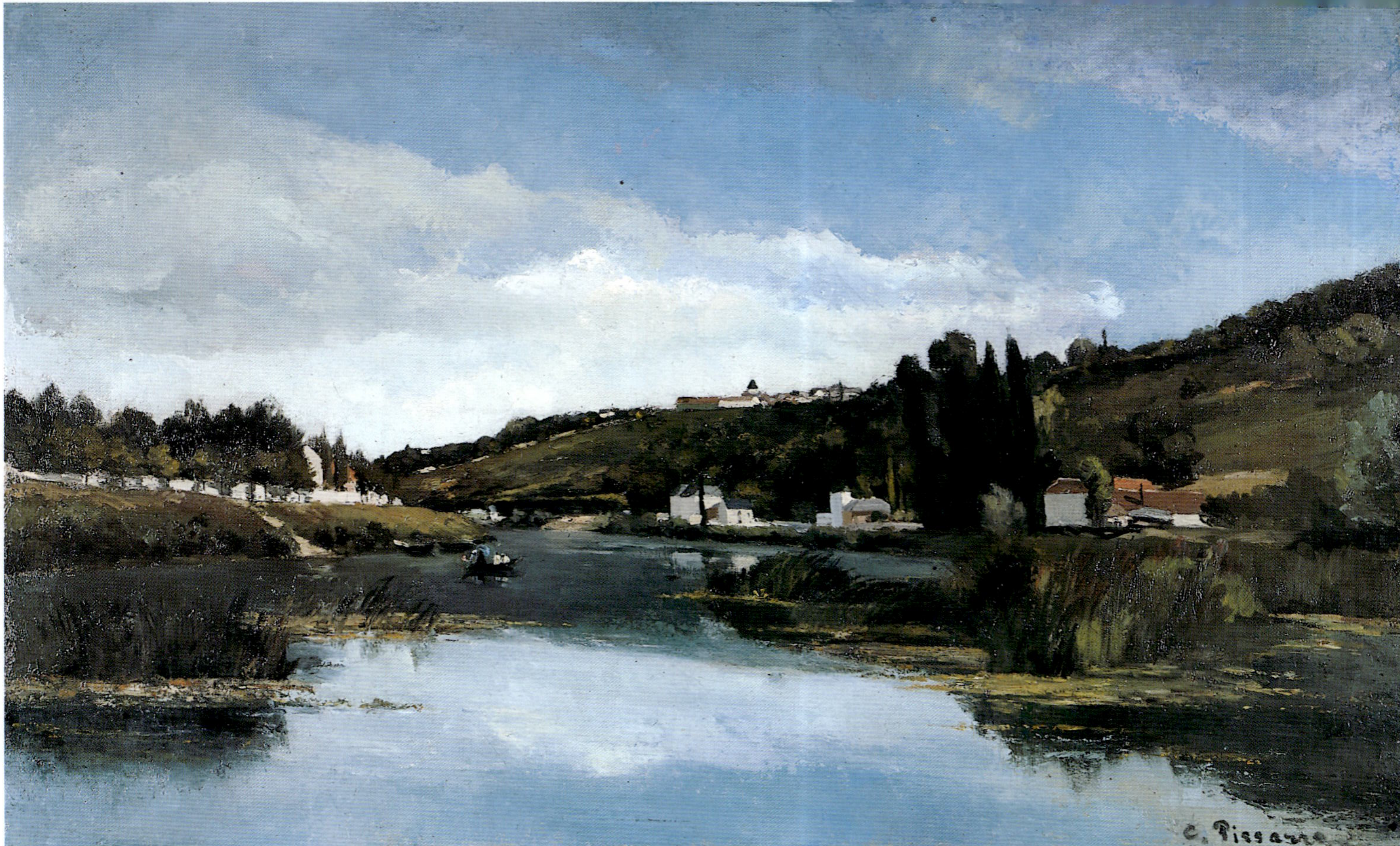

The Marne at Chennevieres (c. 1864-65) by Camille Pissarro
Sold to the National Gallery in Edinburgh from Honeyman's private collection.

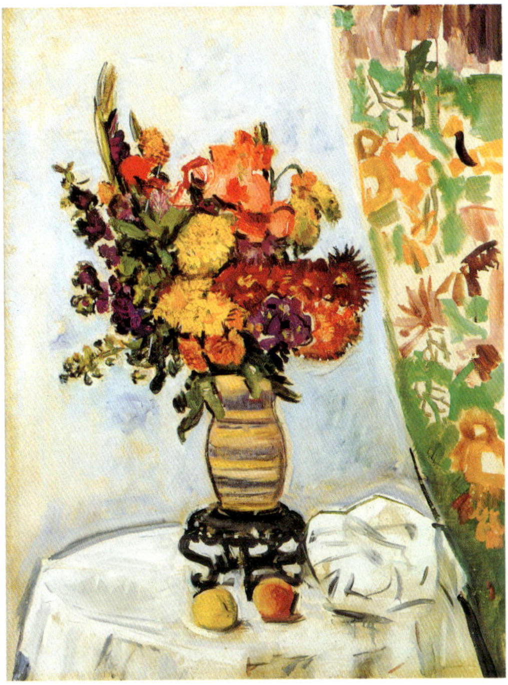

Flowers in a Chinese Vase (1931)
by G. Leslie Hunter
Hunter's last, unfinished, picture,
acquired by Honeyman.

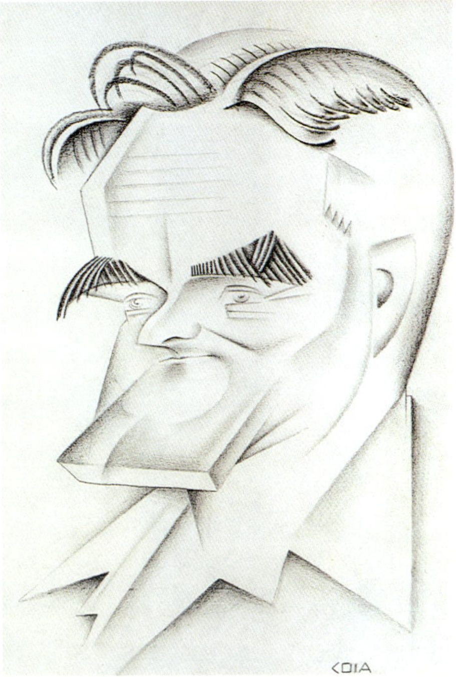

Dr Honeyman (1934) by Emilio Coia.

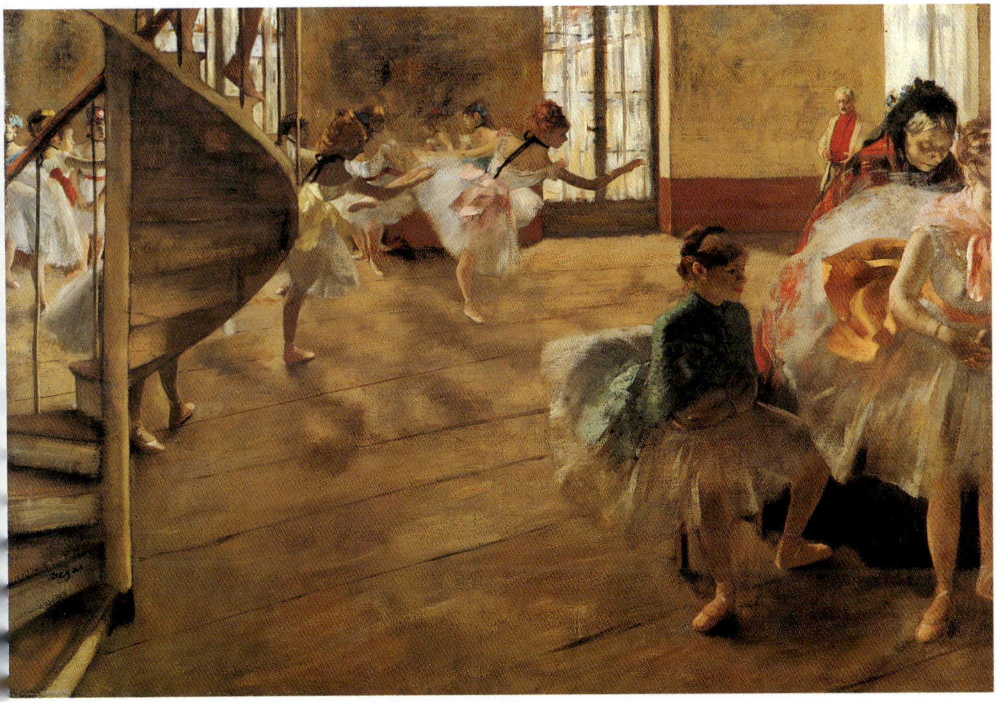

The Rehearsal (c. 1877) by Edgar Degas
Another masterpiece from Sir William Burrell's collection.

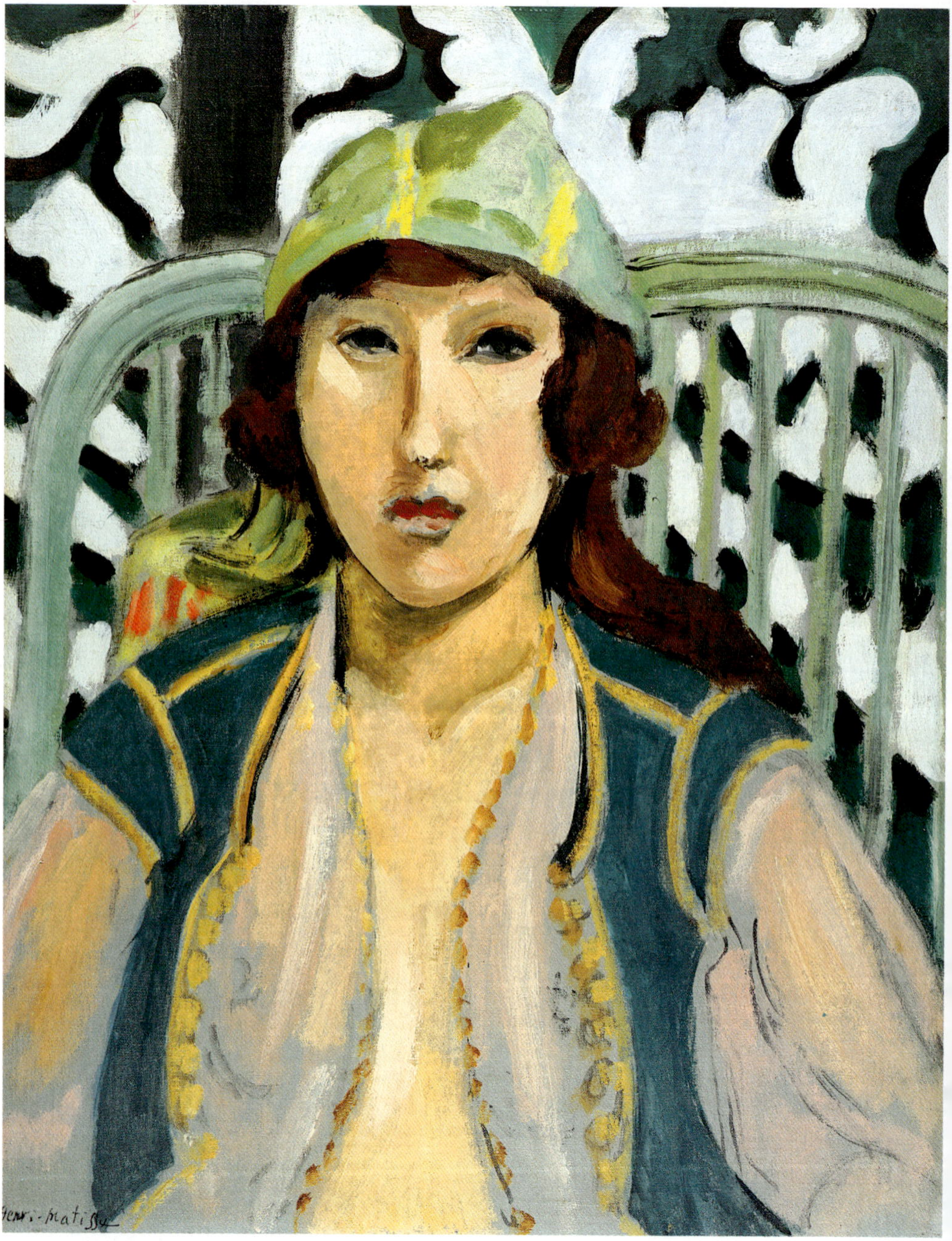

Head of a Young Girl (c. 1919) by Henri Matisse
Presented to Glasgow by William McInnes to mark his approval of Honeyman's appointment as Director.

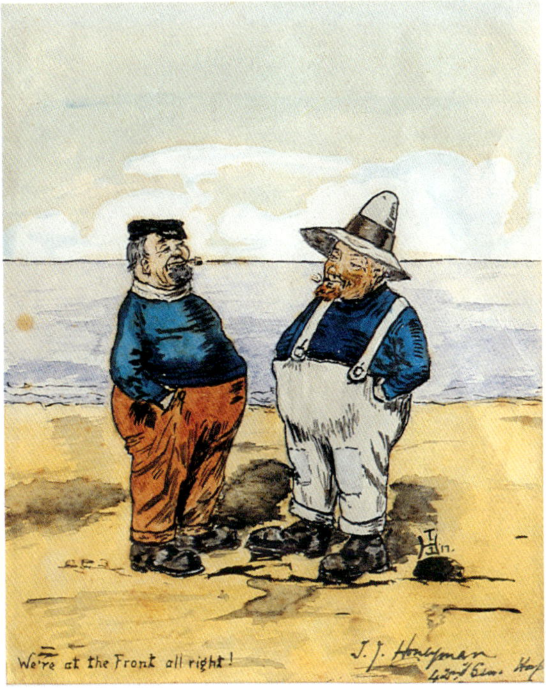

left:
"We're at the Front all right!"
Sketch by Captain Honeyman, RAMC, Salonika 1917.
Honeyman organised an art class for shell-shocked troops.

below:
Portrait of William McInnes (1930)
by G. Leslie Hunter
McInnes was an eminent Glasgow art collector, and a friend both of Honeyman and of Hunter.

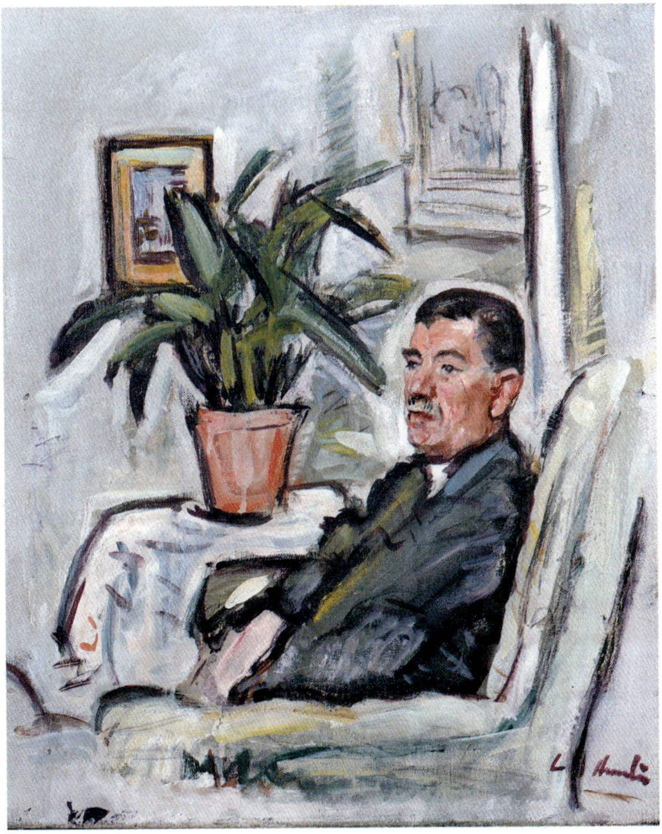

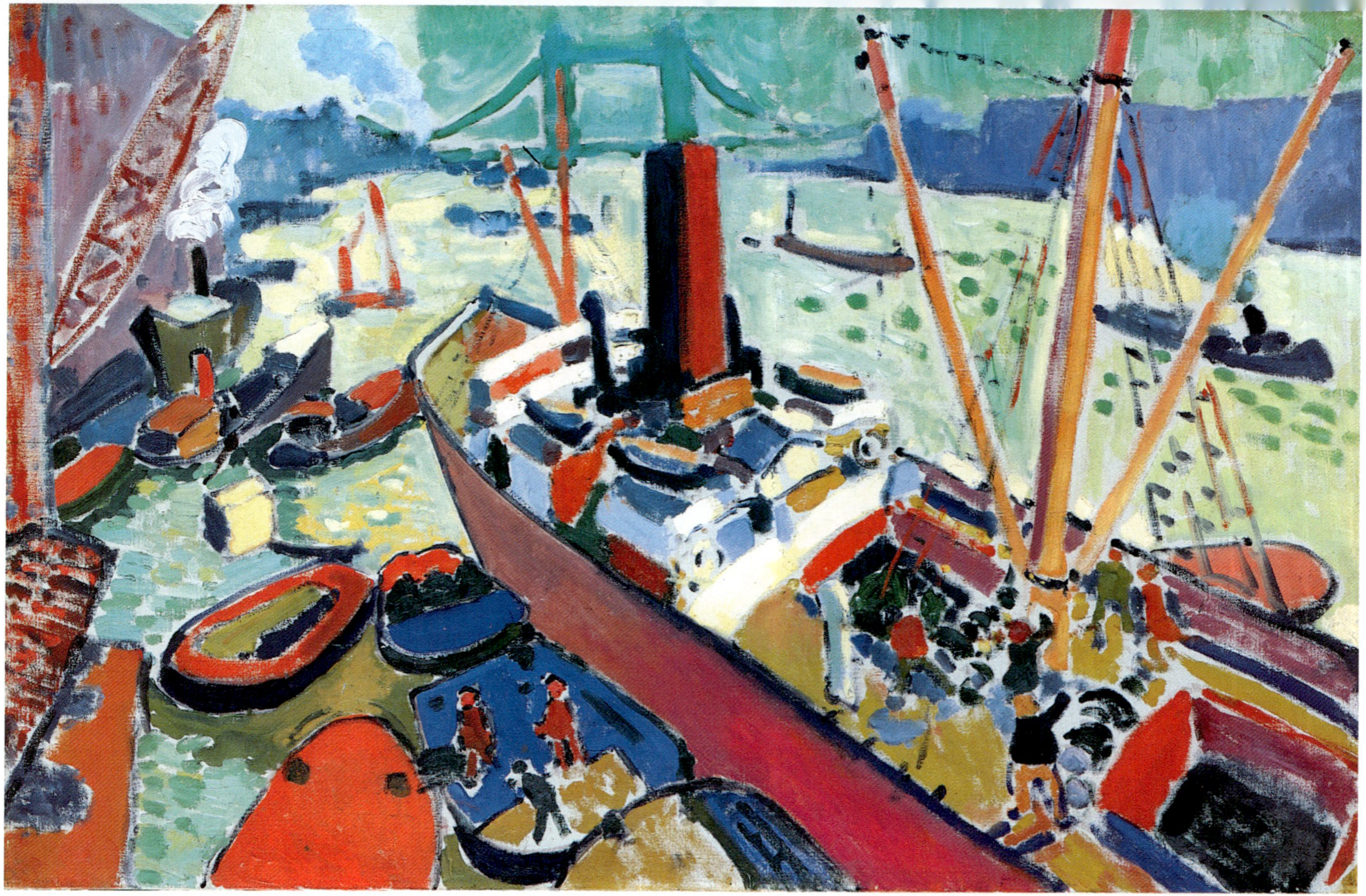

The Pool of London (c. 1906) by André Derain

Another painting from Honeyman's private collection, bought for £45 and later sold to the Tate Gallery.

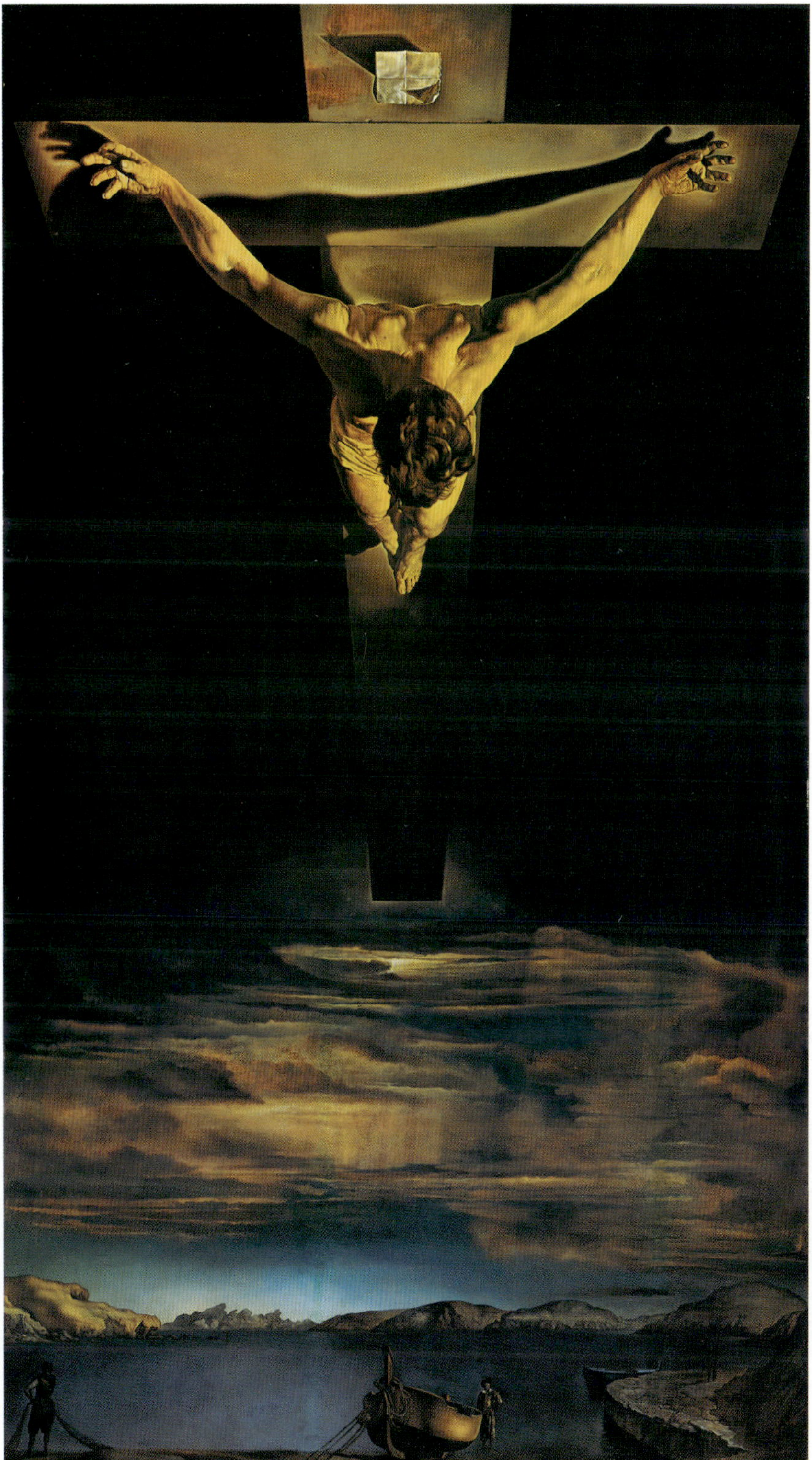

Christ of St John of the Cross (1951) by Salvador Dali
The controversial purchase which proved a wise investment for Glasgow.

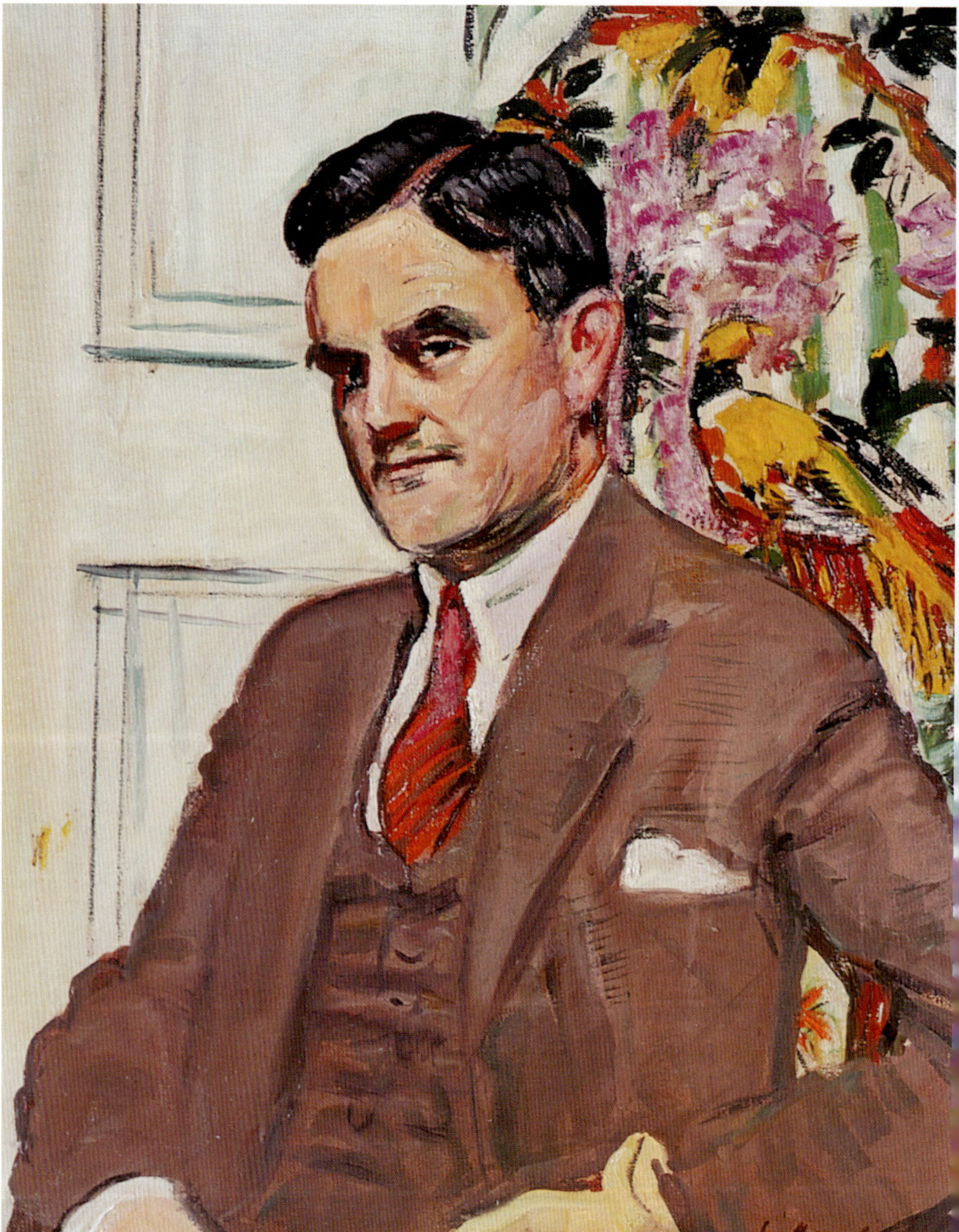

Portrait of T.J. Honeyman (1931) by G. Leslie Hunter

may well have been put there to get at Honeyman. They had been trying to push him out."

Ritchie may not have been the main reason for his departure but he was certainly the last straw. Things went from bad to worse, Honeyman felt he had lost the support of people at the top and he gave a year's notice of his intention to retire in 1954. He also offered any assistance by way of introducing a successor but, as he might have anticipated, that was met with silence.

When he had gone, the council went back on a decision to separate the Art Gallery from the Museums but they did upgrade the latter to the point that the chief official was the Director of Museums, with a deputy director designated as "in charge of Art". The status of the art side had therefore been lowered, though the people of Glasgow would continue to think of Kelvingrove as the Art Gallery.

The council even reversed the name of the department to make it "Glasgow Museums and Art Galleries", with Dr S. M. K. Henderson as the boss. The *Glasgow Herald* lashed out at this "regrettable and retrograde step" and said it was no reflection on Dr Henderson's personal expertness in his own field nor on his administrative ability to say the Corporation had erred. Their error had been to enhance the importance of the museums at the expense of the art side.

Although he was not yet at the age for retiring, Tom Honeyman did have other considerations when deciding to go. He had had two spells in hospital, once for a slipped disc infirmity which was proving a puzzle, and the whole upset of the frustration was causing anxiety at home. As the crisis built up, Cath would notice that he was speaking to himself and became deeply concerned at how the job was upsetting him. Finally his doctor advised him to get out. To the plea that he would qualify for a small pension in two years, the doctor replied bluntly that he might not be there to collect it.

Curiously for a man who had been so well heeled in his earlier days, he was once again worried about his financial position, admitting that his fifteen years in the Glasgow job had seriously depleted his resources. What he regarded as a very inadequate salary had not been enough to maintain his standards, which he believed to be fairly modest.

It was time to think about augmenting the family income to provide for retirement, which meant that something in the private sector must have been in his mind. In more recent times, when people were making much more provision for their old age, one would have expected him to be better prepared.

That disc problem had put him on his back at Glasgow's Western Infirmary at a time when he was forward as a candidate in the university rectorial. Unable to take part in the on-goings, he found himself with a bunch of charming nurses acting as his campaign managers, confronting medical students and others with adhesive tapes declaring "Vote for Honeyman—or I'll melt you".

The opposition was of formidable quality, ranging from Lady Tweedsmuir and Lord Bilsland to John M. Bannerman, Emrys Hughes MP and the eccentric Glasgow character, A. E. Pickard.

To his astonishment he came top of the poll with a vote which was exactly double that of his nearest rival, Lady Tweedsmuir. He was still flat on his back when his jubilant supporters invaded the hospital room and he was expected to make a speech of thanks from a very awkward position. But Tom Honeyman took his subsequent duties very seriously and relished being back at his old university, taking his place on the Court and establishing a rapport with another generation of students.

His substantial rectorial address, which he called "The Clear Horizon", had been met with the usual noisy and irreverent demonstration of student immaturity, which brought a letter from the Very Rev George Johnstone Jeffrey to say: "This is a message of commiseration and congratulation. On the first aspect, I can only say your treatment was an insult to you and yours. Something must be done to prevent a repetition of such an outrage. You stood up to it, as ever, like a man.

"Putting that aside, let me say how acceptably beautiful was the address itself. It torpedoed so much of the pretentiousness of so many of our publicists of today and set forth excellently the claims of the best elements of our human nature."

With more time on his hands, Dr Honeyman had some fun playing the prophet and at a later stage gave us the benefit of his crystal ball as far as the future of Glasgow was concerned. The city would have, on the South Side, an incomparable art and recreational centre sited in Pollok Estate and Rouken Glen. The responsible trustees would give effect to the spirit of Sir William Burrell's conditions and in the new gallery and in Pollok House there would be an abundance of riches for the art lover and scholar and a magnetic attraction for the Glaswegians and their visitors.

In the west there would be the finest university auditorium in Britain—and in the city centre there would rise a magnificent new concert hall with all the complementary facilities for the comfort of musicians and audience. On the banks of the Clyde, reclaimed from the hands of the philistines and vandals, a new civic theatre would be built and named the James Bridie Memorial Theatre. The Mitchell Library would have a much-needed extension and would play a more prominent part in extra-mural research and enlightenment.

Out of the picture stores of the Art Gallery at Kelvingrove would come the hidden treasures, to see again the light of day in a new building, the best in modern architecture, bringing the spectator and the world of art together in an atmosphere of relaxed enjoyment. Glasgow would become internationally known as the Convention City *par excellence* while the day would also come when the Cathedral would cease to be overwhelmed by the sick and the dead; when the Royal Infirmary would be moved out east and the great tumulus of the Necropolis would be reclaimed for recreation, rest and contemplation.

With the nearby Provand's Lordship, Glasgow's oldest house, then safe on its island site, the Cathedral and its precincts would help to renew the hope reflected in St Mungo's prayer, out of which came the civic motto: "Let Glasgow Flourish—by the preaching of Thy Word and the praising of Thy Name." And the statue of David Livingstone would remain as the token of a loud Amen.

Until Dr Honeyman became Lord Rector of Glasgow University in 1953, it had been the custom to confer an honorary Doctor of Laws but it was decided this would no longer be an automatic honour.

In fact it was given to him at the end of his term, in 1956, when the French professor presenting him for his LL.D had a dig at Glasgow Corporation: "When ill-health led Dr Honeyman to resign his post as Director two years ago, many merited tributes were paid to him but one cannot truthfully say that the city in its official capacity showed an adequate realisation of its loss. That loss has been the gain of this university. Though his "preposterous constituents" howled down his address (an admirable plea for the Imagination, whose language is art) . . . he has been a model of what student parlance calls the working Rector."

In 1962 Chief Albert Luthuli was elected Lord Rector and asked Dr Honeyman to be his assessor. In effect, this was to carry out the duties of Rector for a further three years since Chief Luthuli was not allowed by the South African government to leave his native country. He was the son of a Zulu Christian missionary, had led a campaign of non-violent resistance in his country and was awarded the Nobel Peace Prize in 1960.

XXXVIII

WORLD TOURS

TOWARDS RETIREMENT Tom Honeyman would still have his commitment to the Scottish Tourist Board and the Citizens' Theatre as well as his rectorship of Glasgow University. A month before he left his post at the Glasgow Art Gallery there was the promise of yet another interesting career when he was appointed the Scottish representative to the new Independent Television Authority.

Commercial television was on its way and, under the chairmanship of Sir Kenneth Clark, former director of the National Galleries and now chairman of the Arts Council, the new body had a major task in hand. It had to set up transmission stations, frame its own rules of etiquette and permissibility and then scrutinise every programme to see that its own standards were being enforced.

Commercial television was still some time away from being set up in Scotland—that would come when the Canadian Roy Thomson would gain his franchise for Scottish Television—but there was already a large section of responsible and critical opinion which didn't want the commercial sector at all.

With supposedly more time on his hands (that grossly mistaken view of retirement!) Tom Honeyman was even more in demand as a public speaker, facing the tail-end of 1955 with an American tour which would take in the principal toast at the St Andrew's Society dinners in Chicago, Detroit and New York.

In reply to the toast of "The Land o' Cakes", he ranged over his subject in fascinating fashion and drew to a close with this kind of tale to delight his exiled audience:

"Three weeks ago I was in the Highlands and as I came back home, down the West Coast by Loch Ness to Fort William, I nearly went over to see Dame Flora McLeod in Skye, but I knew she was away from home. I was remembering another McLeod, a doctor who, unlike myself, was faithful to the practice of medicine over forty years. He was noted not so much for his medical skill as his common sense. Once an old patient came to him with the complaint that he was going deaf. He said 'Doctor, I seem to be getting a bit hard with the hearing.' Dr McLeod said 'How old are you, Donald?' 'Well now doctor, I'm eighty-eight.' 'Ach Donald,' said the doctor, 'don't you think you've heard enough?' "

And he went on: "By the same token, I'm sure you've heard enough from me. But let me finish my trip. I came down by Ballachulish. You may remember that point in the Pass of Brander where an echo comes back from the hills. Well I tested it with 'Hello' and back came the answer 'Hello'. Then I said 'I'm going to New York. What shall I say?' And in the silence which surrounded me, my imagination played tricks. I thought the hills came back to me whispering 'Tell them that I am something more than a Land o' Cakes. Tell them I am something more than a land where the heather and the bluebells grow, a land of mountains and glens and hills and lochs and wee villages and big towns. Tell them that I am a spirit, the spirit of a race, not infinite, not eternal but unchangeable as long as man lives on the earth. Tell them, my sons and daughters and their sons and daughters, that I know they owe a new and rich allegiance to the land of their adoption, but that I still covet a corner of their hearts. Tell them that in the wind that sweeps over me there is a melody for them:

"Better lo'ed ye canna be
Will ye no come back again?"

The lyrical Honeyman was digging up their emotions and, as you can imagine, there wasn't a throat without a lump. He appeared on television wherever he went and took the chance to promote Scotland at meetings and luncheons organised by the English Speaking Union, a body which gave him many opportunities to boost his native land in foreign parts and which sometimes provided the fees which enabled him to travel so extensively. In fact he became president of the Glasgow and West of Scotland branch of the English Speaking Union and after his death they established a Honeyman Scholarship to enable young Scots to travel abroad. The Honeymans were back in North America at the end of the following year as well, this time visiting their younger son Grant and his wife Monica, who had emigrated to Canada the previous year, as Grant began to establish a reputation as a surgeon.

This trip would also serve to make an extensive study of television methods in the United States and Canada, the land where that dominant figure of Scottish Television, Roy Thomson, had so apprised himself of the opportunities.

Again it was a chance to renew friendships all the way from Ottawa and Montreal to Vermont, Philadelphia and Washington, ending with a reunion dinner in New York with Salvador Dali and his wife. Honeyman wrote in his diary: "Dali very easy to talk to. His English improves and his enthusiasm for his own work is as strong as ever."

The New York visit covered the St Andrew's Night dinner once again, this time as a guest of the society's president, listening with appreciation to that most colourful of statesmen and finest of orators, Scotland's own Lord Boothby, who was in sparkling form. Honeyman was also greatly impressed that evening with the speech of a young Glasgow graduate, Michael Topping, who was spending a year at Columbia University.

Before embarking on yet another American tour, when he would lecture at Yale on the Glasgow School and Charles Rennie Mackintosh, Dr Tom was deeply involved with a BBC series called *Look at This* in which, even in retirement, he was arousing an awareness of art in a wider public which would not normally have regarded it as their subject.

Popular journalist Peggie Phillips wrote: "In bringing back Dr Tom Honeyman in a new Sunday series on art the BBC brings a fresh wind on a subject which had become clogged with an esoteric patter which is off-putting to the ordinary Scot, whose whole inclination is to spurn anything 'precious'. Dr Honeyman, cosy, downright, shunning polysyllabic professionalism, is just the man to set it into its right perspective with the man in the street. In himself he is a bracing rebuke to those intellectuals who are killing the very thing they imagine they are fostering.

"Left to himself, Dr Honeyman, roundly saying he has never met anybody who doesn't know something about art, encourages the housewife who arranges her room—'Art is arrangement'—to feel that in doing so, she proves that she knows something about art."

It was a time when civic development plans seemed hell-bent on pulling down ancient buildings so it was a good time for a man of his enthusiasm to become honorary president of the Provand's Lordship Society, leading a fund-raising campaign to help preserve Glasgow's oldest house, dating back to 1471.

In his retirement, however, the main thrust of his activity was as an art consultant, in demand with collectors who knew that his judgement and integrity could be relied upon completely.

Even after his seventieth birthday in June 1961 his schedule of work and travel would have daunted most younger men. He would try to arrange his London visits to coincide with meetings of the Ansvar Insurance Company, of which he was a director. This unusual company originated in Sweden and was concerned entirely in doing business with total abstainers from alcohol, an interest which Tom Honeyman was naturally keen to encourage.

That life-long concern for temperance was one of the main subjects of his public speaking, along with art and tourism.

But those who observed his hectic round of engagements would have been surprised to know that he was keeping it up while the early signs of heart trouble were beginning to worry him. His was already suffering from angina pectoris and his secretary, Jo Leggat, would notice him quietly slipping a pill under his tongue.

Whereas Isabel Mackintosh had been his secretary throughout his gallery days in Glasgow, that role was taken over by Jo Leggat in those retirement years when he still had so many irons in the fire. Jo had moved from Leicester to be a housewife in East Kilbride and was looking for a part-time job when an agency directed her to a Dr T. J. Honeyman. She expected to be working for a medical man, which of course he was, but much to her surprise the secretarial activities were all to do with the rather different world of art.

He found an office of his own in West Regent Street and that was where she began to serve her new boss for the last eleven years of his life. She was typing correspondence which was destined for a range of personalities, from Dame Sybil Thorndike, the famous actress, to W. A. Cargill, who was being closely advised on his famous art collection by Dr Honeyman.

There were letters on everything from his television connections to his roles at Provand's Lordship and at the Citizens' Theatre. Jo Leggat was also responsible for typing the manuscript of his book, *Art and Audacity*, which had been written in longhand during a voyage to Vancouver and could have been deciphered only by those with skill and intelligence!

Even when she had a family of her own to look after, Dr Tom (as she and many others called him) would travel to East Kilbride with his handwritten letters to save her the journey to Glasgow. Between times, he gave up the West Regent Street office and Jo was based at the Honeyman home in Dowanhill Street. Coming from England, it was the first time she had encountered a Glasgow "wally close", that entrance to a tenement building characterised by the tiles of social superiority. It still surprised her that a shared entrance of limited promise could lead to such a spacious and elegant home, with its mahogany panelling and bannister and large hall opening into a lounge with its double doors, a grand piano and large settees by the fireside. Among the items to catch her eye in Dr Tom's study was a series of small sketches by Salvador Dali, the man whose name had drawn her boss into such widespread controversy.

Moving about in the background, Cath Honeyman struck Jo Leggat as being very much the lady of the house, warm and caring and a truly lovely person. She recalls: "Mrs Honeyman impressed you as a clever woman who could have been a great success in a career of her own. Instead, she devoted herself to the support of her husband, though she was always out at coffee mornings or lunches in aid of one of her charities."

Then Dr Tom would be off on his travels to America or Australia and Jo would be ready to type up his notes on his return.

On a visit to California he brought back a big box of oranges which he distributed all around with great delight. There was a childlike humour in him. Jo reckoned he would kill you with kindness. On those visits to her East Kilbride home there were always bags of sweets for her children. The fact that they were adopted struck a chord with Dr Tom, whose own son Grant had adopted boys in Canada.

On his seventieth birthday, he insisted on giving her seventy shillings, so that she could buy something which would celebrate the occasion.

"It should have been the other way round—but that was the

kind of man he was. I remember I bought a set of grapefruit dishes." Nor did he forget her appreciation of art when he presented her with two worthwhile pictures, including one of the bridges of Paris.

After the Christmas visit to Grant and Monica in 1960, Tom Honeyman thought he might curtail the rest of the tour in view of his health. But with renewed vigour, he and Cath set off for Winnipeg, Calgary, Banff, Vancouver and Victoria returning to Toronto and then on to New York before sailing home in late February.

There were press and television interviews all the way but after an art lecture at the Scottish Auditorium in Vancouver, he recorded in his diary: "I had one of my happiest audiences but . . . pain was acute. Thought I was in for a blackout and don't remember now what I said for about two or three slides after Whistler's 'Carlyle'. I managed to keep going. But this is going to make me decide to stop lecturing. I would hate to do anything sensational in the middle of a public appearance. Better to recognise the risks and avoid them. I still recollect with horror the cold sweating that came over me—but pleased no-one seemed to notice."

Next day he mentioned in his diary that, while lecturing in Vancouver Art Gallery, he got his worst fright: "In the middle of the lecture, felt a tachycardia—pains in the arm." Once the heart scare subsided, however, he carried on as before, still with some years ahead of him and travels which would include visits to Salvador Dali in Spain and journeys to Canada and the United States, Sweden, the Holy Land and Australia.

That journey Down Under was the most restful voyage the Honeymans had ever experienced. It was undertaken on a cargo boat which took four weeks to reach Fremantle, via Port Said, Suez, Aden and Colombo. It was just as well they arrived refreshed for there was yet another punishing schedule ahead, much to do with addressing large gatherings on the subject of temperance. One of the great joys of the Australian trip was that heart-warming reunion with Patricia and John Casson at their home in Melbourne, recalling those post-war days when John was director of the Citizens' Theatre in Glasgow.

Another highlight for Cath Honeyman was the chance to see relations in Brisbane. Indeed, half way through the holiday she stayed with her cousin while Dr Tom broke the visit by flying home to Britain for an art sale! It had to be a major event which brought him all the way back to London and it was indeed the art event of the year—the disposal of the paintings of W. A. Cargill, which fetched over £1 million at Sotheby's. That included a Degas at £105,000.

Not only was this an occasion too exciting to miss but Tom Honeyman had played a major part in building up Cargill's collection and had a kind of agent's role in the disposal. It was said to be the only time in his life that he actually made any real money.

Having come home via Hong Kong and Athens, he flew back to Australia a few days after the sale, this time travelling by New York, San Francisco and Honolulu. In the absence of her mother, daughter Margaret went down from Glasgow to London for the Cargill sale and had a delightful few days keeping her father company.

XXXIX

THE MAN WHO MADE 'THE DAMBUSTERS'

THAT PRESTIGIOUS NIGHT at Sotheby's holds special memories for Colin Clark, a connoisseur of art who is of Scots parentage but lives in London. As a young enthusiast he was taken under the wing of Tom Honeyman and learned so much that he soon came to revere the man.

It was the first time Colin Clark had attended a proper art sale, even if he didn't have access to the main salesroom, for which dinner jacket was obligatory. His contact with Dr Honeyman was through his father, Robert Clark, a remarkable Scot who aspired to art collecting and engaged his distinguished fellow countryman to advise him. The fact that Robert Clark is a name so little known in his native land is yet another example of how often we fail to document the lives of people with fascinating careers. It is all the more strange in this day of apparently blanket publicity.

Robert Clark was born in 1904 at 3 Clavering Street in Paisley, the last of thirteen children in a working-class family. Out of school at fourteen, he was articled to John Maxwell, a Glasgow solicitor whose firm, Maxwell Waddell, still exists in Hope Street today. Young Clark went on to Glasgow University where he took his MA and LL.B and became a fully qualified solicitor. He idolised John Maxwell, a man of vision whose firm was involved in early cinema deals in Glasgow and took a stake in several picture houses, starting with the Prince's in Springburn. He even had a film production company in Scotland (it was called Waverley) but, sensing the potential of this newfangled film industry which was blossoming in the 1920s, Maxwell headed off to London and took over an ailing company which he turned into the Associated British Picture Corporation.

Establishing himself at what became the famous Elstree Studios, he engaged a young director called Alfred Hitchcock to make his first talkie, *Blackmail*, in 1929. In that same year Maxwell sent for young Robert Clark to come south as his assistant. The Paisley lad did not hesitate to renew a working relationship with his old boss but decided that, if he was moving to England, he had better be qualified as an English lawyer, even though that would not be his profession. So the diligent young Scot read for the English Bar.

But his main function was now as a film producer, a new career for which he soon gained a passion. Returning to Paisley to marry his sweetheart, Mary Lang (her family was associated with St Mirren Football Club), Robert Clark set up home at Hendon, which was conveniently situated between London's West End and the film studios at Elstree.

In the 1930s he was involved in putting together films like *Blossom Time*, which led to his friendship with the great Richard Tauber. The Second World War cut into that career when Elstree was requisitioned. That was compounded by the personal tragedy of John Maxwell's premature death in 1940 and it was not until after the war that Robert Clark entered the heyday of his career in films. He landed well, however, for that golden age of British films which ran from around 1947 until the late 1950s.

Now established as a director and driving force of Associated British Pictures, Clark became responsible for a whole string of popular films, ranging from *The Hasty Heart* (it featured Ronald

Reagan) in 1949, to *Laughter in Paradise* with Alastair Sim, *Woman in a Dressing Gown*, Ivor Novello's *The Dancing Years* and the wartime thriller *Ice Cold in Alex*, in which Robert Clark brought together his fellow Scots J. Lee Thompson as director and Tom Morrison to write the screenplay.

A former *Glasgow Herald* reporter, Tom Morrison was one of a family of five from High Burnside, all of whom gained distinction as writers. Two of his sisters were Nancy Brysson Morrison, who wrote *The Gowk Storm*, and March Cost, who gained fame as a novelist in America. Tom became leading screenwriter at Elstree. The film which gave Robert Clark the greatest satisfaction, however, was *The Dambusters*, with Michael Redgrave playing the part of Barnes Wallis, the inventive genius who gave us the bouncing bomb which burst the German dams during the war.

So Robert Clark became a highly significant figure in the British film industry, the man who thought nothing of paying a substantial sum for the film rights of Alistair MacLean's first novel, *HMS Ulysses* in the 1950s, though he never actually made the film. You would find him at ease, having lunch with Marlene Dietrich or putting people like Audrey Hepburn under contract. He also became a director of London Weekend Television.

But the main source of his personal wealth lay outwith films altogether. He was chairman of a major property company in London, Stock Conversion, and was deeply involved in development around the country in that post-war period when names like Charles Clore were much in evidence. The financial world was slow to catch on to the extent of Stock Conversion's ramifications in central London but came to realise that they knew only of the tip of a very large iceberg.

In Scotland, Clark's company used the title Scottish Site Improvements, based at the old Grosvenor Restaurant site in Gordon Street, and developed city centre blocks like Blythswood House in West Regent Street, Trafalgar House in Hope Street and Hamilton House in Waterloo Street, as well as Scottish Life House in St Vincent Street and the Paisley Piazza, back in Clark's home town. His son Robin is still involved in the sector with Taylor Clark Properties Ltd of Renfield Street.

Robert Clark was also a founder-director of Caledonian Associated Cinemas, owners of a large chain of picture houses in Scotland, which brought him into contact with another major figure of cinema, Sir Alexander B. King. King in turn was a founder member of the Scottish Tourist Board, along with none other than Tom Honeyman—and that was how Robert Clark came to meet the former director of Glasgow Art Gallery.

He was reaching that stage when he wanted to possess something more important in the field of painting so he arranged a meeting with Dr Honeyman at the Ritz Hotel in London's Piccadilly. Clark's son Colin had been to Cambridge and was qualified as an accountant but didn't intend to practise. Instead he was extending his passion for music and the theatre to a curiosity about painting so his father suggested he come along to the lunch at the Ritz, where he might learn something.

The main purpose of the meeting was to discuss Robert Clark's ambitions in the art world and as a result of that day he did in fact buy some important pictures over the following year. Caught up in the excitement of his first visit to the Ritz—and hearing so much about art from an expert—son Colin became more seriously concerned with paintings and began attending exhibitions. Robert Clark thought it would be a good idea to adorn his offices with paintings by contemporary Scottish artists and suggested his son should give some attention to the matter.

Colin met up with Tom Honeyman at the Arts Club in Dover Street, London, and that was when he came more under his influence and began to take guidance from a master. Honeyman invited him to Glasgow in January 1964, when he introduced him to the mysteries of contemporary Scottish art. Now in his seventies, he was delighted to impart his knowledge and experience to an enthusiast like Clark who was still in his twenties.

It was the start of a good relationship, with a correspondence which stretched to 123 items between 1964 and Honeyman's death seven years later.

Colin Clark recalled: "My life came to be more and more to do with art. Dr Honeyman took me under his wing and I considered myself to be very much his pupil—a pupil in connoisseurship, learning about art, how to regard it, how to buy it, and being introduced to the personalities."

Dr Honeyman suggested that Colin Clark should pursue research on William Buchanan, the Glasgow man who had gone to London as an art dealer and was responsible for importing so many famous pictures. So Colin embarked on research, intending to write a book on this much-neglected Scot. As it happened, he was diverted from his purpose when he ran across a man in Edinburgh who was also researching Buchanan's letters. But in the 1990s he was turning his thoughts once more to the possibility of writing that book which is still required to do justice to a distinguished Scot.

Meanwhile, Clark was buying pictures for his father's offices, taking advice from Honeyman to go and take a look at such and such.

"Once I began to be aware of the scene and what things cost," he said, "I quickly realised I was able to afford them myself. So I was collecting pictures, though I have never thought of myself as a collector because that implies you know what you are looking for!"

Starting with that contemporary Scottish scene, Colin Clark went back to the days of the Glasgow Boys and built up a collection which ranged from the 18th century until the present day and had a strongly Franco-British influence, taking in drawing, watercolours and oil paintings, with some sculpture.

He had not known much about Leslie Hunter, the Scottish Colourist who was famous for his landscapes and still-life, but the death of Hunter's cousin, J. Gibson Jarvie, chairman of United Dominions Trust, took him on a journey to Suffolk, along with Tom Honeyman, to see some of the work which had remained in the family. He had already attended the public auction at Phillips, where he had made a purchase or two, but he reckons that that was the day when prices for the Scottish Colourists really began to rise. People were surprised at what Hunter's work was fetching.

On the visit to Gedding Hall at Bury St Edmunds, Dr Honeyman and Colin Clark were given lunch by the two daughters of Gibson Jarvie, one of whom had been painted by Hunter, a portrait which they saw that day. They had hoped to buy some of Hunter's work for Robert Clark but, despite a pleasant visit, nothing came of it.

For his most significant acquisitions, Colin Clark waited till a later date when he bought Hunter's "Loch Lomond" at Christie's and a still-life from Ian McNicol in Glasgow.

So Tom Honeyman had turned a young London-Scot of independent means into a substantial private collector. Little could he have guessed, however, of the outcome of events when he first invited Colin Clark to his home at Dowanhill Street, in the West End of Glasgow. That was when the visitor set eyes on the portrait of Cath Honeyman which Dr Tom had commissioned the great Wyndham Lewis to paint in 1936-37. Mrs Honeyman may have been charmed by the sparkling conversation of the artist but she was evidently not exactly at ease with Lewis himself—and some of her discomfort perhaps showed in the portrait, for which she sat in the same chair as subjects like T. S. Eliot and Stephen Spender.

In time, the family collection was divided amicably between their three children, Tim and Margaret in this country and Grant in Canada. The portrait of their mother went to Grant, not inappropriately since the artist had been born in Canada and spent the Second World War there.

Many years later Grant decided to raise some money for his children and, with paintings inclined to be the currency of artistic people, he discussed the possible sale of his mother's portrait with William Hardie, the Glasgow art dealer, when he visited the Honeymans in Ontario. Hardie thought it might be bought by a museum, perhaps the Scottish National Portrait Gallery, and agreed to take delivery in Glasgow. He was standing at the door of his gallery one day when he saw, to his surprise, that Colin Clark was approaching. Colin's visits to the city were fairly rare but he had heard about the Wyndham Lewis and was showing a good deal of interest. He had a good look at the painting again but had to think about the price being asked.

It would be the most he had ever paid but there was so much built into this frame. Here was Cath Honeyman, wife of the man he had come to revere, the lady he had so admired and respected and who had been such a good hostess on his visits to their home in Dowanhill Street. So Colin Clark met the substantial asking price, which would have brought an appreciative response from his old mentor who had paid a very nominal sum to the artist all those years ago.

But if that required a little thought, Tom Honeyman was indirectly responsible for Colin Clark exceeding that price in another purchase, which remains his most valuable.

For Tom was the man who told him that Victor Hugo was a good draughtsman as well as a world-famous writer, responsible for such masterpieces as *Les Misérables*. On one of their holidays the Honeymans had gone to Guernsey in the Channel Islands, to which Hugo had been exiled by Napoleon III, and set out to see some of his work in the local museum.

At a much later date, Colin Clark caught up with the artistic drawing of the great man and wrote a sizeable cheque for an example. One of its charms is the appearance of five lines of verse on the back, duly signed by Victor Hugo. Both items now hang in the elegant surroundings of Colin Clark's home in the exclusive heart of London.

As he casts an eye on Cath Honeyman, he remembers a naturally quiet lady who loved her music and her poetry. With the over-abundant energy of her husband, he felt her role was sometimes a difficult one. She had to keep up her end.

As for any sense of failure on the part of Dr Honeyman, as expressed at the end of his career, Colin Clark felt that had surely been disproved by the events which led to Glasgow becoming the European City of Culture in 1990.

His own father, Robert Clark, died in 1984 at the age of eighty, at that time still chairman of his Stock Conversion company and of Caledonian Associated Cinemas in Scotland. He was also a director of Blackwood Hodge, the earth-moving equipment company.

If Scotland had failed to recognise a distinguished son in London, his *alma mater* did catch up with him at the very end of his life. There is a picture of the day he received an honorary degree of LL.D from Glasgow University in 1984, in which he is seen, appropriately, with the young film-maker of that decade, Bill Forsyth. The man who had recently given films like *Gregory's Girl* and *Local Hero* to a later generation stood proudly with the Scot who had masterminded so many British classics from that golden period of Elstree Studios nearly forty years earlier. The same man had gone on to be governor of the British Film Institute and one of the men appointed to consider the need for a National Film School.

It is all the more an indictment on the journalism of the day that there wasn't a line of obituary about Robert Clark when he died in 1984, not even in *The Times*. The only trace of any article about the man at all seems to have been left to the local paper in his old home town of Paisley, which gave rise in the first place to this inspiring but unheralded tale of a local boy made good.

XL

ART AND AUDACITY

DR HONEYMAN'S last sea voyage began in December 1969, when he sailed from Glasgow on a cargo boat bound for a round trip to Vancouver, which would take two and a half months.

The intention was to draw together his reminiscences of the fifteen years spent as Director of the Glasgow Art Gallery and Museums and to present them as a manuscript. By then he was seventy-eight but, when he arrived back in February 1970, that manuscript was indeed complete and was published under the title of *Art and Audacity* the following year.

He was back in time for a major exhibition of the "Three Scottish Colourists", as he had dubbed them in 1950. It had been his special pleasure to help choose the exhibits, each painter represented by twenty-eight works in a selection covering the period from 1902 until 1933.

In his *Scotsman* review, Emilio Coia wrote: "The selection was made by Dr Honeyman, whose pithy, idiosyncratic writings and reminiscences over the years have contributed greatly to our knowledge of the three and without whose advice and influence, one imagines, this show would have suffered."

In the *Glasgow Herald*, Martin Baillie enthused about the exhibition: "The neutral walls of the gallery show off the paintings to the best advantage. They hang fresh and bright as though they had just left the easel, filling the room with their charm and geniality.

"Light-handed but by no means light-weight painters, all three were serious, dedicated, thoroughly professional men, opposed to the grey mimetics of academicism and responsive to developments in late nineteenth century painting and the School of Paris."

Tom and Cath Honeyman celebrated their fiftieth wedding anniversary on 24 June 1970, which brought some unaccustomed attention to the lady behind the man. For all his own ebullience and extrovert nature, it is fair to say that Tom would have been lost without Katinka, or K, as he used to call her, though to everyone else she was either Cath or Cathie.

Though her husband's life gave her much-envied opportunities to travel and meet interesting people, it said a lot for her adaptability that she followed from one career to the next with such apparent ease. There was a sacrifice of companionship when you consider that, even if they had a free evening at home together, Dr Tom was most likely bound up in his next lecture or newspaper article or sundry adventure.

As was the fashion at the time, it was very much the husband's career which set the pace of their lives and Cath busied herself with creating a home where everybody was welcome. She graced that home with talents which ranged from adventurous cooking to splendid embroidery and there was always the musical background of her skill as a pianist. Cath was also a prolific letter-writer, with a talent for keen observation, vivid description, warmth and wit which made her epistles a joy to a wide circle of family and friends.

At her Dowanhill Street flat you would find her holding a rather special kind of coffee morning in aid of cancer relief, a charity for which she did a great deal.

On one such occasion, described in the *Glasgow Herald*, Cath was joined by two friends, novelist Lavinia Derwent and actress

Molly Weir, in greeting the guests, the perky Molly at that time appearing in *Beneath the Wee Red Lums* at the Metropole Theatre.

As the guests wandered around the house, Dr Tom was on hand to give racy comments on his own art collection, which was unorthodox, catholic and altogether fascinating. There was Graham Sutherland in the hall, a Lurçat tapestry screen in the drawing room, a collection of jewellery by the Scots-American artist, Alexander Calder, inventor of the "mobiles", a Stanley Cursiter seascape from Orkney which was turned to the wall to show the man made out of sea-shells, glued to the back by the artist.

But the *objet d'art* which drew most bemused speculation was "Crossing the Atlantic", an abstract piece of angled sheets of glass over a sinister black sea with a whale cut-out by Marcoussis, a contemporary of Picasso.

A party of forty relatives and closest friends were invited to that golden wedding in June 1970, Grant and his wife Monica bringing their four children from Canada for the occasion.

As they had discovered on a previous occasion, there is no better way to approach a celebration like this than to hire a bus and take everyone there together. So they met up for morning coffee at the Lady Artists' Club in Glasgow before setting out in high spirits for the Lomond Castle Hotel at Loch Lomond. It was a memorable family occasion and they were all relieved that Dr Honeyman stood up to the emotional strain of the day, since a few weeks earlier he had been far from well with heart trouble. Any thought of cancelling the golden wedding party were dismissed on the grounds that, since no-one more enjoyed a family get-together, it would only make him worse to call it off.

By now the proofs of *Art and Audacity* had arrived and the task of correcting them took priority. He was also involved with a BBC television programme about the Three Colourists—Hunter, Peploe and Cadell—giving the *Radio Times* the chance to say:

"Long before he became Director of Glasgow Art Galleries and Museums, Dr Honeyman, then an art dealer, bought and sold the work of the three great Scottish Colourists. He knew them as painters and men. On the eve of the publication of *Art and Audacity* Dr Honeyman remembers these artists who did so much to establish Scottish painting on the European scene."

On 1st April 1971 the first copies of his book arrived and he noted in his diary: "The date is ominous. I hope I'm not entering into a fool's paradise." Three weeks later, on a visit to his publisher at Collins, he further recorded: "On the way upstairs to see Jim Corbett I had a blackout. Thank goodness Donald Sillars was beside me. This is the first complete blackout I have had. It wasn't at all uncomfortable. I was away about a minute. Resisted idea of going to Royal Infirmary and was taken home by Jim Corbett. And so to bed. Was better by evening. I hope my final exit is like this—one moment chatting, then sweet oblivion."

There was much to occupy him, with the publication of *Art and Audacity* and the news that he was to be given an honorary fellowship by the Royal College of Physicians and Surgeons.

Scottish Television was keeping him busy with a programme devoted to his various careers, angled on the fact that he was now approaching his eightieth birthday. That auspicious party was planned by his son Tim, along with some friends of his father—Emilio Coia, Michael Goldberg, George Singleton and Lord Taylor of Gryfe.

Grant and his daughter Pamela arrived from Canada and joined more than 170 guests in the banqueting hall of the Central Hotel for an occasion they would certainly never forget. Tom Honeyman was in sparkling form on his big night and Cath looked radiant. In response to the eulogies, Dr Honeyman directed attention from one person to the next, each of whom had played some part in their lives.

On friendship, he quoted lines which he loved: "A friend is

somebody to whom you can pour out all the contents of your heart—chaff and grain together—knowing that the gentlest of hands will sift it, taking what is worth keeping and with the breath of kindness blowing the rest away."

On that night of warm fellowship who could have guessed that the end was so near? And yet it was probably a fitting climax to such a full and adventurous life.

XLI

THE FINAL CURTAIN

THE HEART TROUBLE had gone respectfully into abeyance while the final curtain was suitably taken. From his big night, Tom Honeyman was still on cloud nine when, three weeks later, he and Cath went to stay with their friends, the Ferguson Smiths, at Strathtay in Perthshire.

During the night he suffered a heart attack and on the following afternoon Mrs Ferguson Smith came to offer him a cup of tea. After a few sips he declined any more and said: "If I could just have a good sleep now, I'd be in Heaven."

The family liked to think that that was what happened for he slipped into unconsciousness and died shortly afterwards. Daughter Margaret travelled to Strathtay with her husband, Jim Wilson, and brother Tim and spent the night there. Unable to sleep, Margaret remembered gazing out at a brightly scintillating star which was framed between two poplars outside the window. She called it to her husband's attention and he expressed her own thought that "It's as if Dad were winking to tell you not to worry. He's all right."

It was a happy funeral at Dowanhill Church as they raised their voices and sang "Praise My Soul the King of Heaven". It had been a long and happy life and the timing of the end was close to perfect.

His life was well summed up in the eulogy of Professor Esmond Wright of Glasgow University, who recalled that he had first met Tom Honeyman during that wartime visit to the deserts of North Africa. Now they were within easy walking distance of his home, his university and his beloved Art Gallery at Kelvingrove.

He said: "Tom Honeyman touched life at so many points that any of his many careers would have been enough for lesser mortals. Doctor of medicine, soldier in Salonika and India, general practitioner, lover of art and art dealer in Glasgow and London, director of Glasgow Art Gallery, publicist, controversialist, radio and television personality, speaker who learned the art of holding audiences as a young man in the St Andrews Halls, *raconteur par excellence*, Fellow of the Educational Institute of Scotland, author, journalist . . .

"Even this list is incomplete for it omits the Citizens' Theatre. He might so easily have become an actor."

So it went on, through university Rector, the Independent Television Authority, the Arts Council, the Provand's Lordship Society, tourism and so much else. Glasgow had given him its accolade, the St Mungo Prize, in 1943 and it was right to do so.

For this was the man who brought it the Burrell Collection, the McInnes Collection, the Dali Crucifixion and so many of its holdings of French Impressionists and the Scottish School.

He said: "We salute a Renaissance figure surging with vitality, rich with curiosity over the human condition, a lover of beauty, wide ranging in his interests and stirred by civic pride, a Renaissance man whose heart belonged to Glasgow."

He had gone from school at Queen's Park to medical practice at Dennistoun and Bridgeton and from there to the wider world but at the core of everything was the dear green place which bred him.

Michael Goldberg, who had followed him at the Citizens', wrote: "Tom Honeyman was the last of a group of unique Glasgow characters who included James Bridie and Walter Elliot. They were men of an unusual and distinctive flavour who enriched and enlivened the Glasgow scene and made it a more exciting and stimulating place to live in."

Sir Denis Brogan, distinguished Glaswegian who became a famous professor at Cambridge, gave the opinion that Honeyman had been the most interesting Glasgow man, active in public life, since the First World War.

Sir Denis wrote: "He had a great virtue of realising that Glasgow had been going downhill ever since that first war and that it must be brought back (and not only the art galleries) to its old and greater days. This naturally involved him in a great many quarrels. I suppose it is possible that he was not always right but his controversial methods caused resentment.

"He knew that many of the examples of Scottish art in the city were trash and he hoped that some of them would be destroyed in the war. 'Alas,' he lamented to me, 'everything was in perfect order!' But some of the paintings given to lunatic asylums for keeping proved to be highly medicinal to the patients.

"He did not revere the baillies as they thought they should be revered. For too many of them, he was simply a not very well paid second-class municipal official. But his fearlessness attracted municipal statesmen of both parties and created or re-created a genuine and passionate devotion to art and to an attitude towards all the arts which had been dying out in the Glasgow of my student days."

Writing in *The Scotsman*, artist Emilio Coia said: "In one important sense at least, Dr Honeyman was the best man for art in Scotland in this century. He never let up. If he knew he was on to something that would further the cause of art by making more people aware of its importance and relevance to their well-being, he would pursue it with a tenacity that was quite unprecedented in these parts—and totally disconcerting to the groaners and Jonahs who stubbornly maintained the principle of *laissez-faire*.

"Dr Honeyman, a great Glaswegian, had to get in there and mix it with the best of them. He did it with the Burrell, to Glasgow's embarrassment, with the cleaning of the Giorgione, with the methods he employed to make sure Glasgow Art Gallery was put on the European map as a place well worth getting to know; and of course he did it with the purchase of the Dali."

In the *Glasgow Illustrated*, W. P. Stewart wrote: "These last few weeks Scotland has lost in Lord Reith, Lord Boyd Orr and now Dr T. J. Honeyman three sons whose eminence would be difficult to parallel in one generation."

That brilliant essayist Wilfred Taylor, writing in his *Scotsman Log*, gave some interesting reminiscences. Those who remember Taylor will know that he wrote with that quaint but effective royal "we":

"One of our happiest recollections is of bumping into Tom Honeyman and his wife one cold afternoon on 57th Street, New York. They were on their way home from one of their visits to Canada. They insisted that we join them in what turned out to be a highly entertaining visit to Salvador Dali in the Carstairs Gallery. We then adjourned to sort out our impressions over cups of tea made from bags."

Taylor made the valid point that nothing like the full force of Honeyman's invincible personality really surfaced in his writings. It was true that he talked much better than he wrote.

He raised another intriguing point: "Whether Tom Honeyman, St Mungo prizeman, Rector of Glasgow University, was ever offered a knighthood or turned one down, we don't know. He, in his unstinted service to the community, certainly merited one. We are pleased that he never became Sir Tom. He didn't need that kind of elevation which, in our view, doesn't sit too well with the efflorescence of the Glasgow ethos, in all its quick captivating humanity at its most irresistible and sometimes disconcerting best."

Did he ever turn down a knighthood? It is hard to imagine.

Given the boyish delight in his achievements—and the vanity which lurks in most human beings—he would surely have accepted such a recognition. Indeed, even if for some extraordinary reason he might have been inclined to turn it down for himself, I cannot believe he would have passed up the opportunity to give some belated glory to his beloved wife. There would have been such domestic teasing over the transformation of his ever-faithful Cath, or Katinka, to the splendour of "Lady Honeyman".

As it happened, plain Mrs Honeyman sat down and wrote her response to the bereavement letters. Some said she was showing signs of a broken heart so perhaps it was a blessing that she did not have long to brood over her loss. Six weeks after Tom's death, daughter Margaret had a memorably warm conversation with her mother. They had not always been on the same wavelength but there was kindness in nature's plan that night.

Suddenly Cath said to Margaret: "You know I'm not afraid of dying. I don't mind whether it is tomorrow or five years hence."

Margaret responded that it would be wonderful, when the time came, to go to bed some night (it had happened with her mother-in-law) and not wake up again. On the very next night, that is exactly what happened. Cath's popularity was reflected in the large turn-out for her funeral. She was cremated at Dalnottar.

In June 1973, almost two years after the Honeymans had gone, a large gathering of relatives and friends assembled in Kelvingrove Park for the formal opening and dedication of a memorial garden. Dr Honeyman had suggested in his will that, instead of flowers at his funeral, donations could be made to the Glasgow Tree Lovers Society. Such was public generosity that the Tree Lovers struck on the idea of a memorial garden, inviting other organisations like the Glasgow Art Galleries and Museums Association to join in the venture.

The Corporation gave an appropriate site between the university and the Art Galleries, overlooking the River Kelvin, symbolising so much of the man's life. Though the garden materialised in the name of Tom Honeyman, the family liked to think that it commemorated both parents. The design allowed for two benches donated by the family themselves, who were delighted that the centrepiece was a statue, "The Palmist" by Benno Schotz, who was a friend. Appropriately, it embraced the theme of music, which was so dear to the heart of Cath Honeyman.

At the formal opening, the address was given by Lord Provost William Gray, who revealed himself as one of that small band of students who approached Dr Honeyman in the first place, with a view to him standing as Rector of the university.

The overall design of the garden was the work of Robert Burnett, a nephew of Cath Honeyman. The memorial plaque was designed by Avril Gibb.

In the dedication, Dr William Morris of Glasgow Cathedral read the 1st Psalm and told of its significance in relation to the young Tom Honeyman. If he could recite that psalm as a boy, his granny used to promise him sweeties from her bottle. After a few verses she would say "That's enough. Just put in your hand and help yourself."

But he would take such a handful that he couldn't get his hand out of the jar. So his granny gave him a little sermon about greed and covetousness. It was the kind of minor incident he would never forget and would repeat with boyish glee in later years.

His little stories were guidelines along the path of his life and, on that dedication day, Dr Morris remembered him above all else as a man who loved beauty and revelled in sharing it with everyone.

XLII

BENNO'S BOMBSHELL

TEN YEARS after Dr Honeyman's death his old friend Benno Schotz, the Queen's Sculptor in Scotland, wrote his memoirs—and sparked fury among the Honeyman offspring for what he said about their father.

Even allowing for family sensitiveness, the remarks of the famous sculptor were certainly outwith the normal bounds of friendship and even revealed an undercurrent of bitterness which was surprising to say the least.

No sooner had she read *Bronze in my Blood* than Margaret Wilson, Honeyman's daughter, was penning a letter of deep hurt to Benno Schotz at his home at 2 Kirklee Road, Glasgow. Complaining of his inaccuracies, unfairness and "disgraceful innuendo", she concluded: "Benno, may I ask, WHY did you do it? WHY?"

But that was mild to the response of her brother Tim, publishing manager of the Church of Scotland's St Andrew's Press, who did not allow his religious stance to inhibit his language. Tim wrote: "I am very sorry indeed that the high regard and affection in which all of our family have held you over these many years should be shattered by a book to which we looked forward with anticipation and which, in the event, turned out to be the pathetic self-bolsterings and aggrandisements of an embittered old man."

Tim had already seen Schotz's reply to his sister and added: "That revealed a viciousness which is totally incomprehensible."

So what did Schotz actually say that could arouse such displeasure? Margaret Wilson's hackles first began to rise with his inference that her father had somehow wormed his way into the role of art dealer at the Reid Gallery by dropping hints about a desire to switch from the medical profession.

Then he suggested that the Glasgow art fraternity may have considered Honeyman "a good doctor but a novice in art and did not have confidence in his judgement." He added: "Dr Honeyman decided to go to London with the firm but for some reason he was not a success there."

The root of the matter, however, may be found in a one-man show of Schotz's work due to be staged at the Reid and Lefevre Gallery in London in 1938. Since Duncan Macdonald, one of the partners, had to be in New York he apparently asked the sculptor if he wished to postpone it till he returned, prompting Schotz to write in his book: "Did he suggest this because he had already taken Dr Honeyman's measure as a dealer?"

Schotz went ahead with the exhibition, apparently unaware of a view among gallery people at the time that artists were often their own worst enemies at press previews and were better kept at a distance. He wrote: "Can you imagine my surprise when Dr Honeyman debarred me from the gallery during the press view to prevent me meeting the critics?"

The *dénouement* of all this was that Benno's one-man show in London was a flop, for whatever reason.

Further derogatory comments in his book were extended to the reply he sent to Margaret, in which he continued the attack of her father, inferring that, in the latter's *Art and Audacity*, he had somehow withheld due praise for the sculptor.

"What did he write?" he asks. "He is loath to mention that I received the LL.D from Strathclyde University. I modelled your father in 1928 and it is considered as fine a portrait as I have done even today. Does your father mention it? Oh no. It might reflect some credit on me. Yet your father writes that I am amongst his oldest friends. So I was; but was he mine? I am afraid that what he wrote denies it."

In fact, in his own book Honeyman did mention the honorary degree from Strathclyde and, although Schotz warranted only a limited place in the manuscript, he wrote of him in the warmest terms, especially in connection with the highly successful lecture-demonstrations in which Benno could model the head of someone taken from the audience and talk wittily on the art of sculpture.

It was a rather sad postscript to what had seemed like a sound friendship between two men who were both born in 1891, Benno in his native Estonia, which he left to study engineering in Glasgow before working in John Brown's shipyard at Clydebank and later rising to prominence as the Queen's Sculptor.

Putting Benno's bombshell aside, Tom Honeyman was being assessed in a more rational manner by others who knew him, looking back from the distance of quarter of a century after his death. Their reflections were varied and interesting.

Emilio Coia, the Scots-Italian who would make his own name in the artistic world, had first encountered Tom Honeyman at Alexander Reid's gallery in Glasgow in the late 1920s but came to know him much better at the Lefevre Gallery in London in the 1930s.

By then Emilio had eloped with a fellow student from Glasgow School of Art, and was making a good living as an artist/cartoonist for Fleet Street newspapers like the old *News Chronicle* and putting on a one-man show at the Lefevre.

The subjects he was encountering in those days ranged from George Bernard Shaw and Rebecca West to T. S. Eliot and Stephen Spender. His observation of the partners at the Lefevre Gallery led him to believe that Duncan Macdonald was the dominant figure, much disliked by portrait painter Wyndham Lewis, who exhibited there only because of Honeyman.

Coia shared Lewis's view of Macdonald and thought him big-headed and rather unpleasant. McNeill Reid, on the other hand, was a likeable man but lacked the strength to withstand the force of Macdonald. As the recent arrival on the art scene, Honeyman was clearly third in line, maintaining a much lower profile than would be the case in years to come. Coia detected a friction among the partners, with McNeill Reid and Honeyman on the same side.

Back in Glasgow, he recalled their meetings at the Art Club where Honeyman would turn up with guests like James Bridie.

Looking back, he said: "We wouldn't have heard of Kelvingrove if it had not been for Tom Honeyman. He bought great French paintings and put life into the gallery, making Kelvingrove what it became. He wasn't a modest man and could be dogmatic but he was a fighter who was trying to put Glasgow on the map—and he succeeded.

"He also had the knack of picking ideas from any source, listening to other people's opinions, absorbing them and making good use of them."

Lord Macfarlane of Bearsden was just plain Norman Macfarlane when he left the forces in 1947 and was home in time to join the queues which stretched endlessly for the famous Van Gogh exhibition.

"Attendances were colossal and I doubt if Glasgow had ever seen an exhibition like that," he said. "Two years earlier Tom Honeyman had brought the Picasso and Matisse exhibition. That was more than fifty years ago but we can now see that they emerged as the two most important artists of the century."

Acquiring a taste for art, the young Macfarlane came to know the bachelor brothers Professor Alex McFee and General Jock McFee from Milngavie, through whom he found himself in the company of Tom Honeyman. Professor McFee was a keen collector whose pictures would eventually go to Glasgow University but he would entrust to the young man the task of checking out works of art.

On one occasion Macfarlane was to pursue two paintings by Stuart Park, a well known West of Scotland artist, which were to be seen at the Fine Arts Society in London. He wanted one for McFee and one for himself, keeping in mind that the former would in time go to the university. Tom Honeyman made the final decision, Macfarlane taking the domestic picture, which he retains to this day.

When Professor McFee died the university showed some hesitancy about accepting the collection. Norman Macfarlane was asked what it was worth and when he casually assessed it at around £500,000 there was a sudden burst of interest!

Recalling Honeyman's influence in landing for Glasgow the collection of William McInnes, Lord Macfarlane said: "It is difficult to imagine that there is somebody like that today who could persuade a businessman like McInnes to give his collection. You needed someone of Honeyman's personality, interest and erudition.

"Intellectually he was very bright and didn't suffer fools gladly. But coming from a well-connected world between medicine and art he found it difficult to work for a local authority. My father was on the town council at the time and got on well with him but he knew that he had the capacity to upset people when he thought it necessary for Glasgow.

"To sum up the man, if I were trying to pinpoint the most important Scotsman in the art world this century, I would find it hard to see past Tom Honeyman."

At his art establishment in Blythswood Square, William Hardie could look back and marvel at his good luck in being able to visit the Honeyman home in Dowanhill Street when he was still a very young man:

"To visit a private house just off Byres Road and find yourself faced with Dali, Marcoussis and Calder was a breathtaking experience never to be forgotten. They were magnificent names which came to be there as a result of Dr Honeyman's days as an art dealer in London and I reckon you couldn't have found that kind of collection anywhere else in Scotland. Those artists displayed in his own home were people he actually knew and his recollection of those people he had met and the paintings he had seen gave him a cachet no-one else in Scotland could approach."

William Hardie remembered the kindly touches, like the day he met Honeyman off the train at Dundee for the opening of the Three Colourists exhibition. His visitor, who had apparently discovered that Hardie had become engaged, was carrying a parcel which, when unwrapped, revealed a colour drawing by Leslie Hunter. Even in the last year of his life he would remember a gift like that.

On that day Hardie was reminded of his skill as a speaker when he addressed a large gathering at Dundee Art Galleries, combining the authority of great knowledge with a spontaneous and informal delivery. Though approaching his eightieth birthday he could still have an audience eating out of his hand.

Being human, however, Honeyman was not infallible as a speaker. William Hardie recalled a less successful performance: "He prided himself in talking from fairly brief notes which would lead him from one point to the next but, in giving his inaugural Cargill Lecture, it didn't work. It went disastrously wrong, as if he wasn't properly prepared, and to make things worse the slides were in the wrong order. I remember sitting in the Lecture Theatre of Glasgow University cringing in the dark."

Coming from different generations, Honeyman and Hardie did not always agree. On the controversial cleaning of the Giorgione, for example, Hardie said: "It was fashionable at the time to clean paintings but I feel it is a mixed blessing. Anything more than the absolute minimum is an intrusion and I felt the way they cleaned at Kelvingrove left something to be desired."

Dr Honeyman's faithful secretary, Isabel Mackintosh, who met husband Harry McLean at the gallery, remained there for twenty-three years after her old boss had retired. Her husband had died prematurely but she was still there in 1977 when she was sixty-four and had completed forty-seven years with the Corporation.

Reminiscing on her years at Kelvingrove, she recalled memorable figures like the lanky Burrell and the rather short McInnes who would come about the place. She remembered how the people in that glorified village of Partick were proud to regard Kelvingrove as their own, supplying most of the ancillary staff and regarding as prestigious posts the most menial of tasks which were passed on from mother to daughter with the pride of tradition.

As for her old boss, she recalled that he was firm in his teetotalism but would make a big play of the fact that he didn't mind other people having a drink. Though politics were seldom raised, Isabel felt he veered towards Labour, always concerned about poverty and saying the Tories never did anything for his family.

"There was a terrible jealousy of him in council circles," she said. "He was a wonderful director but not a wonderful council employee. Having been in business and known that kind of freedom, he was always going to come up against councillors. He was really much too unique to be a council employee."

The Art Gallery director of the 1990s, Julian Spalding, was in no doubt about the stature of his predecessor: "Dr Honeyman began the rebirth of Glasgow and made it the European City of Culture. In coming from art dealer to director he was really the gamekeeper turned poacher. Those jobs were highly respected positions, intended for artists or intellectuals. They might also come from an uppercrust or dilettante background or they were people who had published a few books.

"But in a way it was typical of Glasgow that it was cheeky

enough to appoint an art dealer because art dealing was known to have its shady side. So it was a remarkable appointment. Honeyman was clearly of the personality to persuade them that he could get things done. And he certainly did. He proved that Glasgow had a natural appetite for culture, that it was a naturally creative place, whether it was painting a picture or building the *Queen Mary*. These are not necessarily different things.

"So in a pure way he rang the bell for Glasgow, in a manner which surprised Glasgow itself in the dark years when it was still a slum and industry looked bad after the war. Suddenly they were buying famous pictures!

"The writer John Myerscough said Glasgow was the only post-industrial city in the world which had rebuilt itself on the back of an art gallery."

So they raked over their memories of Tom Honeyman, whose name still gained recognition at the Lefevre Gallery in London, which he left as far back as 1939.

With the outbreak of war, the gallery was closed for a spell before resuming on two days a week. Honeyman was now settled in his Glasgow post, McNeill Reid had joined the Corps of Engineers and Duncan Macdonald was running the Bignou Gallery in New York, along with Georges Keller.

Wisely, the Lefevre stock of pictures and sculptures was evacuated for safety, escaping a bombing raid in 1943 which damaged the original premises at 1a King Street, in the heart of London.

The gallery opened in cramped premises in New Bond Street at the end of 1944 but the prospect was now of a very different world. McNeill Reid resigned as a director in 1947 but returned to give support until he finally left in 1963 at the age of seventy. His son Graham was with the firm for a time.

Duncan Macdonald died suddenly in 1949 and his widow replaced him as a non-active director until her own death in 1958.

Willy Peploe, son of the famous S. J. Peploe, who had joined the firm as a salesman just before the war, returned as a director in 1949, remaining an active force until he died in 1966.

The Lefevre found its present extensive premises in Bruton Street in 1950, by which time Gerald Corcoran had become a director, gradually taking over the management. The pre-war team was now gone and the Corcoran name was the dominant one. Gerald was followed by his son Desmond, who was joined by Martin Summers, and they were still guiding Lefevre in the latter part of the century.

So the firm which owed so much to Alexander Reid was flourishing in London more than a hundred years after the young Glaswegian found himself sharing a flat with Vincent Van Gogh.

XLIII

THE MEMORIAL GARDEN

THE HONEYMANS were survived by their two sons and one daughter. Elder son Tim, who was eighteen when war broke out, ended his service with the Cameronians as a captain and joined Collins the publishers in Glasgow. He moved to the Grant Educational Company but saw the main thrust of his career with the Church of Scotland as publishing manager of its St Andrew's Press.

After his father's death he followed in the footsteps as chairman of Glasgow Art Gallery and Museums Association and of the English Speaking Union in Glasgow. Like his father, he was an accomplished public speaker and a life-long teetotaller. Tim, who was married to Sheila and had four children, died in 1987 at the age of sixty-five, having been predeceased by his only son Tom.

Daughter Margaret, known to the family as Cissa, followed her London schooldays by joining the WAAF in 1942. On demobilisation she became secretary to Craigie Annan, the Glasgow art dealer, before learning about antiques in Inverness and landing in the drama department of the Arts Council in London.

In 1950 she married Jim Wilson, a Glasgow solicitor, and they had two daughters. Margaret is now a widow, living in Glasgow.

Younger son Grant was back from the Hampstead days in time

to complete his schooling at Glasgow Academy before studying medicine at Glasgow University, as his father had done.

He reached the rank of captain during his National Service but emigrated to Canada in 1955, becoming a leading surgeon in Brantford and Brant County, Ontario. A talented musician, and member of the Brantford Symphony Orchestra, he was made Arts Citizen of the Year in 1997. Grant married Monica and they had four children.

Like Tim, Margaret and Grant followed the family tradition of temperance, as part of the general guidelines laid down in a happy home in Glasgow's West End.

With Tim gone and Grant in Canada, Margaret can still be found with her thoughts at the memorial garden in Kelvingrove. And for a final word on Tom Honeyman we can do no better than turn again to the lyrical pen of Wilfred Taylor, who found himself in that garden one day, remembering his chance encounter with the Honeymans in New York, which led to his meeting with Salvador Dali.

Wilfred Taylor wrote: "Our route to the garden took us over Partick bridge, through the Art Gallery, past a croquet lawn and over another bridge. A man was guiding a big grass cutter over a lawn as we turned off Kelvin Way to the little garden.

"It makes an enchanting little island, close to a weir on the river, on one side of which is the gallery Dr Honeyman so vigorously and imaginatively directed, and on the other the university of which he was a graduate and a Rector. With its alfresco sculptures, its flowers, its nursling trees, its two memorial benches within a paved and walled enclosure, the garden is informal and unostentatious compared with the massive nearby figures of Lister and Kelvin. It commemorates Tom Honeyman affectionately and intimately rather as the Peter Pan statue in Kensington Gardens recalls J. M. Barrie.

"We wanted to read the inscription on one of the benches which was occupied by a young couple committed to what looked like a mildly routine amorous embrace. When we asked if they would mind declutching for a moment so that we could read the words they were masking, they asked us who Tom Honeyman was. We then, as an Edinburgh man, had the privilege of telling two young Glaswegians something about a man who had done credit to their city.

"The couple resumed their embrace only momentarily. The boy then stood up, put his arms round the girl's waist, and read out to her the words inscribed on a wall panel. As they wandered off in the direction of the man who was sending green cascades into the metal cow-catcher in front of his machine, a small boy bounded down on to the paving in front of the wall inscription. "What's this, Mister?" he asked. So we told him a little about the man whose memory the garden is fragrantly preserving.

"Tom Honeyman would like all this slightly irreverent and not too respectful attitude to the garden by the water, on the part of lively young Glaswegians."

All within sight of Kelvingrove Art Gallery, it was a suitable note on which to let rest the life and memory of a distinguished son—the man who unwittingly but gloriously paved the way for his beloved Glasgow to become, one day, an international city of culture.

INDEX

INDEX

N

O

P